Wonder-filled WEEKDAYS

for Fall

65 Lesson Plans for Christian Preschool Ministries

Millie S. Goodson, Ph.D.

Abingdon Press
Nashville

Wonder-filled Weekdays for Fall

ISBN 0-687-08211-0

Editor: Daphna Flegal
Designed and Illustrated by: Paige Easter
Page 148: Illustrated by Robert S. Jones
Production Editors: Julie Glass, Leslie Johnson, David Mauldin, and Betsi Smith

99 00 01 02 03 04 05 06 07 08—10 9 8 7 6 5 4 3 2 1

MANUFACTURED IN THE UNITED STATES OF AMERICA

Table of Contents

Introduction

Overview

Wonder-filled Weekdays offers 65 lesson plans for teachers of preschoolers in Christian preschool ministries. These lesson plans integrate developmentally appropriate activities with religious development and are designed to help teachers make faith connections. The lesson plans are organized around monthly seasonal themes with weekly (five-day) lesson plans.

Each lesson contains:

- An outline of the lesson with:
  - Goals
  - Objectives
  - Faith Connections
  - Bible verse
  - Teacher's Prayer
- Center Time
- Wonder Time
- Group Fun
- Goodbye Circle
- Evaluation

It is expected that teachers will choose from the suggested activities and fit them into their unique classroom schedules.

Snack Time

Snack time is an important time for young children. Occasionally you will find a suggestion for a snack which the children make as part of the lesson's activities. These are included because they specifically add to the day's goals and objectives. It is expected that you have snack as part of your regular schedule. Use it as an opportunity to pray. Talk with the children about the day's lessons as you eat together.

Teacher Talk

Several features of *Wonder-filled Weekdays* will help the teacher make faith connections with their children. Verbalizing our faith as the children work and play is what gives an ordinary preschool activity a Christian value. Looking at the veins in fall leaves is not just a science lesson. It is an opportunity to talk about God as Creator and God's plan for the seasons.

Teacher Talk is designed to help the teacher think through the words to say to help children learn about God, Jesus, and our faith in connection to the lesson and to individual activities. Teacher Talk is found on the first page of each lesson along with the goals and objectives. Teacher Talk is also found with each suggested activity during Center Time.

The Bible

Each lesson has a suggested Bible verse for the children to hear and experience. You may want to use each Bible verse as suggested. Or you may want to choose one Bible verse for the week and repeat it each day. There are also suggested Bible stories for each unit. Find these Bible stories in Bible storybooks or in your Sunday school curriculum resources to present the stories in ways the children can understand. *Don't Just Sit There, Bible Stories That Move You for Ages 3-5* (ISBN 0-687-12210-4) is an excellent source of age appropriate Bible stories. You may order *Don't Just Sit There* through your Christian bookstore or by calling 1-800-672-1789.

As you teach your children Bible stories and Bible verses, let them see you handle the Bible. Give the children opportunities to hold the Bible and open its pages. This is the book of our faith. We want to give our children a love for its teachings.

Christian Values

Throughout *Wonder-filled Weekdays* teachers will find Christian values presented as part of the lessons. These values include:

We are created in the image of God.
God loves us.
We can love God.
We can love others.
God is always with us.
We can trust God.
God's world is good.
Jesus loves us.
Jesus taught us about God's love.

Centers for Fall

Home Living Center

- chairs and table
- play appliances
- pretend food
- dishes, pots, and pans
- dress-up clothes
- accessories: belts, hats, ties, jewelry
- phone
- computer

Besides the normal pretend food and dishes, include items that are found in today's homes, such as a television set (you can make one out of a box), a briefcase, and a computer. Some centers include actual living room furniture—soft chairs and sofas. Include items that will represent family chores, such as a plastic waste paper basket, a broom, a stuffed animal with a leash, and pretend pet food and dishes. Also include dress-up clothes that a mother, father, grandmother, and grandfather would wear.

Manipulatives Center

- puzzles
- play dough
- buttons
- lacing beads
- Duplo blocks
- pegboards
- pegs
- small wooden blocks
- foam peanuts
- pompoms
- tongs

This center encourages children to use their small muscles. You will see a marked difference between three-year-olds and five-year-olds in this center. Both younger and older preschoolers need practice using their small muscles.

Manipulating objects also helps children with learning how to pattern, solve problems, and assemble.

Math Center

- small items for counting
- ruler
- measuring cups
- items for sorting and matching
- a counting line with numbers to 25

Math for young children involves counting, sorting and matching, spatial relationships, estimating, and comparing. Avoid worksheets for preschoolers; instead, use actual objects for counting and matching.

Have the children bring items from home for use in the center. Or use items common to most families such as Duplo blocks, stickers, paper clips, animal figures, and so forth.

Music/Movement Center

- cassettes or CDs
- cassette or CD player
- scarfs or ribbons
- rhythm instruments
- headphones

Music can be used for quiet listening or for movement. The activities can be done with one child or with the whole group. Vary the music and movement experiences you provide for your children. Set up a place with headphones, pillows, and blankets for quiet listening. Move furniture out of the way or take the children to a larger space for large muscle play. Remember that music and movement are two important ways children learn.

Art Center

easel and paintbrushes
construction paper (different sizes)
glue
collage materials
scissors
fabric scraps
crayons
magazines
markers
rubber stamps
plain paper
mural paper
manila drawing paper
colored pencils
water colors
art tissue
smocks
table covering

Slowly include items in the art center as children learn how to use the items, to care for them, and to put them back after the children have used them. Children need the opportunity to experiment with a variety of art mediums without trying to create any specific project. The art center can also be used for group activity projects.

Cover the table with rolled paper, newspaper, or a plastic tablecloth to make cleanup easier. Have the children wear smocks to protect their clothing.

Building Center

large wooden blocks
Lincoln Logs building toys
small wooden blocks
Kinex interlocking building toys
small sticks
Duplo blocks

Preschool boys and girls love to construct buildings, houses, roadways, boats, airplanes, and so forth. As with other centers this center needs close supervision, especially at the beginning of the school year. Be sure children know the rules for fun in the center. If play becomes too rough, close the center and tell the children why.

Some children will want to stay in the building center every day for center time. Be sure to have a way of encouraging them to enjoy other centers and letting other children play with building materials. Limit the number of children who can play in the center at one time. This can be done by giving each child a center card. The child puts his or her card in a plastic pocket you have made. Place five pockets in the center and when they are filled no one else can come in until a child leaves.

The building center encourages creative thought as children seek to solve problems in their building. It is a wonderful place for children to learn social skills and to work together. The building center promotes growth of fine and gross motor skills and is a good place for children to practice language skills.

You can reinforce your lesson theme in the building center by using characters that go along with the theme. For example, put family characters in the building center the week you are learning about families.

Centers for Fall

Writing Center

pencils of different lengths and widths
erasers
plain writing paper
lined writing paper
envelopes of different sizes
rulers
posters of the alphabet
stickers
mailboxes for each child and teacher

Basics in this center are paper and pencils. Ask parents to recycle paper from their businesses. Use stamps from magazine promotionals for pretend stamps. Have pencils of varying sizes available so each child can choose the one that feels most controllable and comfortable.

You might want to make a post office as part of the center so children can send messages to others in their class. Be sure to include a name on each box, including each of the adults in the class. Remember, the purpose of this center is for the child to practice writing. For younger children this will probably mean scribbling or writing letters that have no meaning for you. If you are teaching five-year-olds, you may want to have lined paper available and a poster of the alphabet for them to see.

To use the center as a reinforcement for your lessons in the family unit, encourage children to "write" letters to their family members. School-age children are encouraged to write in their journals; therefore, you might want to help older preschoolers get used to this idea by making little books in which children can draw and write. Posting the name of each child, printed so they can copy it, will help older preschoolers with writing their names.

Water/Sand Play Center

water or sand table
dishpan
water
sand
plastic cups and bowls
plastic pitchers
turkey basters
plastic spoons
towels
plastic animals
plastic boats
coffee scoops
colanders
combs
egg beaters
funnels
plastic pails
shells
rocks
sponges
watering cans

Water and sand play is great fun for young children. It can also provide a calming effect and help the children relax. It promotes creativity and provides tactile experiences.

Have towels on hand to clean up water from the floor and from hands and arms. Always sweep up and throw away any sand that lands on the floor.

Science Center

magnifying glass
nature items (rocks, bugs, leaves, and so forth)
class pet
magnets
experiments
writing paper and pencil
photographs of people

Science for young children includes active involvement in collecting specimens, viewing them, and talking and writing about what they see. Encourage children to contribute items to the science table, and be sure all children get a chance to participate in experiments at the center.

Cooking Center

mixing bowls
mixing spoons
measuring cups
baking trays
muffin tins
cupcake liners
plastic bags
oven (or access to one)

Preschoolers love to cook! Have a separate cooking center or combine cooking activities with the home living center. Let the children mix, stir, squish, pound, knead, and of course—taste.

Book Center

books
pictures

Give the book center a little extra attention. Add pillows, blankets, and sleeping bags. Put up a tent or make a reading house from a large appliance box. Hang stars or brightly colored leaves from the ceiling. Rotate stuffed animal characters through the centers as you highlight the books they come from. Make this center a special space for the children to enjoy.

Worship Center

Bible
Bible storybook
nature items (rocks, leaves, shells, and so forth)
flowers or plants
worship cloth
pictures

Worship for young children happens in the midst of everyday life. It is the moment of wonder when a child examines a leaf that has changed from green to red, or the moment of delight when warm, freshly baked bread is tasted on the tongue. Worship happens at wonder time, on the playground, and in the science center. If this is true, then why is a worship center suggested each week? The worship center is designed to give the teacher a planned opportunity to talk and pray with the children. The activities suggested in the worship center will range from art projects to science experiments to games. But each activity has an extra-special ingredient. It suggests ways for you to connect the day's lessons with the faith.

Having a worship center gives your classroom a sacred space. It reminds parents, teachers, and children that God is important in this place.

Preschoolers

Each child in your class is a one-of-a-kind child of God. Each child has his or her own name, background, family situation, and set of experiences. It is important to remember and celebrate the uniqueness of each child. Yet all of these one-of-a-kind children of God have some common needs.

- All children need love.
- All children need a sense of self-worth.
- All children need to feel a sense of accomplishment.
- All children need to have a safe place to be and to express their feelings.
- All children need to be surrounded by adults who love them.
- All children need to experience the love of God.

Preschoolers (children ages 3-5 years old) also have some common characteristics.

Their Bodies

- They do not sit still for very long.
- They have lots of energy.
- They enjoy moving (running, galloping, dancing, jumping, hopping).
- They are developing fine motor skills (learning to cut with scissors, learning to handle a ball, learning to tie their shoes).
- They enjoy using their senses (taste, touch, smell, hearing, seeing).

Their Minds

- They are learning more and more words.
- They enjoy music.
- They are learning to express their feelings.
- They like to laugh and be silly.
- They enjoy nonsense words.
- They are learning to identify colors, sizes, and shapes.
- They have an unclear understanding of time.
- They have a wonderful imagination.

Their Relationships

- They are beginning to interact with others as they play together.
- They are beginning to understand that other people have feelings.
- They are learning to wait for their turn.
- They can have a hard time leaving parents, especially mother.
- They want to help.
- They love to feel important.

Their Hearts

- They need to handle the Bible and see others handle it.
- They need caring adults who model Christian attitudes and behaviors.
- They need to sing, move to, and say Bible verses.
- They need to hear clear, simple stories from the Bible.
- They can express simple prayers.
- They can experience wonder and awe at God's world.
- They can share food and money and make things for others.
- They can experience belonging at church and preschool.

Unit 1

Meet Me and My Family

Goals:

1. The children will identify things about themselves and share their learnings with the class.
2. The children will understand that each family is different and will become aware of the makeup of their own families.
3. The children will learn to verbalize their own likes and dislikes.
4. The children will become aware of ways they are growing.
5. The children will feel comfortable in their new class as they share with others who they are.

Every child needs the chance to celebrate who he or she is and what she or he is able to do. This unit seeks to help the child become aware of his or her own abilities and feel good about them. In addition, the unit celebrates the family that supports this child. It is hoped that through sharing with the class, the child will find her or his place in the group and feel an important part of the whole.

Each week the theme of the unit changes. You can change the learning centers by developing new ones at the beginning of each week or you can add to each center each week—leaving the activities that the children enjoy and removing or adapting the activities that are not used in each center.

Bible Stories for this Unit:

Genesis 1 (The Creation)
Genesis 1:26-31 (The Creation of Humankind)
Luke 2:40 (Jesus Grows)
Matthew 18:12-14 (The Lost Sheep)
Psalm 8
1 Samuel 18:1-4 (David and Jonathan)

I AM SPECIAL

This week the children will feel special, as members of a family and as members of your class. If your class is just beginning, be sure to include get-acquainted activities in these first lessons as well.

Each day of this week children will experience different activities dealing with their names, faces, homes, families, and class that help them see themselves as valued human beings in your sight and in the sight of God. Be sure to carry activities over from one day to the next. Children love repetition and will enjoy doing some of these activities all week.

Lesson 1

My Name

Teacher Talk:

(Child's name), you are important to me.

(Child's name), you are important to God.

(Child's name), I like your name, and I really like you!

Goals:

To help the children learn each other's names.

To know his or her name is important to God.

Objectives:

By the end of this session the children will:

Say the names of their teachers and the other children in the class.

Begin to recognize their own names when they see their names printed.

Faith Connections

Bible verse: God said, "I know you by name." (Exodus 33:17, adapted)

Preschool children need to know that they are special to God, to their families, and to you. Calling a child's name says, "You are special; I know who you are."

Teacher's Prayer

O God, help me to know my children by name. Guide me to pray for them and treat each of them as your child. Amen.

Center Time

Set up your centers as described on pages 6–9. For this lesson add the following:

Writing Center

Teacher Talk

You are important to me.

Resources

cards or self-adhesive notes, pencils, envelopes, notebook paper, stickers

Print each child's name on a card or a self-adhesive note and post it in the writing center. Have pencils and blank cards available on which children can "write" their names and the names of other children in the class.

Math Center

Teacher Talk

I like your name, and I really like you.

Resources

cards, marker, counters of any kind

Write each child's name on a card. Above each letter number the letters so the child can count how many letters are in his or her name.

Example: 1 2 3 4 5
M a r i a

Give the children all the same number of counters to place over each letter. Then have each child count the number in his or her name.

Art Center

Teacher Talk

You are important to God.

Resources

cardboard, marker, awl or paper punch, yarn, tape

Print each child's name on a piece of cardboard. (Empty cereal boxes work well for this.) Punch holes around the lines of the name to make a sewing card. Wrap yarn ends with tape so children can "sew" their name easily. Don't worry if the child loops around the card or does not follow the line. The object is for the children to use their fine muscles to put the yarn through the holes while seeing their names.

Worship Center

Teacher Talk

You are important to God.

Resources

mirrors, nonpermanent ink pads, paper

Place several mirrors in the center so children can see their faces. Place ink pads and paper in the center so children can make prints of their fingers, thumbs, and the sides of their fists. Be sure to use nonpermanent ink pads.

Say: You are unique. There is only one you in the whole world. God loves you.

Pray: Thank you, God, for *(name children)*. Amen.

Home Living Center

Teacher Talk

You are important to God.

Resources

dress-up clothes

Have the children play in the center and pretend to be different persons. Be sure you ask, "What's your name?"

Building Center

Teacher Talk

I like your name, and I really like you.

Resources

blocks

Encourage them to build "houses" for families. If you have children's blocks with letters on them, help the children make their names with the blocks.

Wonder Time

Open the Bible to Exodus 33:17.

Say: "God said, 'I know you by name'" (Exodus 33:17, adapted).

Have the children repeat the Bible verse.

Call the children together with a song or with fingerplays.

Wonder Question: I wonder why we have names?
(Give the children time to think of their own answers.)

Say: We are learning about names today. My name is............. (Introduce the other adults in the classroom by calling their names.)

Play a name game. Have the children sit in a circle on the floor with their legs in a v-shape in front of them. Roll a ball to one of the children and say the child's name. Continue the game until all the children have been named.

Sing: "Will You Be a Friend of Mine?" (*see page 211*).

Read the Bible verse.

Say: God loves each one of us. God knows us by name.

Pray: Thank you, God, for each child here. Thank you, God, for (*name each child*). Thank you, God, for the name our parents gave us. Amen.

Group Fun

Resources

letter-shaped sponges, tempera paint in 3 or 4 colors, shallow containers, construction paper

Explain to the children that they will be printing their own names on paper. Make sure you have all the necessary letters.

Help each child pick out the letters of his or her name from available sponges. Purchase sponges already in letter shapes or cut out letters from sponges. Pour a different color paint in a shallow container that is large enough so the child can put the letter in flat.

Let the children choose the colors they will use with each letter. Help the children spell their names correctly, but do not print the letters for them. Let them choose how they want the letters on their papers. Show the children their name tags or names written but let the letter prints be their own. Lay the pictures flat to dry.

Goodbye Circle

Let the children talk about the things each enjoyed doing today. Let each child tell his or her name to the group. Encourage the children to say each child's name after the child names himself or herself. Repeat the Bible verse with the children.

Pray: Thank you, God, for our names. Amen.

Evaluation

Today's activities will be most helpful in assessing the child's ability to recognize letters and words. Go back over each child's work today and make notes about abilities in writing, recognizing letters, verbalizing in circle time, and fine motor skills.

Lesson 2

My Face

Goals:

To celebrate the self.

To help the children enjoy distinctive features in their own faces.

To understand that even though we all look different, we are all special in God's sight.

Objectives: By the end of this lesson children will:

Look at themselves in the mirror and talk about their own features.

Draw their faces and tell about themselves.

Listen to a story and sing a song about themselves.

Faith Connections

Bible verse: God cares about you. (1 Peter 5:7, adapted)

Our faces help define us. They give us away. They help us to communicate. Children are fascinated with their faces. They study their features and try to do all sorts of things with face muscles. They need to know that God knows them by name and face and that God cares for each of them.

Teacher's Prayer

O God, you know my face—every expression. Etch the faces of your children on my heart. Amen.

Teacher Talk:

Each one of us is different.

Each one of us is special.

God loves each one of us.

You have a great face!

Center Time

Display pictures of different faces. If possible, include photographs of each of your children.

As children arrive, welcome each child as they enter the room by saying their name and "What a great face!"

Math Center

Teacher Talk
God made each one of us different.

Resources
mirrors, drawing paper, crayons, charcoal pencils

Have a mirror, drawing paper, and crayons or charcoal pencils available for each place at this center. Encourage the children to look in the mirror and draw their faces. Remember to provide different shades of drawing paper to match the shades of skin of the children in your class. Post the children's work. This is part of the math center because it deals with spatial relationships and shapes. It could be in the art center instead.

Art Center

Teacher Talk
Each one of us is special.

Resources
paper plates or shapes cut from paper, glue, yarn, crayons or markers

Have different shapes, such as ovals or squares, already cut out for faces. Let each child make a face on a paper shape or paper plate. Allow the children to glue pieces of yarn on the faces to make hair and to decorate the faces with crayons or markers.

Home Living Center

Teacher Talk
Each one of us is different.

Resources
mirror, face cream or after-shave, dolls

Let the children enjoy playing house. You may include a makeup mirror and gentle face cream or watered down after-shave. Have the children look in the mirror and apply the cream or after-shave. Be sure to include dolls with different skin tones and of different ethnic representations.

Writing Center

Teacher Talk
God loves each one of us.

Resources
name cards, half sheets of plain paper, crayons or markers

Keep name cards of the children in the center for them to see and copy. Add the word "Face" in the writing center for the children to see. Include half sheets of plain paper. Let the children use crayons or markers to draw faces on the papers.

Worship Center

Teacher Talk
God loves you just the way you are.

Resources
sugar cookies, icing tubes

Provide plain sugar cookies. Let the children take turns using icing tubes to make faces on their cookies before eating them.

Say: Each one of us has our own face. God made each one of us to look different. God loves us just the way we are.

Pray: Thank you, God, for our faces. Thank you for fun food to eat. Amen.

Wonder Time

Call the children for together time.

Open the Bible to 1 Peter 5:7.

Say: "God cares about you" (1 Peter 5:7, adapted).

Have the children repeat the Bible verse.

Wonder Question: I wonder why God made each of us different?
Say : I see Alicia's face, and Mario's face, and so forth.
Show the faces the children created in the art center. Help the children pick out distinctive features in their faces such as dimples, smiles, blue eyes, rosy cheeks, long eyelashes, and so forth.
Read the Bible verse.
Say: Each one of us is special. God loves and cares about *(name each child)*.
Sing: "God Cares" (*see page 212*).
Pray: Thank you, God, for our faces and all that makes us special. Amen.

Group Fun

Resources

plastic foam cups, markers, potting soil, grass seed, spoon, table covering, watering can, water

Tell the children they will make faces that can grow hair.

Cover the table with newspapers or other table covering. Give each child a plastic foam cup. Let the children use markers to draw faces on the cups. Help the children spoon potting soil into each cup until the cup is about ¾-full. Let the children sprinkle grass seed on the soil. Spoon a little more soil on top of the seeds. Let the children pour a small amount of water on the soil. When the grass seed grows, the faces will have hair.

Goodbye Circle

As you call the children together to say goodbye, ask each child to show you his or her face. Repeat the Bible verse.

Pray: Thank you, God, for our faces. Amen.

Evaluation

How did the children react to their own faces? Are there children who are having trouble adjusting to preschool? Discover their interests from their parents and add centers that they will find interesting. Look back at your objectives to see if each child met each one. Make plans to involve each child in achieving each objective.

Lesson 3

My Home

Teacher Talk:

God plans for all children to have homes and families.

Tell me about your home.

Thank you, God, for our homes.

Goals:

To understand that there are different kinds of homes.

To learn that God plans for all children to have homes and families.

To be thankful for their homes.

Objectives: By the end of this session the children will:

Draw their own homes.

Talk about different homes.

Build homes with blocks.

Faith Connections

Bible verse: God cares about you. (1 Peter 5:7, adapted)

Be aware of the different kinds of homes your children live in. God plans for each one of us to have a home. Every home has value in God's sight. Take time with the children to talk about and to thank God for the things homes do for us like give us shelter, give us a place to sleep, give us a place to eat, and give us a place for our families to live.

Teacher's Prayer

May each child's home be filled with love, O God, and may each child learn of you. Amen.

Center Time

Display pictures of different kinds of homes.

Home Living Center

Teacher Talk

Tell me about your home.

Resources

play items for eating area, sleeping area, and family room; toy cleaning equipment

Expand your home living center to include an eating area, a sleeping area, and a family room with games and a pretend TV. Encourage the children to talk about their homes. Cleaning equipment such as toy mops, brooms, buckets, and so forth can also be used.

Worship Center

Teacher Talk

God plans for all living things to have homes.

Resources

piece of tree trunk or tree bark; plastic container with dirt and earthworms; plastic container with sand, water, and shells

Place a piece of a tree trunk or tree bark; a plastic container with dirt and earthworms; and a plastic container with sand, water, and sea shells on the science table. Let the children explore the different homes represented: wood for beetles and other insects, earth for worms, and water and shells for sea creatures.

Say: God plans for all living things to have homes. What is your home like?

Pray: Thank you, God, for our homes. Amen.

Special Center

Teacher Talk

God plans for different kinds of homes.

Resources

play house or table and sheets, books, soft pillows, doll houses

Set up a play house or construct a pretend house using tables and sheets. Limit the play houses to 3 or 4 children inside at a time. Put books and soft pillows in the house for relaxing.

If you have doll houses, put them out for free time or center time.

Math Center

Teacher Talk

God plans for all children to have homes and families.

Resources

tracing paper or typing paper, different kinds of rulers, pencils, masking tape, pictures of houses

Provide pencils, tracing paper or typing paper, rulers, triangle rulers, and so forth. Let the children play with drawing ruler lines. Use masking tape to hold down the ruler on the paper for younger children. This will make it easier for them to draw the line.

Cut out pictures of houses from your local newspaper or from house magazines. Point out the windows and doors on the pictures.

Building Center

Teacher Talk

Thank you, God, for our homes.

Resources

manipulatives such as Duplo blocks, Lincoln Logs building toys, or wooden blocks

Allow children to build shelters out of whatever manipulatives you have. They can use Duplo blocks to build a house for a Duplo blocks person. They can use Lincoln Logs building toys or wooden blocks to build houses. As the children build, talk about what homes do for us, such as give us shelter, give us a place to sleep, give us a place to eat, give our family a place to live.

Open the Bible to 1 Peter 5:7.

Say: "God cares about you" (1 Peter 5:7, adapted).

Have the children repeat the Bible verse.

Wonder Time

Welcome the children to the circle. Continue to call children by name.

Wonder Question: I wonder what your home is like?
Ask: Who lives in your home? What do you like best about your home?
Talk with the children about different types of homes (apartments, houses, trailers, and so forth). Show the children pictures of different homes. Include pictures of animals' and insects' homes.
Read the Bible verse.
Say: God plans for all children to have homes and families.
Pray: Thank you, God, for my home. Amen.
Sing: "God Cares" (*see page 212*).
Play a movement game. Choose a game that has a "home" place in it, such as "Duck, Duck, Goose."

Group Fun

Resources

large sheets of construction paper, construction paper cut into different shapes, scissors, glue

Cut construction paper into a variety of shapes including triangles, squares, rectangles, and circles. Make sure you have shapes in all sizes and colors. Give each child a large sheet of construction paper for a background. Tell the children that they may use different shapes to build their homes. Let the children glue the shapes to the background pages to make their homes. To add dimension to the houses, show the children how to glue on doors that open.

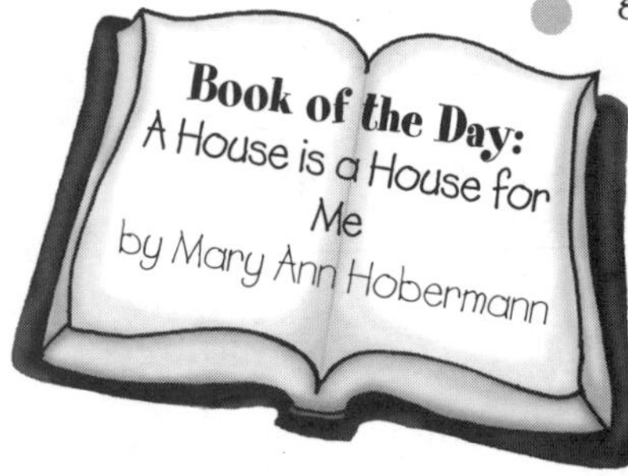

Goodbye Circle

Suggest that children go home and go in every room in their home and say, "What a great place!"

Pray: Thank you, God, for my home. Amen.

Evaluation

Did you meet the objectives? Have you learned information that will help you be a better teacher?

Lesson 4

My Family

Goals:

To celebrate family life.

To learn the importance of family.

To learn what families do.

To understand God's plan for families.

Objectives: By the end of this lesson children will:

Talk about their families.

Act out different people in families.

Make paintings for their families.

Faith Connections

Bible verse: Respect your father and your mother.

(Exodus 20:12, *Good News Bible*)

God plans for family members to take care of one another. Let the children tell you about their families. Remind the children that each family is different, yet all families are loved by God.

Teacher's Prayer

Help me to be open to the parents of the children in my class. Help us to work together for the child's sake. Amen.

Teacher Talk:

God plans for family members to take care of one another.

You are an important part of your family.

Each family is different.

God loves your family.

Center Time

Add pictures that show different kinds of families.

> As children arrive, say, "You are important to your family."

Math Center

Teacher Talk
God plans for families.

Resources
paper, pencils, craft sticks, crayons or markers, fabric squares, magazine pages cut into shapes, glue

Have paper and pencils available for the children to write numbers if they are interested and able.

Have craft sticks available so the children can count out one stick for each family member. Let them include whomever they think of as family members, including those who do not live with the family and pets.

Let the children draw faces on the sticks and then dress them to represent each family member. Dress them by having available fabric and magazine pages cut into squares, rectangles, and triangles. Show the children how to glue the materials onto sticks to make a person.

Home Living Center

Teacher Talk
God plans for family members to take care of one another.

Resources
pictures of families cut from magazines or family pictures from the children

Continue to use items found in the home. You may want to do your cooking for today *(see cooking center)* in the home living center. Locate pictures of families or have the children bring family pictures to put in the family center.

As the children play in the home living center, encourage them to play family by asking them who is the mother or the baby or the grandmother.

Worship Center

Teacher Talk
God loves all families.

Resources
drawing paper or construction paper, leaves cut from construction paper, glue, marker

Draw a tree trunk on a piece of paper for each child. Cut leaf shapes from construction paper. Write the name of one family member on each leaf. Let the child glue the leaves onto the tree.

Say: Each family is different. God loves all families.

Pray: Thank you, God, for families. Amen.

Cooking Center

Teacher Talk
Families work and play together.

Resources
ingredients for rice treats, saucepan, mixing bowl, large spoon, measuring cups and spoons, plastic resealable bags, stove

Let the children take turns measuring, pouring, and stirring to make rice treats for a snack and to take home to their families.

Rice Treats

12 ounces semi-sweet chocolate chips
1 stick margarine
½ cup peanut butter
12 ounces Rice Chex cereal
2 cups powdered sugar

Melt the margarine in a saucepan. Add the peanut butter and chocolate chips and stir them together until everything is melted and mixed together. Remove pan from stove.

Add the melted ingredients and the Rice Chex cereal together in a bowl. Let the children mix. Put the powdered sugar into a plastic bag. Let the children take turns putting some of the mixture into the bag and shaking the bag to coat the mixture. Scoop some of the rice treats into small plastic bags for the children to take home.

Wonder Time

Call the children together.

Wonder Question: I wonder what it means to be a family?
Ask: Who is in your family?
Talk about different kinds of families.
Say: Families are people who care about each other and usually live together. *(Be sure to include in your examples of families all the different types of families today: men and women with no children, mothers and fathers with children, mothers with children, fathers with children, and grandmothers and/or grandfathers raising children. Be sure to include examples of your children's families.)*
Read the Bible verse.
Say: Each family is different. God plans for children to live in families.
Sing: "Thank You, God, for Loving Me" *(see page 212).*
Pray: Thank you, God, for *(name each child)*'s family. Amen.

Open the Bible to Exodus 20:12.

Say: "Respect your father and your mother" (Exodus 20:12, *Good News Bible*).

Have the children repeat the Bible verse.

Group Fun

Resources

watercolors; watercolor paintbrushes; plastic containers of water; paper; bowl of fruit, vase of flowers, or stuffed bear

Ask the children if their families have any paintings or pictures hanging in their homes. Tell them they are going to get to paint beautiful pictures for their families.

Have watercolors for each child or every two children. Give each child a piece of plain paper. Show the children how to use the paints and to clean their brushes in the clear water. You may also have a bowl of fruit, a vase of flowers, or a stuffed bear in the middle of each table for children to use in their paintings.

Goodbye Circle

Let children share their art work. Teach the rhyme:

F - A - M - I - L - Y (spell letters once)
Family, Family
You and I

Say this several times and encourage children to say it to their family members when they go home.

Pray: Thank you, God, for our families. Amen.

Evaluation

Are there ways you can help the families of your children? Are you having trouble in any center? You might want to close it for a while and then slowly introduce it to the children.

Lesson 5

My Class

Teacher Talk:

You are an important part of our class.

I'm glad you are here today.

You are special to God.

I like the way you are working together.

Goals:

To understand that each child is an important part of the class.

To get to know the other children in the class.

To know the teachers' names and their jobs.

Objectives: By the end of this session the children will:

Say the name of each classmate and each teacher.

Join with the whole class in an art project.

Play a singing game with class members.

Go on a walk with class members.

Faith Connections

Bible verse: For we are partners working together for God.

(1 Corinthians 3:9, *Good News Bible*)

Preschool children are beginning to move from playing side-by-side to playing with friends. Sharing is still hard, but it needs to be encouraged. "Catch" your children sharing. Compliment them on how well they are working together. Help your children see that everyone in your class is important to you, to the other teachers, and to God.

Teacher's Prayer

O God, these are my children. Help me to shape this class into a family. Amen.

Center Time

Display a class picture where the children will see it when they enter the room.

Math Center

Teacher Talk

You are an important part of our class.

Resources

items for counting, counting board

Have items such as plastic counting bears available for counting out the number of children in your class. You can have three different colored items to count; for example, red for boys, green for girls, and yellow for teachers. Make a counting board with dots for each person so the children can cover the dots with the counters.

Manipulatives Center

Teacher Talk

I like the way you are working together.

Resources

play dough, cutting and rolling instruments

To encourage conversation with classmates, have play dough (*see recipe below*) available with cutting and rolling instruments. As the children play with the dough be sure to use their names and encourage them to talk with each other with comments such as, "Ellen, did you see Alex's dog?" or "Our class is so much fun."

Play Dough

1 cup flour
1 cup water
½ cup salt
1 tablespoon cream of tartar
few drops of food coloring

Mix dry ingredients together. Mix water and food coloring together. Combine dry and wet ingredients together in a pan and cook on high. Stir constantly. Remove from heat when play dough becomes rubbery with a slightly salty crust. Cool. Knead until smooth. Store in plastic bag or other airtight container.

Worship Center

Teacher Talk

We can thank God for our class.

Resources

cardboard pieces to make a pie or pizza; an edible pie or pizza; or puzzles

Use items to show parts and whole such as pieces of a pie or a pizza or a puzzle. Make pie or pizza puzzles from round cardboard. Cut the pie or pizza into pieces. Talk about how all the pieces go together to make the whole. Let children put the puzzle together.

Say: We are all part of our class. Everyone is important.

Pray: Thank you, God, for our class. Thank you for (*name each child and teacher*). Amen.

Art Center

Teacher Talk

You are special to God.

Resources

strips of white paper, crayons or multicultural crayons, tape or glue

Cut white paper into two-inch-wide strips. Give each child a strip of paper. Have the child write his or her name on the strip. Or have the child color the strip with crayons. Let the children choose their favorite colors, or have the children choose the color that matches their skin color or eye color. Help the children work together to loop the strips together to form a class chain. Secure each loop with tape or glue. Let the children help you decide where to display the class chain in your room.

Open the Bible to 1 Corinthians 3:9.

Say: "For we are partners working together for God" (1 Corinthians 3:9, *Good News Bible*).

Have the children repeat the Bible verse.

Wonder Time

As the children gather, make comments about the class.

Wonder Question: I wonder why our class is so special?

Say: We have so many creative boys and girls in our class. We will wait for each child in our class to come to the carpet because each of you is important.

Talk about what the children did in the centers. As a review, you can talk about homes and families, their faces, or their names.

Say: You are a very special group of boys and girls; there is no other class in the whole world exactly like ours. Why is it special? Because each person in it is special to God.

Sing: "I Want a Friend" *(see page 211).*

Read the Bible verse.

Say: We are all special in our class. We can all work together.

Pray: Thank you, God, for our class. Thank you for (*name each child and teacher*).

Take a walk. Encourage each child to find a partner to walk with on a class outing. If you cannot walk outside today, just walk through your building.

Group Fun

Resources

mural paper, crayons or markers, collage materials, glue

When you return from your walk let the children tell you what they saw on the walk. After your discussion, introduce the group activity. Tell the children that they are going to work together to make a class mural.

Place mural paper on the table or floor. Ask the children what they would like to draw that they saw on the walk. Younger children will need a separate place on the mural paper to draw their pictures; or you can give each child a piece of drawing paper, and then post the pictures on a class mural. Five-year-olds can tell you what they want to include in the mural and then choose a part to draw. Remember, grass and sky and clouds are all important parts of a mural. Make the mural three-dimensional by having the children glue on collage materials such as cotton balls, fringed paper, and cupcake papers.

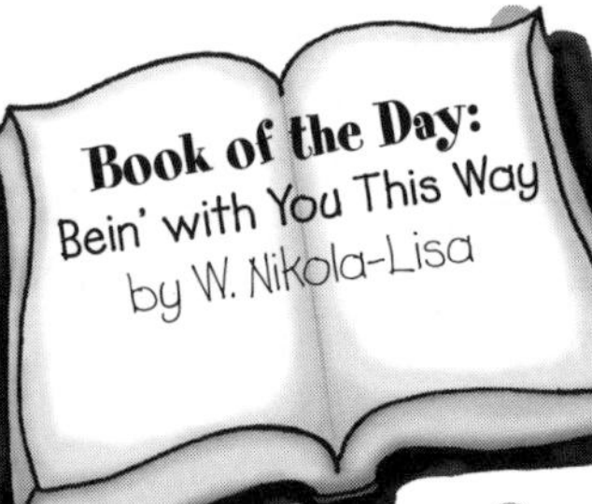

Goodbye Circle

Sing "Will You Be a Friend of Mine?" (*see page 211*). Be sure you include each child in the song. Have the children sit in a circle and hold hands to pray.

Pray: Thank you, God, for our class. Thank you for (*name each child and teacher*).

Evaluation

How is it going? Are all the children feeling that they are part of the whole class? Do the children know your name? Do they know the names of their classmates?

MEET ME

This week the children will share with each other their likes and dislikes. Help them see that as they tell what they like and dislike, others in the class get to know them better. Also, as the children discover and express their likes and dislikes, they are learning about the items they experience. This week they will discover a variety of foods, a variety of places, a variety of fun things to do, and what it means to be a friend.

Be sure to check your application blanks for food and other allergies as you allow the children to experience different things this week.

I Like to Eat

Goals:

To help the children discover and express their likes and dislikes.

To experience different kinds of foods.

Objectives: By the end of this session the children will:

Taste different foods and tell about foods they like and dislike.

Hear about foods that are healthy.

Teacher Talk:

We thank God for good things to eat.

What's your favorite food to eat?

Faith Connections

Bible verse: O taste and see that the LORD is good. (Psalm 34:8)

Even young children have definite preferences for what they like to eat. Help your children experience different kinds of food. Help the children see that God made many good foods. Since we are all different we will all like different things to eat.

Teacher's Prayer

Help me to know these children better that I may be a better teacher. Amen.

Center Time

Set up your centers as described at the beginning of this unit. For this lesson add the following:

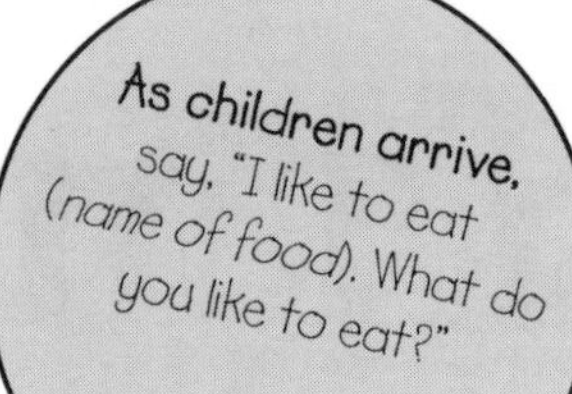

Math Center

Teacher Talk

We can thank God for different kinds of food.

Resources

small carrots, celery chunks, cheese chunks, or other finger foods

Include a variety of foods for the children to prepare and taste: small carrots, celery chunks, cheese chunks, apples, bananas, and so forth. Encourage the children to use vegetable brushes to wash the fruit and vegetables. Let them help you prepare the food. Slice each piece so that the children can see the patterns and seeds inside. Then have the children count or categorize the different foods.

Science Center

Teacher Talk

We can grow food that is good to eat.

Resources

bean seeds, paper towel, water, glass jar

Let the children plant bean seeds. Put a piece of paper towel around the inside of a small glass jar. Put about a half inch of water in the bottom of the jar. Plant the seeds between the paper and the side of the jar. The paper will absorb the water and nourish the plants. The children can watch their seeds grow.

Art Center

Teacher Talk

We can thank God for good things to eat.

Resources

play dough

Allow children to play with play dough. Encourage them to make their favorite foods.

Home Living Center

Teacher Talk

We thank God for good things to eat.

Resources

play foods

Let the children pretend to shop and then to serve the play foods to one another.

Cooking Center

Teacher Talk

God gives us healthy things to eat.

Resources

ingredients for dip

Let the children make a dip for the vegetables they washed in the Math Center.

Vegetable Dip

1 cup cottage cheese
⅓ cup grated cheddar cheese
1 teaspoon dried dillweed
2 teaspoons Worcestershire sauce
½ teaspoon salt

Mix cottage cheese and cheddar cheese in a large bowl. Let the children take turns stirring. Add the dillweed, Worcestershire sauce, and salt. Mix together again.

Worship Center

Teacher Talk

Thank you, God, for good things to eat.

Resources

pictures of food from magazines.

Let the children talk about the foods they like and dislike.

Say: God planned for many different kinds of food.

Pray: Thank you, God, for food. It makes us strong and healthy. Amen.

Wonder Time

As the children gather in the circle, talk with them about the foods they tasted.

Open the Bible to Psalm 34:8.

Say: "O taste and see that the LORD is good" (Psalm 34:8).

Have the children repeat the Bible verse.

Wonder Question: How do you know if you like or dislike a food?

Provide an unusual food for the children to taste and tell whether they like or dislike it.

Make a graph. Show the children a graph you have made on a large piece of mural paper. Place a picture and the name of each of the foods at the top of the paper. Under the name of each food make two columns, one for like and one for dislike. Draw a line down the page so like and dislike are separated from each other. Give each child a sticker and ask him or her whether he or she likes or dislikes a food. Be sure to allow each child to say the word "like" or "dislike." After each child has stated his or her choice, ask all the likes to come and put their stickers in the like column. Ask the dis likes to put their stickers in the dislike column. Some children will change their mind, which is okay. After all the children have registered their preferences, ask the children to count with you the number of stickers in each column.

Sing: "I'm Thankful," verse 1 (*see page 215*).

Read the Bible verse.

Say: God is good. God has given us many different kinds of food to eat.

Pray. Tell the children your prayer is a thank you to God for special foods we eat. You say, "Thank you God for food to eat, for..." Then encourage each child to say the name of a food for which she or he is thankful.

Group Fun

Resources

food utensils such as spoons, potato mashers, vegetable brushes, scrubbers, sponges, and so forth; paint, shallow trays, construction paper, table covering, smocks

Cover the table and have the children wear smocks. Provide a variety of food utensils and construction paper. Have two or three colors of paint in shallow trays on each table. Allow the children to dip the utensils into the paint and use them to make prints on the construction paper.

Goodbye Circle

Show the food graph to them again. Encourage them to find a new food to taste before tomorrow.

Pray: Thank you, God, for good food to eat. Amen.

Evaluation

Did the children share their likes and dislikes? Do you think they feel special in your class? Did you discover any "likes" you can serve for snacks another day? Pray for God's help in understanding and helping each child.

Lesson 7

I Like to Play

Teacher Talk:

Playing is fun.

God plans for us to have time to play.

Playing helps us grow and learn.

We thank God for time to play.

Goal:

To help children feel good about their play.

Objectives: By the end of this session the children will:

Play alone and play with each other.

Talk about the games they play.

Play inside and outside.

Faith Connections

Bible verse: Be happy and glad. (Matthew 5:12, *Good News Bible*)

The session should include fun activities the children enjoy. Play is one way children learn to practice kindness, sharing, cooperation, and patience. As they play they learn to be peacemakers; they learn to express their feelings; and they learn how to overcome obstacles without becoming discouraged.

Teacher's Prayer

O God, help me learn when to intervene and when to stay back so that the children can learn from their play. Amen.

Center Time

Have a new toy or toys that are not available for the children to play with all the time out in your center area today.

As children arrive, use phrases such as "playing is fun," "playing is hard work," and "playing helps us to grow."

Home Living Center

Teacher Talk

Playing is fun.

Resources

family clothes, party clothes, clown costumes, party hats, party decorations, dolls, pretend or real birthday cake

Include family clothes and party clothes for the children to play dress-up. Add clown costumes, party hats, and party decorations. Help the children pretend to have a birthday party for one of the dolls in the center. They can even wrap pretend presents for the party. Bake a cake (pretend or real).

Science Center

Teacher Talk

God plans for us to have time to play.

Resources

large clock face with moving hands

Show the children the times when they do different things. Tell them when it is "time for centers" or "time to come to the circle." **Ask:** "How long do we have for play?"

Math Center

Teacher Talk

We can learn when we play.

Resources

numbers cut from posterboard or foam board, paper, crayons

Let the children play with numbers. You can cut numbers from zero through nine out of posterboard or foam board. Let the children make designs with the numbers, put them in order, stack them, or draw them on paper—whatever is fun for each child.

Building Center

Teacher Talk

Play helps us grow and learn.

Resources

blocks, cardboard people figures, toy cars, plastic or wooden zoo animals, play items

Enhance the center today with toy cars, cardboard people figures, zoo animals, or other play items. Instead of the usual block play, encourage children to build a particular item such as a boat, plane, or zoo. Have your snack time at the place the children have built.

Art Center

Teacher Talk

God plans for us to play.

Resources

pictures from school supply catalogue, construction paper, glue

Cut out pictures of various items the children might like to play with. Have them choose which would be their favorites. Give each child a piece of construction paper. Let the children glue the pictures onto their paper.

Worship Center

Teacher Talk

We thank God for time to play.

Resources

play dough, Duplo blocks, table games, and so forth

Choose some of the children's favorite table toys for play today.

Say: God plans for us to have time to play. When we play by ourselves and with our friends we are learning and growing.

Pray: Thank you, God, for time to play. Amen.

Open the Bible to Matthew 5:12.

Say: "Be happy and glad" (Matthew 5:12, *Good News Bible*).

Have the children repeat the Bible verse.

Wonder Time

Invite the children to together time.

Wonder Question: *What do you like to play?*
Talk about the importance of moving our bodies. Help the children see the difference between watching television or videos and playing.
Sing: "Will You Be a Friend of Mine?" (*see page 211*).
Read the Bible verse.
Say: *God plans for us to have happy times when we can play.*
Pray: *Thank you, God, for play. Amen.*
Encourage the children to help you make a list of the rules of play.
Ask: *What must we do to make our play safe and happy?*

RULES FOR SAFE PLAY

- Always tell your parents or your teacher where you are playing.
- Take care of your toys and the toys of other children.
- Follow playground rules for the equipment, such as going up the slide only by the ladder.
- Never talk to strangers when you are playing.
- Keep outdoor plants and things on the ground out of your mouth.
- Throwing sand and rocks hurts; don't do it.
- Listen to your teachers and parents for safe play.
- Share your toys with other children.
- Give everyone a chance to play.
- Be kind.

Group Fun

Resources

tent, books, blankets or sleeping bags, toy musical instruments; buckets of water, paint-brushes; mural paper tempera paint, paint-brushes, paper towels

Plan to have an extended play time outside or inside. Add new items to the playground such as a tent with books in it, blankets or sleeping bags for the children to lie on and look at the sky, or toy musical instruments for a parade. If it is warm enough outside, enjoy water play with buckets of water and paintbrushes used to "paint" the fence, the sidewalk, or the building.

You can also attach mural paper to the fence in the playground and let the children paint with tempera paints and brushes. Just be sure to have a bucket of water to rinse hands and lots of paper towels.

Goodbye Circle

Tell the children you had fun playing with them today and to remember that play is important.

Pray: *Thank you, God, for play. Amen.*

Evaluation

Do some children have an easier time playing than others? Help those who stand back and have difficulty jumping in.

Lesson 8

I Like My Friends

Goals:

To help the children think about what it means to be a friend.

To enjoy doing things with their friends.

To help the children discover that friends come in all ages.

Objectives: By the end of this session the children will:

Enjoy the friendship of an older person, a teen, or an adult.

Talk about how to be a good friend.

Make a friendship bracelet.

Thank God for friends.

Faith Connections

Bible verse: A friend loves at all times. (Proverbs 17:17)

Preschoolers love to have friends. They may proclaim another child as their friend one day and not their friend the next. They need help in learning the loving qualities of friendship.

Teacher's Prayer

O God, some of my children make friends so easily and some have a more difficult time. Help them to be open to others. Amen.

Teacher Talk:

A friend is a gift from God.

I'm glad you're my friend.

We have lots of friends in our class.

God plans for us to have friends.

Thank you, God, for friends.

Center Time

Display pictures of children playing and working together.

As children arrive, say, "Look who's here. It's our friend (*child's name*)!"

Math Center

Teacher Talk

God gave us friends.

Resources

jars, peanuts in the shell or individually-wrapped candies, napkins

Ask the children to get a friend to help them. One child will place peanuts in the jar while the other child counts. Or one will put peanuts in the jar in secret, and the other will try to guess how many there are. After counting them, divide the peanuts and eat them. For children who are allergic to peanuts, you may substitute individually-wrapped candies.

Art Center

Teacher Talk

We have many friends here at school.

Resources

crayons, mural paper or construction paper

Draw outlines of the children. Let them lie on large mural paper and pose any way they wish. After their outlines are drawn, let the children draw in their faces and their hair. These portraits will be available for the children to work on next week.

Music Center

Teacher Talk

I like to play with my friends.

Resources

cassettes or CDs, cassette or CD player

Play music and let the children move to the music with a partner. Choose different varieties of music.

Choose one child to be the leader and one to be the mirror. Have the leader move his or her arms or legs. Have the mirror move his or her arms or legs the same way.

Worship Center

Teacher Talk

We thank God for our friends.

Resources

blank tape, cassette recorder

Have the children come one at a time and say his or her name into the cassette recorder. Rewind the tape.

Pray: Thank you, God for (*play the tape and listen to the children say their names*).

Building Center

Teacher Talk

Friends help each other.

Resources

blocks

Direct block play today by telling the children that we are building a big boat that all of us can ride in. Encourage the children to do creative problem solving to plan and build the boat. As they build, use phrases such as, "Josh needs a friend to help him hold up the corner" or "Sarah Anne and her friends are making seats for everyone."

Manipulatives Center

Teacher Talk

Friends work together.

Resources

paper squares (red, blue, green, yellow), glue, drawing paper

With a partner, have each child use the colored squares of paper to make a pattern. One child will get blue and green; the other child will get red and yellow. Have the children glue their colored squares of paper to drawing paper to make a pattern.

Wonder Time

Invite an older adult, a teen, or if you are in a large school, an older elementary child to come and visit with the children.

Wonder Question: *What does it mean to be a good friend?*

Have your guest read the book of the day.

Thank the person reading the story. *Tell the children this person is their friend who cares about them and has done something nice for them.*

Sing: *"I Want a Friend"* *(see page 211).*

Read the Bible verse.

Let the children tell you how to be a good friend.

Pray: *Thank you, God, for our friends. Amen.*

Open the Bible to Proverbs 17:17.

Say: "A friend loves at all times" (Proverbs 17:17).

Have the children repeat the Bible verse.

Group Fun

Resources

construction paper or file folders, magazine pictures of personal items and clothes, scissors, glue, pretend boat, bowl, name cards, simple snack

Tell the children they are going on a pretend trip with their friends and that they need to get their suitcases ready.

Give each child a piece of construction paper. Show the children how to fold their papers in half to make a pretend suitcase. Provide pre-cut magazine pictures of personal items and clothes that people might take on trips. Let the children choose from the pictures and glue their choices on their paper suitcases. Older children may cut out the pictures themselves. (Option: Use a file folder and add yarn for the handle.)

Say: *"Now we are ready for our trip. We get to take a friend on our trip."*

Help the children choose a partner by drawing names from a bowl. (Beforehand, put half the group's names in a bowl. Let the other half draw out the names until everyone has a partner.) Have the children hold their suitcases and stand with their partners. Lead the pairs around the room to the boat made during center time (*see building center*). Ask your guest to take up pretend tickets as each child gets on the boat. Pretend to see things such as bridges, animals, people, and buildings from the boat. Talk about what the children put in their suitcases. Serve a simple snack on the boat.

Goodbye Circle

After your busy day you may wish to say goodbye in the boat.

Pray: *Thank you, God, for all our friends at school and all our friends at home. Amen.*

Evaluation

Think of ways you can help the children make friends.

Lesson 9

I Like to Explore

Teacher Talk:

God has made a wonderful world.

Thank you, God, for everything you have made.

Let's explore!

Goals:

To encourage the children to explore the world outside.

To encourage the children to ask questions.

To encourage the children to think about a variety of answers to questions.

Objectives: By the end of this session the children will:

Enjoy exploring the out-of-doors.

Ask questions about things important to them.

Wonder about creation.

Faith Connections

Bible verse: I will tell of all the wonderful things God has done. (Psalm 9:1, *Good News Bible*, adapted)

God created a wonderful world. Preschoolers learn best when they are able to experience God's world with all of their being. They can experience the joy of discovery and share it with others.

Teacher's Prayer

Teach me to explore more, O God. Help me to be willing to try new things. Amen.

Center Time

Prepare the centers with lots of new things for the children to explore.

As children arrive, say, "Come and see what we have in our class today!"

Picture Table

Teacher Talk

I can learn about God's world.

Resources

magazine pictures, scissors, envelopes

Cut large pictures out of magazines. Pictures of creation, nature, plants, and animals will best fit the theme for the day. Cut each picture into four or five puzzle pieces. Put only one piece in the center, put the others in an envelope. Let the children choose a piece and talk about what might be in the whole picture. Reveal the whole pictures at Wonder Time.

Building Center

Teacher Talk

God's world is fun to explore.

Resources

building toys with batteries, Duplo blocks, butcher paper, crayons

Make a neighborhood to explore. Use blocks for buildings. Use butcher paper. Put houses on the butcher paper. Draw in the streets and so forth.

Science Center

Teacher Talk

I learn about God's world by asking questions.

Resources

magnets and various items that are attracted to magnets and items that are not attracted to magnets

Provide magnets of different strengths and sizes. Put various items that are attracted to magnets and various items that are not in this center. Let the children tell why they think some things "stick" to the magnet and other things don't.

Art Center

Teacher Talk

I enjoy exploring colors in God's world.

Resources

tempera paint, water, construction paper, spoons, table coverings, smocks

Cover the table and have the children wear smocks. Give each children a piece of construction paper. Thin tempera paint with water. Spoon two or three globs of different colors of paint onto each child's paper. Have the children twist their papers back and forth to make the paint run in different directions.

Let the children continue to work on their paper outlines (*see Art Center, page 34*).

Home Living Center

Teacher Talk

I can be an explorer.

Resources

costumes or clothing worn by explorers, astronauts, and scientists

Have the children pretend to be the person that might wear those clothes. Think about and then act out what that person might do and what they might explore.

Worship Center

Teacher Talk

Thank you, God, for a world to explore.

Resources

various items from nature (rocks, shells, leaves, sand, seeds, and so forth)

Have the children explore the different textures and surfaces of the various objects on the table.

Say: God has made a wonderful world.

Pray: Thank you, God, for a world to explore. Amen.

Open the Bible to Psalm 9:1.

Say: "I will tell of all the wonderful things God has done" (Psalms 9:1, *Good News Bible*, adapted).

Have the children repeat the Bible verse.

Wonder Time

As the children gather, talk about the things they did in their centers. Help to clear up any misinformation which might have occurred as the children explored new items. Reveal the rest of the pictures from the Picture Table.

Wonder Question: I wonder how it feels to do something for the very first time?

Talk with the children about what it means to explore. Help them think of people who are explorers such as scientists, astronauts, and historical figures.

Read the Bible verse.

Sing the Bible verse to the tune of "The Wheels on the Bus" (see right).

> Oh, come tell the things
> that God has done,
> God has done,
> God has done,
> Oh, come tell the things
> that God has done,
> Wonderful things.
>
>

Pray: Thank you, God, for the many wonderful things we can explore in your world. Amen.

Group Fun

Resources

paper bags

Tell the children that God's world is for them to explore and that you are all going on an exploration walk. Talk about some of the things they might discover on the walk. Tell the children that they may pick up things from God's world and put them in their paper bags. Tell the children the types of nature items you are seeking. Discourage them from picking up any items that are not natural to the world, such as bottle caps, pieces of glass, cigarette butts, and so forth.

Go over safety rules before your walk. Give each child a paper bag. Encourage the children to place their items in the bags. The children can start collecting items as soon as they get outside. Do not rush them, but let them enjoy their discoveries. If it's a nice day, walk to a convenient spot and have a time of worship. Look at the children's discoveries and thank God for each one. Encourage questions and wondering about the objects they find.

Goodbye Circle

Tell the children we are all explorers in God's world. Ask them to tell you about their discoveries today.

Pray: Thank you, God, for the many wonderful things we can explore in your world. Amen.

Evaluation

Are there ways you can let the children explore in your class rather than telling them everything? As you develop centers, try to make them easy for the children to explore independently.

Lesson 10

I Like Me

Goals:

To review the past two weeks.

To remind the children of the things they like.

To help the children feel special in their homes and in your class.

To help the children appreciate their uniqueness.

Objectives: By the end of this session the children will:

Describe themselves.

Enjoy centers from past lessons.

Celebrate their uniqueness.

Faith Connections

Bible verse: We are God's children. (1 John 3:2)

We are created in the image of God. This makes us special. If we accept this as true, then how can we say that any person is not good enough? Each child is a gift and brings his or her own special talents to God's world.

Teacher's Prayer

O God, what gifts you have given me! How wonderful they are! Amen.

Note: Send a note home asking parents to send in baby pictures of the children to use with Lesson 11.

Teacher Talk:

You are a child of God.

You are special to me.

You are special to God.

I like you!

Center Time

Have mirrors around the room in which the children can see themselves.

Art Center

Teacher Talk

God made each person special.

Resources

fabric scraps, glue, paper outlines *(see page 34)*, construction paper, crayons or markers, scissors, tape, stapler, staples

Let the children who are interested glue fabric scraps on their paper outlines to make clothes.

Let the children make "I'm Special" crowns. Give each child two pieces of construction paper. Let the children decorate the strips with crayons or markers. Trace the child's handprint three or four times in a row across the long edge of one piece of paper. Place the second sheet of paper behind the tracing. Cut out both sheets around the fingertips. Leave the bottoms of the tracings uncut to make two crown strips. Write "I'm Special" across one strip. Tape or staple the strips together to make a crown. Remind the children that they are all children of God. Each one of them is special.

Writing Center

Teacher Talk

God made you special.

Resources

paper, markers, paper outline *(see page 34)*

As a child comes to the center, ask him or her, "Who are you?" Write down the child's name and the description they give you about what they like and who their family members are. These descriptions can be displayed beside the child's paper outline that was started in Lesson 8 (*see page* 34).

Worship Center

Teacher Talk

I am glad God made me.

Resources

tape recorder, mirror, blank tape

Have each child look in the mirror. Sing the song "Look in the Mirror" to the tune of "London Bridge."

Look in the Mirror

Look in the mirror, I see me.
I see me, I see me.
Look in the mirror, God made me.
I'm someone special.

Say: God made you. You see a special child of God in the mirror.

Pray: Thank you, God, for (*child's name*).

Manipulatives Center

Teacher Talk

God knows you and loves you just the way you are.

Resources

letter beads, plain beads, plastic lacing

Let the children make necklaces with letter beads. Letter beads and plastic lacing are available from your local craft store or the craft area in discount stores. Help the children find the letters in their names and place them on the table. Let the children make patterns for their necklaces by adding plain colored beads with their letter beads.

Give each child a piece of plastic lacing about 24 inches long. Tie a knot in one end of the lacing. Let each child string the beads on the lacing. Tie a knot in the other end of the lacing when the child is finished stringing beads. Tie the ends of the lacings together to finish the necklace.

Wonder Time

As the children gather ask them to be thinking about their friends and about something they know about their friends.

Wonder Question: I wonder why everyone is not alike?

Ask: What makes us different from one another? Let the children talk about the differences they recognize.

Say the action poem *(see box)* **with the children.**

Sing: "Just the Way I Am" (*see page 214*).

Read the Bible verse.

Say: Each one of you is a child of God.

Pray: Thank you, God, for (*name each child and yourself*). Amen.

I like my eyes
(Point to eyes.)
And the nose on my face.
(Point to nose.)
I like my legs.
(Touch legs.)
See how they race?
(Run in place.)
I like my fingers;
(Hold up fingers.)
They can wave and wiggle.
(Wiggle fingers.)
I like my smile.
(Point to smile.)
I like my giggle.
(Hold hands over stomach; shake.)
God made me special
(Place hands over heart.)
As you can see.
(Point to eyes.)
God made me special,
(Place hands over heart.)
And I like me!
(Hug self.)

Words: Daphna Flegal

Open the Bible to 1 John 3:2.

Say: "We are God's children" (1 John 3:2).

Have the children repeat the Bible verse.

Group Fun

Resources

white T-shirts (one per child), large pieces of cardboard, three-dimensional fabric paint (various colors), wooden craft stick, wet paper towels, black permanent marker, recycled newspaper

Cover the tables with recycled newspaper. Slide a piece of cardboard inside the T-shirt between the front and the back to protect the paint from bleeding through. Write each child's name on the front of their T-shirt with the permanent marker. Have the children hold out their hands. Squirt the paint over their hands and fingers. Spread with a wooden craft stick. Then have the children press their hands onto the T-shirt around their names. Let the children choose the colors they want to use. Allow to dry. The paint will set after 24 hours and will be machine washable.

Goodbye Circle

Play a guessing game with the children. Say, "I am thinking about a special person who has a baby sister, who loves to play in the block center, and who has on brown pants." Let the children guess who you are describing. Older preschoolers will enjoy being the ones who describe the person.

Pray: Thank you, God, for each one of us. Amen.

Evaluation

Are there children you have difficulty liking? Try to get to know these children better. They may be feeling the same way about you.

I AM GROWING

This week we move beyond helping children know who they are by physical features and likes and dislikes to helping them see their abilities to make a difference in the life of their families and their class. This week we will talk about potentials. Help the children see ways of being caring, helpful children of God.

Lesson 11

Teacher Talk:

God plans for you to grow.

Look at how much you have grown.

You can do many things.

Thank you, God, for all the ways we are growing.

I Am Big

Goal:

To help the children see that they are growing big and strong.

To help the children discover that they are able to do many things.

Objectives: By the end of this session the children will:

Make their own growth charts.

Compare their sizes with something smaller and something larger.

Faith Connections

Bible verse: The child grew and became strong. (Luke 2:40)

Children like to see how much they have grown and are likely to enjoy showing you new skills as they develop. Talk about growth as part of God's plan for all things.

Teacher's Prayer

O God, as the children grow tall, help them to grow spiritually as well. Amen.

Center Time

If the children brought baby pictures, display them in the worship center.

As children arrive, weigh and measure each child. Write the weight and height on a 3"x 5" card. Cut a piece of ribbon as long as the child is tall. Encourage the children to take their ribbons and cards to the art center to make a growth chart.

Science Center

Teacher Talk
You are growing stronger.

Resources
variety of weights or plastic bottles and sand

Set out the weights (hand, ankle, or wrist weights). (Option: Fill plastic bottles with different amounts of sand so they will have different weights.) Let the children lift the different weights. Let them guess what weighs the most and what weighs the least.

Math Center

Teacher Talk
You are growing bigger.

Resources
Five to ten objects of different sizes

Have five to ten objects for the children to put in order from smallest to biggest. You can cut out different-sized circles, different-sized paper dolls, or use different sizes of crayons or chalk. Younger preschoolers can be given five objects to put in order.

Home Living Center

Teacher Talk
You are growing bigger and stronger.

Resources
clothes in different sizes

Include clothes of different sizes in the center from baby clothes to adult clothes. As the children play and discover the baby clothes, tell them they are big now and have grown from baby size to child size. When they try on the larger clothes, remind them that even though they are big now, God plans for them to grow bigger.

Building Center

Teacher Talk
God plans for you to grow bigger and stronger.

Resources
large and small blocks

Talk about how strong the children are to be able to lift and place blocks. Encourage the children to compare the big and small blocks.

Art Center

Teacher Talk
Growing big and strong are a part of God's plan.

Resources
height ribbons, rolled paper, glue, stickers, pre-cut magazine pictures, crayons

Cut a length of rolled paper a little longer than each child's height ribbon (*see "As children arrive" at top of page*). Encourage the children to glue their height ribbons to the paper to make a growth chart. Let the children decorate their charts with stickers, pre-cut magazine pictures, or crayons.

Worship Center

Teacher Talk
We can thank God that we grow.

Resources
baby pictures of children

Let the children look at the various baby pictures. Talk about what babies can do and what they cannot do.

Say: You can do many things now that you could not do when you were a baby.

Pray: Dear God, thank you for the ways we have grown. Amen.

Wonder Time

Open the Bible to Luke 2:40.

Say: "The child grew and became strong" (Luke 2:40).

Have the children repeat the Bible verse.

Have the children pretend to be babies and crawl to wonder time.

Wonder Question: *What can you do now that you couldn't do when you were babies?*
Say: God plans for each of us to grow and grow.
Sing: "God Plans for Many Growing Things" (*see page 213*). Have the children crouch down and slowly stand with arms above head.
Pray: Thank you, God, that (*name each child*) is growing big and strong. Amen.
Play a movement game. Say the following statements for the children, and have the children do the motions.

God loves us when we are babies. Let's crawl like babies. (*Crawl around the room.*)
God plans for us to grow. (*Crouch down and slowly stand with arms over head.*)
God loves us when we take our first steps. Let's walk with baby steps. (*Take baby steps around the room.*)
God plans for us to grow. (*Crouch down and slowly stand with arms over head.*)
God loves us when we grow big enough to march. Let's march! (*March around the room.*)
God plans for us to grow. (*Crouch down and slowly stand with arms over head.*)
God loves us when we grow big enough to hop. Let's hop! (*Hop around the room.*)
God plans for us to grow. (*Crouch down and slowly stand with arms over head.*)

Group Fun

Resources
balls, playground equipment

Plan some special outdoor activities in which the children can show their abilities: running, kicking a ball, or playing on playground equipment. Make sure the children know the safety rules.

Talk with the children about things they can do now that they couldn't do when they were smaller. Talk with the children about how dangerous it is to try to do things that we see bigger kids doing when we are not quite big enough.

Goodbye Circle

Ask the children how big boys and big girls help at home. Encourage them to find some ways to help at home tonight.

Pray: Thank you, God, for helping us grow big and strong. Amen.

Evaluation

Do the children realize that every day they are growing and changing and are able to do more and more? Do you encourage them to try new things?

Lesson 12

I Can Help

Goal:

For the children to think of themselves as persons who help others.

Objectives: By the end of this session the children will:

Help in their class.

Hear ways they can help at home and school.

Make cookies to share.

Make helping hands.

Faith Connections

Bible verse: Be kind to one another. (Ephesians 4:32)

Talk with the children about how Jesus must have helped his father Joseph in the carpenter's shop. Help the children think about the gifts they have been given to help others: hands to help, eyes to see when someone needs help, and so forth.

Teacher's Prayer

I need patience, O God, to let the children help as much as they can. Help me to wait. Amen.

Teacher Talk:

I like the way you are helping.

We can help in our classroom.

We can thank God for helpers.

Center Time

Have a variety of tasks that need to be completed in different places around the room

As children arrive, ask them to be your helpers. Direct each child to one of the tasks you have set up in today's centers.

Home Living Center

Teacher Talk

We can help in our classroom.

Resources

cleaning supplies such as child-size brooms, dustpans, dust cloths or paper towels, sponges

Provide cleaning supplies such as brooms and dustpans, dust cloths or paper towels, and sponges. One child might sweep the floor, one might dust the window sills or shelves, and one might wipe tables and chairs.

Science Center

Teacher Talk

Helping is fun.

Resources

smocks, scented shaving cream, sponges, dishpan, dishpan with water or sink

Have the children wear smocks to protect their clothing. Put scented shaving cream directly on the table top. Let the children enjoy fingerpainting with the shaving cream. Then give the children damp sponges to wipe the shaving cream off the tables into a dishpan. Rinse out the sponges in the sink or in a dishpan of water. Continue until the shaving cream is cleaned off. The table will be left clean.

Cooking Center

Teacher Talk

We can help others.

Resources

ingredients for peanut butter cookies, mixing bowl, mixing spoon, measuring cups and spoons, baking sheet, resealable plastic bags

Let the children make peanut butter balls to help someone on your staff feel special. Make enough for the children to enjoy some also.

Peanut Butter Balls

3 cups peanut butter
1⅓ cups honey
3½ cups graham cracker crumbs
2 cups raisins
2 cups dry milk

Mix 3 cups crumbs with dry milk and raisins. Save ½ cup of the crumbs to use later. Mix in honey and peanut butter (or orange juice). Roll into small balls. Place ½ cup of the crumbs into a large resealable plastic bag. Place three or four balls into the bag and seal shut. Shake the bag to cover the balls with the cracker crumbs. Remove the balls and place them on a baking sheet. Chill.

Art Center

Teacher Talk

God wants us to help others.

Resources

construction paper or foam sheets, scissors, collage materials, glue, clothesline, clothespins, marker

Give each child a piece of construction paper or a foam sheet. Have the child place a hand on the paper or sheet. Draw around the child's hand. Older children may cut out the handprints. Have glue and collage material available for each child to decorate his or her handprint. Hang the hand prints on a line with clothespins and label, "Our Helping Hands."

Worship Center

Teacher Talk

We can thank God for helpers.

Let the children act out ways they can help. One child might pretend to take out the trash, set the table, or pick up toys.

After each child performs a task, **Pray:** Thank you God for (*child's name*) who can (*name the activity the child acted out*).

Wonder Time

Invite the children to join you in your circle.

Wonder Question: What did you do to help in our class today?

Ask: Why did you help? (It gets things done. Others need our help. It's more fun to do things together. There are tasks that aren't really fun but need to be done.)

Sing: Have the children stand in a circle. Sing the words printed at the right to the tune of "This Is the Way." Choose a child to pantomime a way to help at home or at school such as sweeping, taking out the trash, washing dishes, or wiping tables. Then have everyone do the motion. Be sure to let the child tell you what he or she was doing when the verse is finished.

This is the way we help our moms,
Help our moms, help our moms.
This is the way we help our moms
So early in the morning.

This is the way we help our dads,
Help our dads, help our dads.
This is the way we help our dads
So early in the morning.

This is the way we help our teachers,
Help our teachers, help our teachers.
This is the way we help our teachers
So early in the morning.

Ask: What do you do to help at home? Who needs our help?

Talk with the children about looking for ways to help others.

Read the Bible verse.

Say: When we help others we are being kind.

Pray: Thank you, God, for every helper in our class. Teach us all to help others. Amen.

Open the Bible to Ephesians 4:32.

Say: "Be kind to one another" (Ephesians 4:32).

Have the children repeat the Bible verse.

Group Fun

Resources

box with lid, plain paper, stickers

Say: "We are going to help someone feel special by taking *(name of person)* some of the peanut butter balls that we made in center time. Let's all help decorate a box to put the balls in." Provide a box with a lid. If the box has writing on the outside, cover the box with plain paper. Cover the lid separately. Let the children decorate the box by placing stickers over the box and lid. Deliver the treat.

Goodbye Circle

Let the children tell you one thing they will do to help when they go home today. Look around your room and remind the children of all they have done to help today. Clap for a job well done.

Pray: Thank you, God, for every helper in our class. Teach us all to help others. Amen.

Evaluation

Think about the children who loved helping and those who were not interested in helping. Plan ways to encourage those children who don't like helping.

Lesson 13

I Can Move

Teacher Talk:

Joints help our bodies care for themselves. Knees help us walk and run and march. Elbows help us feed ourselves and wash ourselves.

Dance and twirl and feel your body move.

You are moving beautifully.

God plans for our bodies to move.

Goals:

To help the children enjoy the experience of moving their bodies.

To help the children learn that moving helps keep us healthy.

Objectives: By the end of this session the children will:

Sing and dance.

Stretch their muscles to music.

Play an active game.

Name moving as a way to keep their bodies healthy.

Faith Connections

Bible Verse: "I am wonderfully made." (Psalm 139:14, adapted)

Tell the children that God planned for us to have healthy bodies. Remind the children that they can use their bodies, their hands, and their feet to help others.

Teacher's Prayer

Remind me, O God, that I too can move. Give me strength to move with the children. Amen.

Center Time

Move furniture to make floor space for movement and dance. Play quiet music as the children arrive.

Art Center

Teacher Talk

You can move your fingers to make a picture.

Resources

smocks, table covering, fingerpaints, fingerpaint paper, large mirror

Have the children wear smocks and cover the table. Let the children fingerpaint to the music you are playing in the classroom. Place a large mirror flat on a table. Add fingerpaint to the mirror and let the children paint on the mirror. Or have fingerpaint and paper for each child at the center to make his or her own painting.

Fingerpaint Variations

• Tape wax paper to a cafeteria tray. Let the children apply paints.

• Pour a blob of liquid starch on the fingerpaint paper. Let the child sprinkle powdered paints into the starch and then paint.

• Allow the children to paint with their fingers, fists, lower arms, and elbows.

• Approach fingerpainting with the attitude that it is a process rather than a finished product.

• Use different mediums for painting: fingerpaints, hand cream, or shaving cream.

• Avoid using pudding, catsup, or other liquid foodstuff. Bacteria develops in the food when it is left to dry

• Encourage the children to make prints of their fingerpaints by placing a clean piece of paper over their design, lifting it, and then letting the print dry.

• Give the children a variety of utensils with which to etch designs into the fingerpaint. The end of the handle of a paintbrush, unsharpened pencils, kitchen utensils, and so forth make great designs.

Science Center

Teacher Talk

Your body can do so many things.

Resources

locks or lock boxes, shoes with laces, clothing with buttons or zippers

Place a variety of small muscle tasks in the center. Label it: What can your body do? Include a variety of locks, a lock box if available, shoes to tie, buttons to be buttoned, zippers, and so forth. You can use this center to assess each child's fine motor skills. Allow the children to perform the different tasks and make a chart to record what tasks the child has mastered, almost mastered, is just beginning to master, and not yet able to do.

Math Center

Teacher Talk

Our bodies move in so many different ways.

Resources

Three-minute timer

Let the children see how many different ways they can move before the sand runs out (or the bell rings).

Worship Center

Teacher Talk

God plans for our bodies to move.

Resources

cassette or CD, cassette or CD player, scarfs

Encourage the children to dance to the music that is playing. Have lightweight scarfs available for them to wave in the air as they dance.

Say: I like the way you move!

Pray: Thank you, God, for our moving bodies.

Open the Bible to Psalm 139:14.

Say: "I am wonderfully made" (Psalm 139:14, adapted).

Have the children repeat the Bible verse.

Wonder Time

Encourage all the children to dance to the music.

Wonder Question: I wonder what it would be like to move as a tree?

Lower the volume on the music and direct the children's movements. Have the children sway like a tree, with arms out as branches swaying in the wind. Have them stand with their feet planted like a tree trunk, reach up to the sun, wiggle as if a squirrel is running up their trunk, and then gently rock a nest of baby birds in their branches. Have them slowly sit down and quietly rock the baby birds to sleep.

Say: Don't say a word or make a sound. I want you to watch me and move as I move.

Go through a series of movements of the fingers, hands, head, and upper body to quiet music. Be sure to use large sweeping movements with your arms and small movements with your eyes and eyebrows.

Turn off the music. Ask the children to name a body part that they just moved. Talk with the children about why moving is important. (It helps our blood inside of us move; it makes our muscles strong; it helps us grow; it keeps us from gaining too much weight.)

Sing and Move: "I Want a Friend" (*see page 211*). Have the children stand in a circle. Choose a child to begin the game. Have the child skip around the circle and then stop at the child named. Let the two children change places and sing the song again.

Read the Bible verse.

Say: God made our wonderful bodies.

Pray: Thank you, God, for our bodies that move and run and jump and play. Amen.

Group Fun

Resources

construction paper, crayons or markers, ribbon, paper punch, cassette or CD, cassette or CD player

Tell the children you are going to make flags and have a parade to celebrate the human body.

Give each child a piece of construction paper for the flag. Let the children decorate the papers with crayons or markers however they wish. Use a paper punch to make two holes in the edge of each paper and tie just enough ribbon in each hole so the child's hand fits through the ribbon like a bracelet. Tell the children they are moving flag poles. Show them how to wave their arms up and down to make their flags move. (Pieces of lightweight fabric in bright colors can be used instead of paper for flags.) After the flags are made, march outside as you play music on a cassette or CD player.

Goodbye Circle

Let the children tell you the things their bodies did that was the most fun this day.

Pray: Thank you, God, for all the ways our bodies move. Amen.

Evaluation

Did you notice the children who have a hard time moving? These are the children who will need more encouragement to move and try large muscle activities.

Lesson 14

I Can Think

Goals:

For the children to use critical thinking skills.

To help the children discover how important the brain is.

Objectives: By the end of this session the children will:

Put together puzzles.

Solve a problem in the math center.

Go on a nut hunt.

Make patterned artwork.

Faith Connections

Bible Verse: If there is anything worthy of praise, think about these things. (Philippians 4:8)

Tell the children that Jesus loved to make people think new thoughts and solve puzzles. He told parables or stories that the people had to think about to understand what Jesus meant. Share with the children the parable of the lost sheep (Matthew 18:12-14). Tell them that Jesus wanted people to know that everyone is important to God.

Teacher's Prayer

O Lord, my brain needs oiling too. Help me search and explore to solve problems. Amen.

Note: Send a note home telling parents that the children may bring an item for show-and-tell for the next class.

Teacher Talk:

Use your brain.

Our brain is our control center. It tells us when to go and when to stop.

Thinking stretches our brain. Think, think. Stretch that brain.

God made our bodies with brains.

Center Time

Let the children think through their own solutions when solving puzzles or planning art projects.

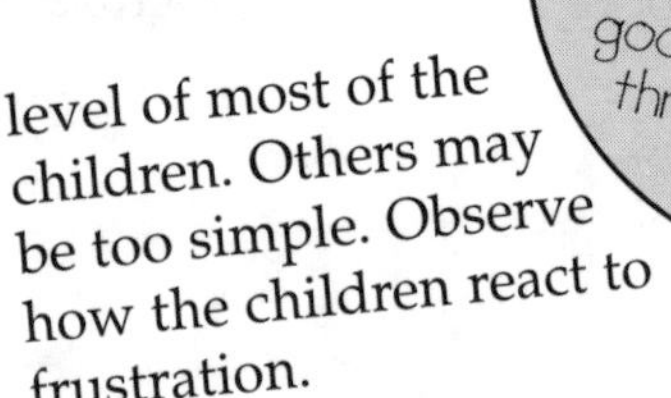

As children arrive, say something such as, "You are a good thinker. I am glad you are here today" or "I have three good thinkers coming through the door."

Writing Center

Teacher Talk

Use your brain.

Resources

plain paper with a hole cut in each sheet, crayons or markers

Before class cut a hole somewhere in a piece of plain paper for each child. Give the children the paper. Let the children decorate the paper the crayons and markers. Some children will incorporate the hole into their drawings. Other children will simply ignore the hole.

Math Center

Teacher Talk

Thinking stretches your brain.

Resources

ten sticks of different lengths, cardboard box, knife (for adult use only), objects

Present problems to be solved on the child's level. Some suggestions:

- Include ten sticks of different lengths. Ask the children to put them in some kind of order.
- On a cardboard box, trace around various unbreakable items (shampoo bottles, wooden blocks, balls, detergent bottles, wooden spoons). Cut out the shapes from the box. Then have the children drop the item into the box by matching the object to the opening.

Manipulatives Center

Teacher Talk

Our brains are our control center.

Resources

variety of puzzles from easy to hard

Set out the puzzles for the children to use. Some might be difficult and above the skill level of most of the children. Others may be too simple. Observe how the children react to frustration.

Art Center

Teacher Talk

We can use our brain to solve problems.

Resources

long piece of mural paper, easel brushes, lots of aluminum pie tins or muffin pans; large jars of red, blue, and yellow paint

Place a long piece of mural paper on the floor. Before the children arrive, mix just a small amount of yellow and blue paint to make green. Mix a small amount of red and blue paint to make purple. Paint a green line and a purple line across the length of the mural paper.

Give each child an aluminum pie or muffin pan. Have the children mix paints in their tins and paint the colors they create on the paper. Some children might be upset that the painting is not a picture of some kind. Let them paint a picture on other paper if they need to. Praise the children for the process and the effort more than for the result, as this is a difficult task.

Worship Center

Teacher Talk

God gives us a brain to think and solve problems.

Resources

cassette, cassette player, headphones

Record a variety of different sounds and let the children try to guess what sounds they are hearing.

Say: Isn't it wonderful that God plans for us to have brains that can help us guess?

Pray: Thank you, God, for our brains that help us solve problems. Amen.

Wonder Time

As the children come together, show them the picture of the human brain from an encyclopedia, library book, or teaching picture.

Wonder Question: What has your brain been doing since you came to class?
Help the children learn that their brains help them solve problems. Talk about the problems they encountered in the centers and how their brains helped solve them.
Play an "I'm thinking of. . ." game: Let different children choose something they see and describe it for the other children without telling them what the object is. Allow the children to guess what the child is thinking of. Play this game again during the day and tomorrow so all the children will get to play.
Sing: "God Cares" (*see page 212*).
Read the Bible verse.
Say: Our Bible verse means that we can use our brains to think about good things. What are some good things you like to think about?
Pray: Thank you, God, for brains that help us think. Amen.

Open the Bible to Philippians 4:8.

Say: "If there is anything worthy of praise, think about these things" (Philippians 4:8).

Have the children repeat the Bible verse.

Group Fun

Resources
nuts, lunch-size paper bags, crayons or markers

Prepare the children for your nut hunt. Purchase nuts in the shell or collect nuts (acorns, walnuts, hickory nuts, and so forth) native to your area. Hide the nuts in an area where it is safe for the children to have a hunt. Talk with the children about how to have a safe hunt.

Give the children paper bags and let them color the bags as they wish. Walk to the hunting place and take the children to the center of it before starting the hunt. This will allow the children to walk in different directions. Have the children find the nuts and place them in their bags. The children can take their nuts home to hide or give to their parents to use in cooking something special.

Goodbye Circle

Remind the children of ways they have used their brains today. Remembering to wash their hands or saying thank you, solving a problem or saying the right thing are all products of our wonderful brains.

Play "Simon Says" until parents arrive. Ask the children to bring something to share with the rest of the class tomorrow.

Pray: Thank you, God, for brains that help us think. Amen.

Evaluation

Allowing children to solve problems on their own makes for a more stressful class. It is easier for us to do things for the children than to tell them how to do them. Were you able to let them do the solving today?

Lesson 15

I Can Share

Teacher Talk:

When we share with others, we help them to be happy and we are happy too.

Sharing is caring.

The Bible teaches us to share with others.

Goal:

To help the children experience the joy of sharing.

Objectives: By the end of this session the children will:

Create artwork to share with others.

Make food to share with others.

Faith Connections

Bible Verse: "Share what you have." (Hebrews 13:16)

Jesus taught us to love and to care for one another and to share what we have with others. Sharing is difficult for some children. Toddlers are learning to say "mine." By the time they are four, we want them to give the "mine" to someone else! Help them feel the joy in sharing. As children become older, they begin to move out of their self-centered world and begin to realize that others have needs and wants. Then sharing becomes easier.

Teacher's Prayer

I have so much, O God. What do you wish me to share? Amen.

Note: Send a note home to ask parents to send family photographs with their children to the next class.

Center Time

Intentionally set centers up so each child will be encouraged to work with another child to successfully complete a task.

As children arrive, place any show-and-tell items on a special table. Cover the items with a sheet.

Art Center

Teacher Talk

We can share with our friends.

Resources

smocks, 3 plastic squeeze bottles, measuring cups, salt, sheets of cardboard or paper plates, newspaper, 3 bowls and spoons, flour, 3 different colors of food coloring

In three separate bowls,mix together 1 cup of all-purpose flour, 1 cup of salt, and 1 cup of water colored with a different color of food coloring. Stir the mixtures well and pour each color into one of the squeeze bottles. If the mixtures are too runny, add more flour. Let the children share the paints. Show the children how to squeeze the mixtures onto the cardboard sheets or paper plates in a design. Make two designs, one to keep and one to share. When the creations are dry, the mixture hardens and sparkles.

Worship Center

Teacher Talk

The Bible teaches us to share with others.

Resources

grocery bags, crayons, bottle of glue, blocks, play dough, Bible or Bible storybook

Have four or five different grocery bags. Place a different item in each bag. The item needs to be something that the children usually share in the classroom such as a box of crayons, a bottle of glue, blocks, a ball or can of play dough, and so forth. Place a Bible or a Bible storybook in one of the bags.

Let the children feel inside each bag and try to guess what the item is. After each child has a turn guessing, show the children the items.

Say: These are all things we share in our class.

Pray: Thank you, God, for things to share. Amen.

Building Center

Teacher Talk

We can share and work together.

Resources

blocks

Emphasize sharing as the children create their own structures.

Book Center

Teacher Talk

Sharing is fun.

Resources

books

Make a place for two to four children to share books with one another. Provide a variety of books about diverse populations and activities.

Cooking Center

Teacher Talk

Sharing makes us happy too.

Resources

ingredients for chocolate pie, utensils

Allow the children to make a pie that they can share with others. Makes enough for twelve people to share.

Chocolate Cream Pie

1 pkg. instant chocolate pudding and pie filling
milk
6 individual graham pie crusts
whipped topping
mini chocolate chips

Prepare the pie filling as directed on the box. Spoon the mixture into the individual pie crusts. Top with whipped topping and mini chocolate chips. Chill until set.

Open the Bible to Hebrews 13:16.

Say: "Share what you have" (Hebrews 13:16).

Have the children repeat the Bible verse.

Wonder Time

Invite the children to bring the things they brought to share and join you for wonder time.

Wonder Question: Why do you think we share?

Help the children see that sharing often helps another person and helps us feel good too. Talk about some of the ways they can share.

Enjoy show-and-tell. Limit the number of items shared so circle time doesn't get too long and lose the children's interest.

Sing: "Will You Be a Friend of Mine?" (see page 211).

Read the Bible verse.

Say: The Bible tells us to share with others.

Pray: Dear God, help us learn to share. Amen.

Easy Steps For a Successful Show-and-Tell

- Have the children put their items on a table as they enter the room. Cover the items with a sheet.
- Allow each child to tell about his or her item and encourage others to listen first and then ask questions.
- Five children at about 3–5 minutes each are more than enough to present at one time.
- Plan for several show-and-tell times during the day. They are wonderful transitions as the children wait for lunch or playtime.
- Allow the children to actually play with their items with their friends as they sit on the carpet and wait for their parents.
- Send a note home to parents to explain to them rules about show-and-tell items.
- Thank the children for sharing their special things with the class.

Group Fun

Resources

pies made during center time, napkins, plates, plasticware

The individual crust pies are large enough that two children can share a pie. Have the children invite a person (or persons) from the staff of the church to share the pies. This might be the director, the custodian, the support staff, or other teachers.

Goodbye Circle

Ask the children to find a way to share when they go home.

Pray: Dear God, help us learn to share. Amen.

Evaluation

Were there opportunities for each child to share? Was sharing difficult for some?

MEET MY FAMILY

We will celebrate the people in our families this week. The word family has taken on a new meaning as the structure of family has changed over the years. Family to one child might be a father and grandmother; to another child family might be Dad's wife and her children and Mom's husband and his children. Children will learn that *family* means those persons who live with them and care for them. Remember, "living with" includes weekend changes, weekly changes, or other varieties for blended families.

We will talk about people in the home and people who love and care for the children. We will help children learn how to be a good member of the family. We will also talk about families all over the world and what they do.

Lesson 16

The People in My Home

Teacher Talk:

God plans for families to love and care for us.

All families are different.

Each family is special.

Goal:

For the children to realize that they have families that love and care for them.

Objectives: By the end of this session the children will:

Name the people in their families.

Hear a definition of family.

Faith Connections

Bible verse: Children are a gift from the LORD.

(Psalm 127:3, Good News Bible)

Families are important to young children. Take the time to listen to each child tell you about his or her family.

Teacher's Prayer

Help me be sensitive, dear God, to the differences in families. Amen.

Center Time

Add any family photographs to the Worship Center.

As children arrive, greet each child. Be sure to speak to family members today.

Writing Center

Teacher Talk

Your family loves and cares for you.

Resources

invitations to an open house, paper, crayons, pencils

Let the children "write" an invitation to give to their parents for an open house. Write and photocopy invitations for the children to decorate. Add writing materials so that the children can write letters to members of their families.

Home Living Center

Teacher Talk

God plans for families to love and care for us.

Resources

box, small sofa, artificial turf, tissue paper

Add a pretend family room this week. Include a small sofa if available. You might also create a pretend garden next to the home living center with artificial turf. Let the children make tissue paper flowers to "plant" in their garden.

Art Center

Teacher Talk

All families are different; each one is special.

Resources

doll pattern (*see page 218*), cardboard, scissors, push pins, drawing paper, carpet pieces, masking tape, collage materials, glue

Photocopy and cut out the doll pattern (*see page 218*). Cut several copies of the doll from cardboard before class starts. Give each child a push pin and a piece of thick carpet. Let the child make a doll to represent each person in his or her family. Let the child choose a piece of drawing paper. Have a variety of colors of paper so each child can match the skin color of family members. Place the paper on the carpet piece. Secure the cardboard pattern on the paper with loops of masking tape. Show the children how to press the pin over and over again around the outline of the pattern. When the child is finished he or she should be able to carefully tear out the doll. Let the children dress the dolls with collage material.

Math Center

Teacher Talk

Each family is different.

Resources

large paper, markers

Count the number of members in each child's family. Use a piece of large paper to make a chart or graph of the numbers.

Worship Center

Teacher Talk

God plans for families to love and care for us.

Resources

family photographs

Display pictures the children have brought of their families.

Say: Each of our families is different. God loves all families.

Pray: Thank you, dear God, for the people who take care of me. Thank you for all of our families. Amen.

Building Center

Teacher Talk

Our families love and care for us.

Resources

wooden blocks, toy people, toy cars

Encourage the children to use wooden blocks to build homes for small plastic people. Add toy cars.

Wonder Time

As the children gather in the circle, talk with them about the things they did in the centers.

Open the Bible to Psalm 127:3

Say: "Children are a gift from the LORD" (Psalm 127:3).

Have the children repeat the Bible verse.

Wonder Question: I wonder what a family is?

Listen to their answers. Add to their ideas the fact that families are the people who love and care for us. Families usually live together and eat together. The people in our families are the people whom we feel close to. Sometimes a family member lives away from us, but we try to let them know we love them by talking on the phone and sending them letters. Sometimes grandparents live away from us.

Sing: "Thank You, God, for Loving Me" *(see page 212).*

Read the Bible verse.

Pray: Thank you, God, for families. Amen.

Have each child name the people in his or her family. Have all the children clap and say, "Thank you, God, for families" after each child has named his or her family members.

Tell the children you will have a party for their families on Friday. Show them the invitation and encourage the children to write their names on the invitations. Send these home with the children today.

Group Fun

Resources

sponges, clothespins, paper towels, shallow trays, tempera paint, mural paper, smocks

Let the children make sponge prints on a large mural to decorate your room for the open house. Have the children wear smocks. Place mural paper on a table or on the floor. Place folded paper towels in shallow trays. Pour tempera paint onto the paper towels. Clip clothespins onto sponges. Show the children how to hold the clothespins, dip the sponges into the paint, and then press the sponges onto the mural paper.

Cut out letters for the words, "Welcome, Families." Let the paint dry, then glue the letters on the mural. Display the mural in your room.

Goodbye Circle

Play a game with the children. Instruct the children to stand. Have all the children with a younger brother or sister clap their hands. Have all the children with older brothers or sisters stomp their feet. Have all the children with no brothers or sisters touch their toes.

Pray: Thank you, God, for families. Amen.

Evaluation

Some families are not a safe haven for children. Some families are stressed and too busy for the child. Give extra care to those children whose families are too busy. Your classroom can serve as a safe haven for them.

Lesson 17

The People in My Family

Teacher Talk:

God plans for people to live in a family.

We thank God for our families.

I live in a family who takes care of me.

Goal:

To help the children see that there are many people who love them and who care for them.

Objectives: By the end of this session the children will:

Begin making a book telling about their family.

Name the people who love them and care for them.

Remember and continue to talk about the meaning of family.

Continue to work on family paper dolls.

Faith Connections

Bible verse: Let all that you do be done in love.

(1 Corinthians 16:14).

God plans for us to live in families that love and care for us. We are aware that in today's world this is not always the case. Be aware of your children's family situations. Offer help when asked or when situations may cause the children harm.

Teacher's Prayer

Dear God, help me remember the others who surround this child and keep them in my prayers. Amen.

Center Time

Continue centers suggested for this unit. In addition you might include the following:

As children arrive, greet children and members of their families. Send the children to explore in today's centers.

Manipulatives Center

Teacher Talk

God plans for people to live in a family.

Resources

Duplo blocks

Encourage the children to build houses with Duplo blocks.

Art Center

Teacher Talk

All families are different; each one is special.

Resources

doll pattern *(see page 218)*, cardboard, scissors, push pins, drawing paper, carpet pieces, masking tape, collage materials, glue, easel, paint, brushes, paper, smocks

Some children will continue to work on their family dolls. Add an easel, paints, and brushes so the children can paint pictures of their families having fun together.

Writing Center

Teacher Talk

God plans for us to live in families. Our families take care of us.

Resources

paper, stapler, staples, pencils, crayons

Make small booklets with 4–6 pages for each child. Station a teacher or volunteer at the writing center. Let each child dictate a story about her or his family as the adult writes the story in the small book. Encourage the child to tell about members of the family who do not live with the child. During the rest of the day and the week encourage the children to illustrate their stories.

Book Center

Teacher Talk

God plans for people to live in families. Each family is special.

Resources

pictures of families from around the world

Explore social sciences at the center today by including pictures of families from around the world. Magazines, newspapers, *World, Kid's Discover* and *National Geographic* magazines are good sources for pictures. Invite the children to look at the pictures. **Ask:** "What are the people in this family doing? Do we do the same things in our families?"

Worship Center

Teacher Talk

We thank God for our families.

Resources

plastic microphone or paper tube, aluminum foil, tape

Use a plastic microphone or make a pretend microphone with a paper tube and foil. Shape aluminum foil into an 8-inch tube with a ball at one end. Push the end of the foil tube (without the ball) into one end of a paper tube. Secure with tape.

Use the pretend microphone to let the children take turns telling about members of their families.

Ask: Who is in your family? Does *(name a family member the child named)* live with you? What does *(name a family member the child named)* do to show love for you? What do you do to show love for *(name a family member the child named)*?

You may need to help the children think about ways family members show love, such as cooking food, giving hugs, washing clothes, reading stories, playing quietly, or saying "I love you."

Pray: O God, thank you for our families. Each one is special. Amen.

Open the Bible to 1 Corinthians 16:14.

Say: "Let all that you do be done in love" (1 Corinthians 16:14).

Have the children repeat the Bible verse.

Wonder Time

As you call the children together, talk about families.

Wonder Question: I wonder who is in your family, but does not live with you?
Share stories. Encourage the children to tell about family members who do not live with them such as grandparents and aunts and uncles.
Say: God plans for us to have people who love us and who care for us. We are all part of the family of God.
Read the Bible verse.
Sing: "Thank you, God, for Loving Me" *(see page 212).*
Pray: Thank you, God, for all those whom we love and who love us. Amen.

Group Fun

Resources

small balloons, bag, paintbrushes, liquid starch, shallow containers, art tissue

Let the children make miniature piñatas. Blow up small balloons before class. Keep the balloons in a bag. Give each child a balloon and a brush. Pour liquid starch into shallow containers. Show the children how to dip their brushes into the starch, paint the balloons, and then attach squares of art tissue on the balloons. Write the child's name on one piece of paper and paint it on the balloon. Hang balloons on a line to dry.

Successful Papier-mâché

- Papier-mâché can be a nightmare with preschoolers if you try to use lightweight paper and sticky paste.
- Four- and five-year-olds are able to paint liquid starch on balloons or cardboard boxes and then rub a piece of art tissue in the space they painted. They will need encouragement to cover the whole area.
- Do not use light bulbs as children can break the bulbs and become injured.
- Make only small individual papier-mâché projects, or let the class participate in covering a larger piece.
- Children can construct items with boxes, then papier-mâché.
- Wait until the project has dried, then paint with acrylics.

Goodbye Circle

Book of the Day:
Just Grandpa and Me
by Mercer Mayer

Talk with children about how some family members do not live with them. Aunts and uncles, grandparents, and parents who are separated are all part of a family even though they do not live at home. Ask the children to find out from their parents the name of a person in their family who doesn't live with them.

Pray: Thank you, God, for families. Amen.

Evaluation

Make extra miniature piñatas for the children who are not in class or let the children make piñatas tomorrow. Do the children seem to understand the larger idea of family?

Lesson 18

Being a Family

Goal:

To help the children feel they are a part of a family at school.

Objectives: By the end of this session the children will:

Have fun in the classroom.

Take a picnic lunch outside and enjoy eating together.

Finish their piñatas and family paper dolls.

Work in their family books.

Faith Connections

Bible verse: Keep yourselves in the love of God.

(Jude 21)

Young children are beginning to experience caring for others as they care for the members of their families. Help them understand that their class is like a family, and the classroom is a place where they can work and play together.

Teacher's Prayer

Dear God, help us to learn how to care for one another in our class the same way we care for members of our families. Amen.

Teacher Talk:

God plans for families to love and care for one another.

Our class is like a family.

Our class works and plays together.

Center Time

Set up your centers as described at the beginning of this unit. For this lesson add the following:

As children arrive, greet each child as another part of the preschool family.

Home Living Center

Teacher Talk

Our class is like a family. We can do things together that families do.

Resources

peanut butter, jelly, bread, table knives, wax paper, name stickers, picnic basket

Add an extra table to the home living center. Help the children make their own peanut butter and jelly sandwiches for a picnic. After a child makes his or her sandwich, wrap it in wax paper and put on a sticker with the child's name. Place the sandwiches in a picnic basket. If the children bring their own sack lunches for the picnic, let them wash apples or do some other housekeeping chore to prepare for the picnic.

Art Center

Teacher Talk

God plans for families; each family is special.

Resources

doll pattern (*see page 218*), cardboard, scissors, push pins, drawing paper, carpet pieces, masking tape, collage materials, glue; crayons, balloons, art tissue, liquid starch, shallow trays, paintbrushes, small wrapped candies or prizes

Allow children to complete the variety of projects begun this week:

Color and dress the family paper dolls.

Complete the piñatas. When dry, the balloon should be popped and small wrapped candies or prizes placed in each piñata.

Invite the children to continue illustrating their family books.

Math Center

Teacher Talk

God plans for families to work together; our class is like a family.

Resources

napkins, paper cups, paper plates

Let the children count out the number of napkins, cups, and plates needed on the picnic and put them in the basket.

Building Center

Teacher Talk

Our class is like a family; we work and play together.

Resources

blocks

Encourage the children to work together, and comment on how much fun they have playing with their friends.

Worship Center

Teacher Talk

Our class is like a family.

Resources

mural paper, tempera paint, shallow pans or foam meat trays, paper towels, markers

Create a class family tree. Use markers to draw a tree on mural paper. Make a paint pad by pouring tempera paint onto folded paper towels placed in a shallow pan or foam tray. Have the children press their hands onto the paint pad; then press their handprints onto the mural. Write each child's name on or beside the handprints when dry. Label the mural "Our Class Family Tree."

Say: Our class is like a family.

Pray: Thank you, God, for our class family. Amen.

Wonder Time

As you call the children together, talk with them about how much you look forward to each day with them.

Wonder Question: I wonder how our class is like a family?
Say: Our class is like a family. We work and play together. We love and care for each other.
Read the Bible verse.
Sing: "Thank You, God, for Loving Me" (see page 212).
Pray: Thank you, God, for our class family. Amen.

Open the Bible to Jude 21.

Say: "Keep yourselves in the love of God" (Jude 21).

Have the children repeat the Bible verse.

Group Fun

Resources
food for picnic, blanket or sheet

If possible, take the children outside for the picnic. Ask the children to help you think about what they need to do so they and their preschool friends have a good time.

Spread a blanket or sheet on the ground. If you are unable to go outside, spread the blanket or sheet on the classroom floor. Let the children sit together and eat the peanut butter sandwiches made during center time. Say a thank-you prayer. After the children have finished eating,

Say: Families work and play together. Let's have fun playing games with our friends in our preschool family.

Play one or two of the children's favorite games such as "Duck, Duck, Goose" or "I Spy."

Goodbye Circle

Remind children that you will have a party on Friday to celebrate families. Ask the children if their parents are coming. Tell the children that you love each of them and that you look forward to seeing them tomorrow. Tell the children that you are glad they are part of your preschool family.

Pray: Thank you, God, for all our preschool family. Amen.

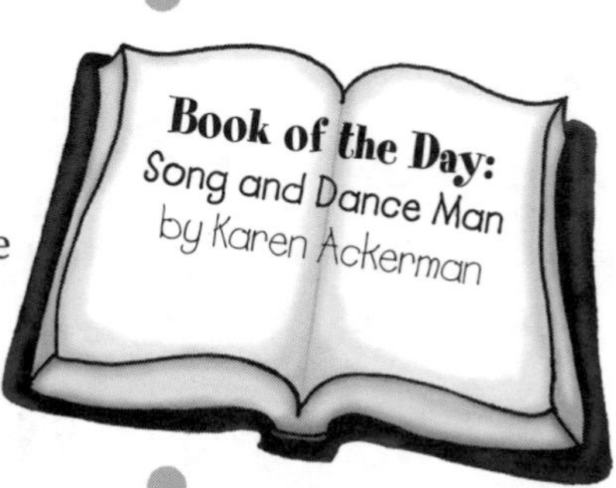

Evaluation

Do you need to call families to tell them about the party? Ask one or two parents to bring some punch and cookies.

Lesson 19

Families of the World

Teacher Talk:

God plans for families all over the world.

We all belong to the family of God.

We can love and care for all persons.

Goal:

To help the children discover that there are children and families all over the world.

Objectives:

By the end of this session the children will:

Look at pictures of families from around the world.

Finish preparations for the family celebration tomorrow.

Make family dancing sticks.

Faith Connections

Bible verse: God is love.

(1 John 4:8)

Children need to see other children different from themselves to see that all persons are loved and accepted by God. Knowing that God cares for other children can help your children feel secure in God's love for them and understand that God wants us to love and care for one another.

Teacher's Prayer

Dear God, your love reaches around the world and into our classroom. Thank you for families everywhere. Amen

Center Time

Continue centers suggested for this unit. In addition you might include the following:

As children arrive, greet the children. Tell the children that we have lots to do to prepare for the family celebration.

Art Center

Teacher Talk

God created families all over the world to be special. Many families have special things they enjoy doing together.

Resources

wooden dowels or bamboo sticks or paper towel cardboard rolls at least 12-inches long, yarn, strips of fabric

Invite the children to begin making family dancing sticks. Provide sticks at least 12-inches long. You can use thick or thin dowels, bamboo, or paper towel cardboard rolls. The longer and wider the stick, the easier it is for the children to wrap them. Cut pieces of yarn and strips of colorful fabric into 18-inch lengths. Show the children how to wrap the materials around and around the stick until it is covered. Write the children's names somewhere on the sticks. Explain that tomorrow they will help their family put bells on the sticks.

This activity is best done at a table. Putting the stick on the table and rolling it helps the child accomplish the wrapping more easily.

Math Center

Teacher Talk

God plans for families all over the world. God loves all persons.

Resources

doll pattern (*see page 218*), scissors, tape, wall map of the world, marker

Put up a wall map where the children can easily reach it. Photocopy and cut out ten doll patterns (*see page 218*). Number the dolls from one to ten. Spread out the dolls. Call out a number. Have the children take turns finding the doll with that number and taping the doll to the map.

Book Center

Teacher Talk

God created families all over the world.

Resources

pictures, books that show families from countries around the world (for example, *People* by Peter Spier), clothing and other touchable items from countries around the world

Display pictures and books that show families from countries around the world. Have available clothing and other items from countries around the world that children can touch and perhaps use or wear.

Worship Center

Teacher Talk

God loves all persons. We can love and care for all persons.

Resources

multicultural crayons, mural paper, Bible and/or cross

Invite the children to make a cover for the worship table. Let them use the multicultural crayons to color the mural paper. When finished, place the paper on the worship table. Place a Bible and/or a cross on the table.

Say: God loves all persons. The multicultural crayons show us many of the beautiful colors of skin God has created for people all over the world.

Pray: Thank you, God, for families all around the world. Amen.

Open the Bible to 1 John 4:8.

Say: "God is love" (1 John 4:8).

Have the children repeat the Bible verse.

Wonder Time

Cover a long stick with strips of yarn and cloth *(see Art Center)*. Add bells to the stick *(see page 70)*. Call the children together by shaking the dancing stick.

Wonder Question: I wonder if every family is just like mine or yours?
Ask: What is something new you learned about families today?
Have the pictures from the book center available. Talk with the children about the activities of families in countries around the world.
Read the Bible verse.
Say. God loves and cares for each person on earth.
Sing: "Thank You, God, for Loving Me" *(see page 212)*.
Pray: Thank you, God, for families all around the world. Amen.

Group Fun

Resources

music from different countries, cassette/CD player, grocery-size paper bags, crayons or markers or stickers

Talk about chores that must be completed before the family celebration. Encourage the children to help clean the room, put up murals, and finish their family paper dolls and family books. Play music from countries around the world as the children work.

Let the children make family bags. They will use the bags to take home their things from the family celebration. Give each child a grocery-size bag. Let the children decorate the bags with crayons or markers or stickers. Write (*Child's name*)'s Family on the outside of the bag.

Goodbye Circle

Send reminder notices home today giving the date and time of the family celebration. Write a note to those who have volunteered to bring food or help in some way. Talk with the children about how to be good hosts and hostesses at the party (see list at right).

Pray: Thank you, God, for families. Amen.

- Keep our hands to ourselves.
- Be nice and greet each visitor and tell them you are glad they came to the party.
- When it is time to eat, serve the guests first.
- Walk in the room, since it might be crowded and someone could get hurt if we are in a big hurry.
- Show your family the room and the things we have been making.

Evaluation

Did the children understand that the people in your pictures were real people who lived far away? How can you continue to help them get a sense of the world?

Are you ready for the party? Be sure there are dancing sticks and miniature piñatas for every child. Move furniture out of the way to make a place for sitting and a place for dancing.

Lesson 20

A Family Celebration

Goal:

To have fun celebrating families. Whether you have invited families to the celebration or you are just celebrating with the children, today will be a day of fun.

Objectives:

By the end of this session the children will:

Sing and dance to songs and dances they have learned.

Talk about their families and why they love their families.

Finish making their dancing sticks.

Celebrate their families.

Teacher Talk:

We all belong to the family of God.

God plans for each family to be special.

My family is special.

Faith Connections

Bible verse: We are God's people.

(Psalm 100:3, adapted)

Each child's family is important to him or her. Be sure to greet each family and try to spend equal time with all parents.

Teacher's Prayer

Dear God, help me bring joy to each person who comes today. Help us to have a true celebration of all our special families. Amen.

Celebration of the Family

Everyone seems to have their own idea of how to have a good party and how to involve parents. Be sure you have planned ways of involving everyone, children and adults. Be sensitive to any children whose families could not come. Plan for them to join another family or to spend time with you as part of your family.

Center Time

Set up each center with items the children have enjoyed throughout this unit. Have enough activities out for the children to have fun before the party begins. Sometimes our tendency is to concentrate on the party and forget to engage the children before the party begins. This can lead to discipline problems and boredom. Be sure to include the activities in the centers that the children have enjoyed, and give families time to enjoy them together.

As children arrive, check with the children to see if family members are coming to the party. Encourage the children to become involved in the centers.

Art Center

Teacher Talk

God plans for each family to be special.

Resources

dancing sticks, ribbons, bells

Show the dancing sticks to the parents and tell them how to thread the ribbons through the top of the stick and tie bells to them. Encourage parents to help their child make the stick.

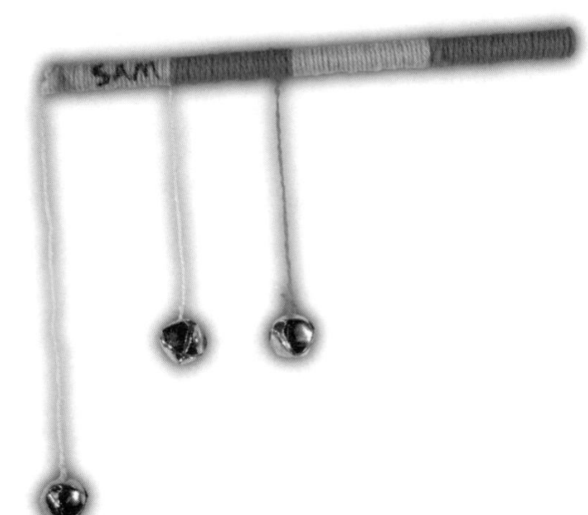

Building Center

Teacher Talk

God plans for each family to be special.

Resources

blocks, sticks, pictures of houses from around the world

Invite parents to work with the children to plan and build houses. Suggest they build ones like their own, ones that are different, or ones that are seen in different parts of the world. Display pictures of houses made differently from those in the United States. *National Geographic* and *World* magazines and travel magazines are a good source for these pictures.

Math Center

Teacher Talk

Each of our families is special.

Resources

small jar for each family containing individually wrapped candies

Have each child select a jar and try to guess how many candies are in it. Then have the parents open the jars and let the children count the candies. Invite the families to share the candy.

Worship Center

Teacher Talk

We all belong to the family of God.

Resources

pictures, books that show families from countries around the world, clothing, other touchable items from countries around the world.

Let the children show their parents and each other the pictures of different families. Encourage them to touch the clothes and other items and to talk about the ways the items are the same and different from ones in their families.

Pray: Dear God, we thank you for our families. Each family is special. We are happy that we are also part of your special family, the family of God. Amen.

Wonder Time

Use your dancing stick to call everyone together. Talk about families.

Wonder Question: I wonder what makes each family special?

Tell parents and children what you have learned about families this week.
Let the children tell you what a family is.

Say: We all belong to the family of God.

Have the pictures from the worship center available. Talk with the children about the activities of families in countries around the world. Put the pictures down side by side on the floor and tell the children that all the families in the pictures and all the families of everyone in the room make one big family, the family of God.

Discuss what it means to be a part of God's family. God loves and cares for each person on earth. We help other people on earth because God wants us to treat everyone as if they are our brothers and sisters.

Read the Bible verse.

Sing: "Thank You, God for Loving Me" (*see page 212*).

Pray: Thank you for families who love and care for one another. Amen.

Open the Bible to Psalm 100:3.

Say: "We are God's people" (Psalm 100:3, adapted).

Have the children repeat the Bible verse.

Group Fun

Resources

music, cassette/CD player, family dancing sticks, refreshments, napkins, cups

Move furniture to make a space for dancing. Play the music and let the children enjoy dancing. Encourage parents to dance with their children. Suggest they use their family dancing sticks.

Enjoy refreshments with each other. Say a thank-you prayer.

Invite the children and their parents to share with the group the family books and the family dolls the children made.

Let each child show his or her piñata to the group.

Goodbye Circle

Have the children put their piñatas, family books, family dolls, and jars of candy *(see math center)* in the family bags they decorated yesterday *(see page 68)*.

Thank the parents for coming and helping with the celebration.

Pray: Thank you, God, for families. Amen.

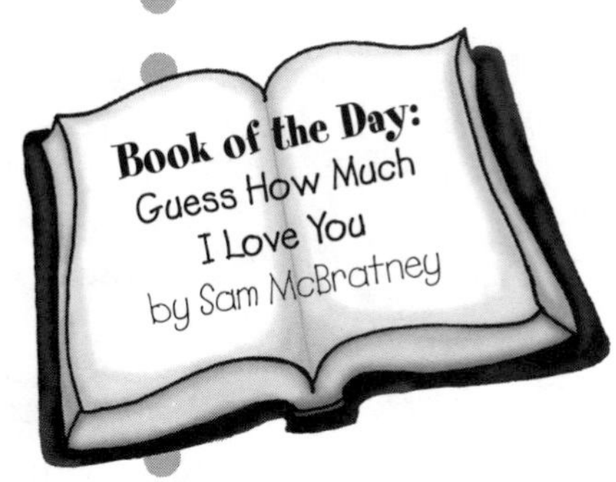

Evaluation

What did you learn about the children today? Did they have a good time? Are there ways of involving parents that you learned about today?

Unit 2

My Wonderful Body

Goals:

1. The children will learn that God planned for us to have a variety of feelings and will learn what to do when they are angry or sad.

2. The children will explore their five senses and learn ways their senses help them.

3. The children will learn more about their hearts, what foods to eat, and ways to exercise so that their hearts stay healthy.

4. The children will understand the importance of caring for themselves, for others, and for all of God's world.

This month the children will learn even more about their bodies and abilities. Be sure that you have planned activities in which children can experience on their own their hearts, feelings, senses, and ways to care.

If you feel that a topic needs more attention than the one lesson here, extend the lesson to other days. As you plan your curriculum, adapt the lessons in this book to your own class. You may need more time on the heart and less time on feelings. You and your coworkers can better judge what to emphasize. There are many different activities listed, and since preschoolers like repetition, you may wish to repeat some activities and omit others. Use the lessons to your own advantage.

Bible Stories for this Unit:
Genesis 1:26-31 (The Creation of Humankind)
Ruth (Ruth and Naomi)
Genesis 37; 43–48 (Joseph and His Brothers)
Luke 10:25-37 (The Good Samaritan)
John 12:1-8 (Mary Anoints Jesus)
Luke 10:38-42 (Mary and Martha)

I HAVE FEELINGS

This week the children will explore some of their feelings. Help them know it is okay to have feelings; we just have to learn how to manage our feelings. Help the children use words to name their feelings rather than using their bodies to express their frustration.

Most preschoolers are just beginning to learn to keep from showing their emotions entirely through their bodies. If outbursts occur, ask yourself it there is anything you can do to arrange your classroom or schedule to ease the frustration. As the children learn to use words, you can help them deal better with emotions.

Lesson 21

Love

Goals:

To help the children learn about love and loving feelings.

To help the children learn that God loves them and their families.

Objectives: By the end of this session the children will:

Talk about love and how it feels.

Show love toward their friends and be recognized for it.

Make something for someone to show their love.

Faith Connections

Bible verse: Love is kind. (1 Corinthians 13:4)

Children experience God's love through the love and care of teachers, parents, and friends. Help the children recognize those who love them.

Teacher's Prayer

O God, please help me to show love to each child in everything I do. Amen.

Teacher Talk:

I love you!

I want you to be loving toward your friends in preschool.

God loves you!

Today will be an especially loving day!

Center Time

Compliment each child who shows love by sharing or being kind as the children work in the centers today.

> **As children arrive,** say: "Now here is a child we love . . . (say child's name)!"

Book Center

Teacher Talk

We have many special feelings. One of those feelings is love.

Resources

glue, construction paper, crayons, precut pictures of people showing different feelings

Let the children begin making a book of feelings. Explain that each day this week they will add pictures showing different feelings. Today they will put pictures of people who are showing love in their books. Precut from magazines pictures of people showing a variety of emotions. Let the children choose pictures of people with expressions that seem to the child to be loving. If you wonder about some of their choices, talk with the children about them, remembering that each child experiences love differently. Give each child a piece of construction paper. Let the children glue the pictures to the pieces of construction paper. Write the children's names on their pictures so that they can add to their books.

Art Center

Teacher Talk

We can be loving to others.

Resources

easel, easel paints, paint containers, brushes, paper, smocks

Have the children wear paint smocks. Cut easel paper into the shape hearts. Let the children paint the hearts however they wish.

Let two children work together at the easel to paint one heart. Remind the children that one way we show love is by sharing with each other. Write both children's names across the bottom of the heart.

Manipulatives Center

Teacher Talk

We can be loving to our friends.

Resources

play dough, heart-shaped cookie cutters, rolling pins

Place heart cookie cutters, play dough, and rolling pins on a table. Have five or six chairs around the table. Encourage the children to take turns and share the play dough. Recognize each child as you see him or her be loving to another child.

Blocks Center

Teacher Talk

We can be loving to our friends.

Resources

blocks

Encourage the children to build something together with blocks. Recognize their loving acts by saying, "I like the way Lee is being a loving friend to Ansari."

Worship Center

Teacher Talk

God loves us.

Resources

none

Sing "God Loves" to the tune of "Hot Cross Buns."

God loves me.
God loves me.
I am happy, oh so happy.
God loves me.

Pray: Thank you, God, for loving me. Amen.

Wonder Time

Draw a large heart shape on a sheet and place the sheet on the floor. Or use masking tape to make the outline of a heart on the floor. Place books and floor puzzles in the heart. Let the children look at the books and puzzles as they gather for together time.

Wonder Question: I wonder how love feels?

Ask: What are some feelings you have? (Happy, sad, angry, or surprised.)

Play a game. Whisper to one child a feeling to act out using face expressions. Let the other children guess the feeling.

Sing: "Faces" *(see page 213).*

Say: Today we are talking about a feeling called love. How does it feel to love someone? How do we know when someone loves us?

Help the children see that, although you cannot see the feeling of love, you can see the things a loving person does. Have the children name some ways we show love.

Read the Bible verse.

Say: When we are kind to one another, we are showing love.

Name for the children the loving acts you saw as they played with one another.

Let them think of ways your class can show love today.

Pray: "Thank you, God, for our feelings. Thank you for your love and for all the people who love us. Amen.

Open the Bible to 1 Corinthians 13:4.

Say: "Love is kind" (1 Corinthians 13:4).

Have the children repeat the Bible verse.

Group Fun

Resources

collage materials, glue, the letters L-O-V-E cut from posterboard or large construction paper

Create four activity stations in your room. Place one large letter from the word *love* in each station. Have each child go to one of the stations. Let the children decorate the letters with collage materials. When the children have finished, show the children how the letters spell the word love. Let the children help you decide who should receive their gift of *love.* Mount the letters in the hall, give them to another class, or take them to a nursing home.

Goodbye Circle

Ask the children what they have learned about love today. As they leave, tell each child that you love him or her.

Pray: Thank you, God, for your love. Help us show love to one another. Amen.

Evaluation

Do the children have a little better idea of love after today's session? Do you?

Lesson 22

Happy and Sad

Teacher Talk:

God loves you when you are happy.

God loves you when you are sad.

God loves you all the time.

You look happy!

Goals:

For the children to realize that everyone has happy feelings and everyone has sad feelings.

To help the children think about their own feelings.

Objectives: By the end of this session children will:

Talk about happy and sad.

Make faces on cardboard and cover them with foil.

Tell the class what emotions they are feeling.

Name some happy times and some sad times.

Faith Connections

Bible verse: Be happy and glad.

(Matthew 5:12, *Good News Bible*)

A preschooler's smiles and tears come and go, but the way we receive them has lasting effects on their lives. Children need to know that God loves them no matter how they feel, when they are happy and when they are sad.

Teacher's Prayer

O God, help me to move beyond any sadness in my life to make this a happy classroom. Amen.

Center Time

Encourage the children to be involved in one of the centers you have planned.

As children arrive, tell them you are happy to see them.

Math Center

Teacher Talk

Sometimes we feel happy. Sometimes we feel sad. God loves us all the time.

Resources

cardboard, marker, scissors

Draw a happy face on a large cardboard circle. Cut out the circle and cut it into simple puzzle pieces. Do the same to make a sad face. Mix up the puzzle pieces and encourage the children to put the faces together.

Book Center

Teacher Talk

We have many special feelings. Two of those feelings are happy and sad.

Resources

precut pictures of happy and sad people, construction paper, glue, crayons

Let the children add another page to their books on feelings. Provide precut pictures of people. Give each child a piece of construction paper. Let the children glue on pictures of people showing happy and sad feelings. Write the children's names on their pictures. Save these pages with the pages on love.

Art Center

Teacher Talk

Sometimes we feel happy. Sometimes we feel sad. God loves us all the time.

Resources

small piece of cardboard (side of a cereal box will do), scissors, facial features cut out of thick cardboard, masking tape, glue, heavy duty foil, blue or black tempera paint, shallow trays, paper towels

Before class cut an oval and facial features out of cardboard for each child. Cut a piece of heavy duty foil a little larger than the oval for each child. Let each child make a face, happy or sad, on the piece of cardboard by gluing on facial features. Help the children cover their cardboard faces with the foil. Tape or glue the foil to the back of the cardboard. Show the children how to rub the foil softly so that the facial features show up. Pour blue or black tempera paint into shallow trays. Let the children dip paper towels in tempera paint and rub it over the whole surface of the foil, which makes an antiqued effect.

Building Center

Teacher Talk

You look happy when you are playing and having fun.

Resources

blocks

Be sure to comment on children's feelings as they play in the building center.

Music Center

Teacher Talk

Sometimes when we listen to music, it makes us feel happy or sad.

Resources

happy and sad music, cassette/CD player, earphones

Let the children listen to the music. Ask them if they think the music is happy or sad.

Worship Center

Teacher Talk

God loves us when we are happy and when we are sad.

Resources

none

Invite the children to use their faces and bodies to show you feeling sad and feeling happy.

Pray: Thank you, God, for our feelings. Thank you for loving us when we are happy and when we are sad. Amen.

Open the Bible to Matthew 5:12.

Say: "Be happy and glad" (Matthew 5:12, *Good News Bible*).

Have the children repeat the Bible verse.

Wonder Time

As children come together, talk about the expressions on their faces.

Wonder Question: I wonder why we feel happy sometimes and sad sometimes?
Play music. Talk with the whole group about how the music makes them feel.
Say: Sometimes we all feel happy and sometimes we feel sad.
(Let them tell you a time when they were sad; then talk about happy times. Remember together times in your class when you were happy and sad.)
Say: God planned for feelings. It is all right for you to feel the way you do. When feelings aren't comfortable, we should talk with a grownup we can trust about them.
Read the Bible verse.
Say: God loves us when we are happy and glad. God loves us when we are sad. God always loves us.
Sing: "Faces" *(see page 213)*.
Pray: Thank you, God, for happy times and for friends to help us through the sad times. Amen.

Group Fun

Resources

colored chalk, damp sponge, drawing paper, cardboard boxes, brightly colored paper, strapping tape

Prepare the children for the group activity by helping them think of a happy time. Ask them to close their eyes and think of a time when they were very happy. Wait a few minutes. Then tell them to open their eyes and, without telling anyone the picture in their mind, to go to the table and draw it.

Let each child use chalk to draw a picture of a happy time. You may want them to wipe their papers with a damp sponge before drawing.

Make an art tower out of cardboard boxes by wrapping the boxes with brightly colored paper and stacking them into a tower. Secure the boxes with strapping tape. Display the pictures on the art tower.

Goodbye Circle

Review the activities of the day and point out happy and sad times to the children. Have the children name things that make them happy, then **say:** "Thank you, God, for all these things."

Pray: Thank you, God, for all these things that make us happy. Amen.

Evaluation

Did you learn anything during the session that will help you plan for individual children?

Lesson 23

Angry and Frustrated

Goals:

To help the children recognize that we all get angry and frustrated.

To help the children learn that they can make choices when they are angry and frustrated.

Objectives: By the end of this session the children will:

Tell you what makes them angry.

Make a paper strip sculpture.

Express their feelings as they play with clay.

Name acceptable ways they can handle their angry feelings.

Faith Connections

Bible verse: Do not be quick to anger.

(Ecclesiastes 7:9)

Children often feel that anger and frustration are wrong and that they are bad for having these feelings. They need to learn that we all feel frustrated and upset and that there are things we can do to help ourselves when our feelings are too strong for us to handle. Remember preschoolers have been on this earth three to five years. They have not learned to control their feelings and actions. It takes a lifetime!

Teacher's Prayer

O God, let my patience soothe the frustration of these children. Help me to love and understand them when they are angry and frustrated. Amen.

Teacher Talk:

I can tell you are feeling angry.

It is all right for you to feel frustrated.

Relax. Take a deep breath.

God loves you.

Center Time

Encourage the children to be involved in one of the centers you have planned.

As children arrive, tell them the sand and water area is open for five children, and everyone will get a turn.

Music Center

Teacher Talk

When we are angry or frustrated, we can try to relax.

Resources

cassette/CD of soothing classical music, cassette/CD player

Have the children remove their shoes and socks and lie on their backs with their eyes closed. Turn off the lights in the room. As you play the classical music, lead the children through several exercises:

Wiggle your toes. Tighten them up very tight. Tighter. Now let them relax.

Wiggle your feet. Tighten them up very tight. Tighter. Now let them relax.

Continue giving instructions for legs, hands, arms, neck, head, and finally the whole body. Afterward, have the children lie still and relax for a few minutes.

Water/Sand Play Center

Teacher Talk

Sometimes when we are frustrated, we can do something that helps us feel better.

Resources

plastic dishpans, sand, water, scoops, plastic sheeting funnels, measuring cups, plastic sheeting

If you have a sand and water table, bring it out today and for the rest of this week. The coolness of the water and texture of the sand are calming and help children "feel" better if they are having a frustrating day. Doing something comforting is one choice they can make when they are frustrated. If you do not have a ready-made sand and water table, you can use plastic dishpans partially filled with sand or water. Add plastic scoops, funnels, and measuring cups. Put plastic sheeting under the table and where the children stand at the table so they do not have to worry about being messy.

Art Center

Teacher Talk

Sometimes we feel angry or frustrated.

Resources

strips of paper (different widths and lengths), glue sticks, construction paper

Give each child a piece of construction paper. Show the children how to make paper strip sculptures by gluing strips of paper to the construction paper base, then gluing the strips to each other. Invite the children to make their own designs to show you feelings of anger or frustration.

Book Center

Teacher Talk

We have many special feelings. Two of those feelings are feeling angry or frustrated.

Resources

precut pictures of angry or frustrated people, construction paper, glue, crayons

Let the children add another page to their books on feelings. Provide precut pictures of people. Give each child a piece of construction paper. Let the children glue on pictures of people showing feelings of anger or frustration. Write the children's names on their pages. Save these pages to add to each child's book.

Worship Center

Teacher Talk

God loves each of us. We love each other.

Resources

none

Have the children stand in a line with their hands on the shoulders of the person in front of them. Show the children how to massage the person's shoulders.

Pray: Dear God, thank you for friends who help us feel better when we are angry or frustrated. Amen.

Wonder Time

Call the children to together time.

Wonder Question: I wonder what I can do when I am angry or frustrated?

Ask: What makes you feel angry or frustrated? Did any of the activities in center time make you feel frustrated? What did you do?
(If a child successfully solved his or her problem, talk with the whole class about what the child did. If not, talk about ways children can successfully deal with their frustrations. See the list at right for suggestions.)

Sing: "Faces" *(see page 213).*

Read the Bible verse.

Pray: Help us, God, when we are angry. Help us to remember that you always love us. Amen

What to Do When You Feel Angry or Frustrated

- Walk away from the situation and come back to it later.
- Get some help from someone.
- Try doing what you are doing in a different way.
- Relax. Sing a song, take a deep breath, get some water, take a walk.
- Use words rather than hitting or screaming or pushing. Let your words tell how angry you are.

Open the Bible to Ecclesiastes 7:9.

Say: "Do not be quick to anger" (Ecclesiastes 7:9).

Have the children repeat the Bible verse.

Group Fun

Resources

oil-based modeling clay, plastic baggies, paper towels, place mats

Let the children manipulate clay. Show the children how to pull a shape out of the clay rather than to make it separately and attach it. Encourage them to soften the clay by working it (squeezing, rolling, pounding). After softening the clay, they can make any shapes they wish. Encourage the children to talk about their feelings while they are working with the clay. When they are finished working with the clay, put their shapes in plastic bags to take home. Note: Oil-based modeling clay cleans up better without water. Just let the children wipe their spaces with paper towels. Or give each child a place mat on which to work; then wipe the place mat with a paper towel.

Goodbye Circle

Use this time to review what children have learned about how to deal with their anger and frustration. Let them tell you what they will try next time they are angry.

Pray: Dear God, help us remember what to do when we are angry. Amen.

Evaluation

How did the day go? Think about your schedule and activities. Is there anything in your schedule or activities that causes frustration for the children or for you? Try to rearrange schedule, activities, or even the room so that frustration is at a minimum.

Lesson 24

Afraid

Teacher Talk:

God is with us when we are afraid.

We can talk to others when we are afraid.

Whenever we are afraid, we can ask God for help.

Goals:

To help the children know that God is with us when we are afraid.

To help children know that they can ask God to help them when they are afraid.

To help the children find ways to express their fears.

Objectives: By the end of this session children will:

Talk about their fears.

Make day/night pictures.

Make paper bag monster faces.

Make scary spider pictures.

Create a Feel Good Collage.

Faith Connections

Bible verse: Do not fear, for God is with you.

(Isaiah 41:10, adapted)

Children need to be able to express their fears and be taken seriously. Whether the fear is real or imaginary, it is real to the child. Make your classroom a safe place where your children can talk about their feelings. Listen carefully to each child to discern if there is something you need to do beyond listening about their fears.

Teacher's Prayer

Dear God, please be with my children when they are afraid. Please help me deal with my own fears and trust in you to be with me. Amen.

Center Time

Encourage the children to be involved in one of the centers you have planned.

As children arrive, have soft classical music playing. Make sure it is background music and that it doesn't overpower their thoughts or conversation.

Science Center

Teacher Talk

God is always with us, day and night.

Resources

newspapers, smocks, construction paper, wax crayons, paintbrushes, thin black tempera paint, shallow containers

Cover the table with newspapers and have the children wear smocks to protect their clothing. Give each child a sheet of construction paper. Invite the children to use the crayons to draw daytime pictures. Suggest they draw pictures of things they like to do during the day such as playing outside or helping Mom or Dad in the kitchen.

When the children have finished, invite them to make their daytime pictures into nighttime pictures. Thin black tempera paint by mixing it with water. Pour the paint into shallow containers. Show the children how to dip their paintbrushes into the thinned paint and then wash the paintbrushes over their pictures.

Talk with the children about the things they do at nighttime, such as taking a bath or listening to a bedtime story. Assure them that God is always with them, day and night.

Art Center

Teacher Talk

Everyone is afraid sometimes.

Resources

paper bags, markers, crayons, yarn, scraps of fabric and paper, newspaper, buttons, glue or tape

Invite the children to make paper bag monster faces. Suggest they color the paper bags to look very scary. Have them add yarn, buttons, and scraps of paper and fabric to the faces. When they are finished, show the children how to wad up newspaper and stuff the bags. Use yarn to tie the bags closed.

Math Center

Teacher Talk

Some people are afraid of spiders and bugs.

Resources

non-permanent ink pads, paper, crayons or markers

Show the children how to press their thumbs on the ink pads and then onto pieces of paper to make thumbprints. Let each child use a marker or crayon to add legs to the thumbprint to create a scary spider. Encourage the children to make several scary spiders on their papers. When they are finished, have the children count their spiders and write the numbers on their papers. Write the children's names on their papers. Save these pages to add to the children's books of feelings.

Worship Center

Teacher Talk

When we are afraid, we can ask God to help us.

Resources

cassette, cassette player

Before class record sounds that might be frightening to children: dog barking, siren, people yelling, scary music. Have the children listen and tell you what the sounds are. Encourage them to tell you which ones make them feel afraid.

Pray: Dear God, sometimes we are afraid. Sometimes we are afraid of *(name some of the things the children are afraid of)*. Please help us not to be afraid. Thank you for being with us, even when we are afraid. Amen.

Open the Bible to Isaiah 41:10.

Say: "Do not fear, for God is with you" (Isaiah 41:10, adapted).

Have the children repeat the Bible verse.

Wonder Time

Have all the children join you.

Wonder Question: I wonder what I can do when I am afraid?
Talk with the children. Ask them to name some of the things that scare them.
Play a game. Name several things that might scare the children. Ask them to cover their eyes if they would be afraid. Ask them to smile a big smile if they would not be afraid. Name things such as: seeing a rainbow, hearing a loud noise, a big dog barking, a spider, watching a scary movie, hugging Mom or Dad, getting lost in a store, waking up in the dark, playing with friends, watching cartoons, falling off of a swing.
Ask: How do you feel when you are afraid?
Read the Bible verse.
Sing, "God Cares" *(see page 212).*
Say: Everyone is afraid sometimes. When we are afraid, we can do some things to feel better. We can tell an adult we trust what is making us afraid. We can pray to God and ask God to help us. God is always with us, even when we are afraid.
Pray: Thank you, God, for adults we can talk to when we are afraid. Thank you for being with us when we are afraid. Amen.

Group Fun

Resources

mural paper, magazine pictures of stuffed animals and adults with caring expressions, small squares of fabric, glue or paste

Have precut pictures of stuffed animals and adults with caring expressions. Also provide small squares of fabric that resemble blanket material. Invite the children to select pictures of things that make them feel better when they are afraid. Have them create a Feel Good Collage by gluing the pictures and fabric to the mural paper.

Book of the Day:
There's a Nightmare in My Closet
by Mercer Mayer

Goodbye Circle

Talk with the children about being afraid. Ask them what they can do to feel better when they are afraid.

Pray: Thank you, God, for being with us when we are afraid. Amen.

Evaluation

Were the children able to express their fears? Do you have concerns about any child that you need to discuss confidentially with another adult? Who in your class needs extra care from you?

Lesson 25

Joy

Goals:

To help the children express the joy they feel inside.

To review and celebrate all the feelings we have talked about this week.

Objectives:

By the end of this session children will:

Sing joyous songs.

Move to music.

Celebrate all their feelings.

Faith Connections

Bible verse: Make a joyful noise to the LORD, all the earth.

(Psalm 100:1)

Children are naturally joyous. Their excitement for the newness of life fills them, and the movement of their bodies is a prayer of praise to God. Help the children name this feeling of joy and to name their songs as songs of praise to God.

Teacher's Prayer

O God, bring back to me the joy of childhood. As I open myself to these children, let the joy of your love surround us all. Amen.

Teacher Talk:

What a joyful noise!

I feel like dancing with joy.

I hear lots of joyful noise.

Thank you, God, for the feeling called joy.

Center Time

Have joyful music playing as the children work in today's centers.

As children arrive, tell them there are activities from earlier in the week out for them to enjoy.

Science Center

Teacher Talk

We feel joy when something gives us great happiness.

Resources

dishwashing liquid, straws, plastic tubs, water, plastic to cover table, white drawing paper, food coloring

Cover the table with plastic. Place a large bowl or plastic tub partially filled with water on the plastic. Add several drops of food coloring to the water. Pour in several squirts of dishwashing liquid. Give each child a straw. Have the children practice blowing, not sucking, through the straw. Then let the children put their straws into the the tub of water and blow. As they blow, bubbles will form.

Give each child a piece of paper to make bubble prints. Show the children how to place their papers gently on top of the bubbles to make the prints. The print is often a light pastel color. Let the children experiment with this process to see if they can do it differently. The joy is in the experimentation!

Music Center

Teacher Talk

We can dance with joy.

Resources

construction paper strips, crepe paper rolls, scissors, tape, music, cassette/CD player

Precut construction paper into 2-by-12-inch strips. Let the children make wrist bracelets out of the strips by taping the paper strips into circles. Let the children cut or tear strips from the crepe paper roll and tape the strips of crepe paper to the bracelets. Show the children how to slide the bracelets over their wrists. Play music and let the children enjoy moving and dancing to music.

Book Center

Teacher Talk

We have many special feelings. One of those feelings is joy.

Resources

precut pictures of joyful people, construction paper, glue, crayons, tape or stapler and staples

Have the children create the last page for their books on feelings by gluing pictures of people showing joy onto pieces of construction paper. Tape or staple each child's pages together to form a book. Be certain each child's name is on his or her book.

Art Center

Teacher Talk

We can show joy in many ways.

Resources

watercolor markers, mural paper

Write the word *joy* on a piece of mural paper. Have the children draw lines, squiggles, dashes, dots, and curves on the paper. If they are able, ask them to write the word *joy* near their drawings.

Worship Center

Teacher Talk

We can thank God for all of our feelings.

Resources

none

Lead the children in singing a version of "If You're Happy and You Know It" using the following suggestions: loved…hug yourself; happy…clap your hands; sad…rub your eyes; angry…stomp your feet; scared…say a prayer; joyful…jump up and down.

Pray: Thank you, God, for all of our feelings. Thank you for all the ways we can show our feelings. Amen.

Wonder Time

Invite the the children to join you for together time. Have the children place their wrist bracelets on the floor beside them or in their laps.

Wonder Question: I wonder what a joyful noise sounds like?
Talk with the children. Ask them to tell you about all the fun things they have done this week. Help them remember that they have learned God plans for feelings.
Read the Bible verse.
Ask: What do you think a joyful noise sounds like?
(Tell the children what you think it means. Talk to them about how the noise in your classroom when they are busy and having fun learning is a joyful noise to God.)
Sing: "Clap, Clap" *(see page 211).*
Pray: Thank you, God, for the things we love to do in our class. Amen.

Open the Bible to Psalm 100:1.

Say: "Make a joyful noise to the LORD, all the earth" (Psalm 100:1).

Have the children repeat the Bible verse.

Group Fun

Resources
wrist bracelets, music, cassette/CD player, rhythm instruments

Tell the children they have been preparing to make a joyful noise. Move furniture to create an open space for dancing or move to another room. Encourage the children to put on their wrist bracelets. Sing the song "Psalm 100" to the tune of "She'll Be Coming 'Round the Mountain." Let the children dance and sway to the song.

Give the children rhythm instruments. Play music and let the children enjoy using the rhythm instruments.

Psalm 100

O-o make a joyful noise
unto the Lord.
O-o make a joyful noise
unto the Lord.
O let's worship God with
gladness.
O let's worship God with
gladness.
O-o make a joyful noise
unto the Lord.

Words: Daphna Flegal and Sharilyn S. Adair

Goodbye Circle

Ask each child to show you without using words how joy feels. Tell them all that you wish them joy today. Be certain each child has his or her feelings book to take home.

Pray: Thank you, God, for our feelings. Thank you for joy. Amen.

Evaluation

Were all of today's objectives met? What happened in your class this week that was positive for the children? Is there a way to repeat or continue that?

Begin planning for next week's lesson.

I HAVE FIVE SENSES

This week the children will explore their five senses. The lessons attempt to bring surprise and joy to the children as they touch and see and smell new things. You know what would be exciting to your children; add to the centers items which are particular to your area and items which will be new to children.

Each day this week children will experience activities which challenge their senses: touching, hearing, smelling, tasting, and seeing. As you explore the Scriptures, help young children see that even long ago when the Bible was written, people were using their senses and learning that God planned for senses.

Lesson 26

I Can Touch

Teacher Talk:

Thank you, God, for our senses.

God plans for our fingers to touch and feel.

Please touch!

Goal:

For the children to learn that their ability to touch is one of their senses.

Objectives: By the end of this session the children will:

Touch and guess what they are touching.

Feel and describe different textures.

Make a caterfeeler.

Faith Connections

Bible verse: Then Jesus asked, "Who touched me?" (Luke 8:45)

Children need to know that their sense of touch is a gift from God. God's love is spread through your gentle touch.

Teacher's Prayer

O God, help me keep in mind that there are many different kinds of touches. Help me to only touch the children with gentleness and caring. Amen.

Center Time

Encourage the children to use their sense of touch as they work in the centers today.

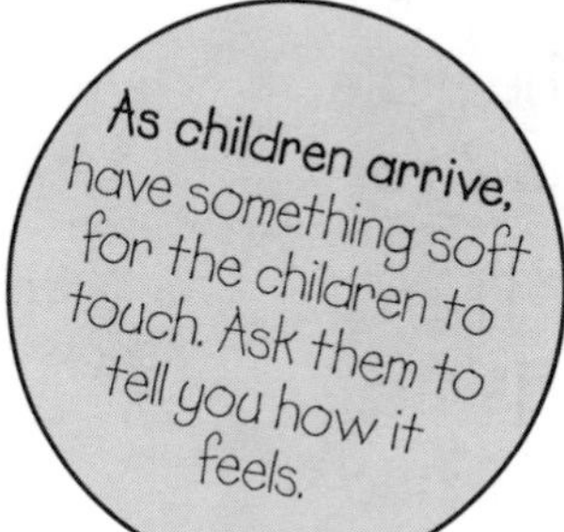

Writing Center

Teacher Talk

God plans for us to touch and feel.

Resources

3 x 5 cards, glue, colored sand, trays, alphabet chart

Place an alphabet chart in the writing center. Have each child use glue to write one letter on a card. Place each card in a tray. Let the child sprinkle sand over the wet glue. When the glue dries, have the children trace the letters with their fingers.

Worship Center

Teacher Talk

Thank you, God, for fingers that can touch.

Resources

sand or water tables or a dishpan partially filled with water or sand, shells, rocks

Use the sand or water tables or the dishpan partially filled with water or sand. Include various textured items such as smooth shells, pointed shells, rough rocks, and so forth. Let the children handle the objects.

Pray: God, I thank you for my fingers that can touch so many wonderful things. Amen.

Science Center

Teacher Talk

It's fun to touch different things.

Resources

old clean socks, objects with a variety of shapes and textures, string

Place each object in a separate sock and tie a knot in the top of the sock. Hang the socks separately from the ceiling across one wall or place them on a table. Let the children feel the socks and guess what is in each one.

Art Center

Teacher Talk

We can use our sense of touch.

Resources

cardboard, sandpaper, fabric, burlap, velvet, cotton balls, glue, construction paper, chenille sticks, paper punch, markers, scissors

Before class cut cardboard, construction paper, sandpaper, and fabrics of different textures into 2-inch circles. Let the children choose four to six cardboard circles to make "caterfeelers." Have the children glue sandpaper, fabric circles, and cotton balls on the cardboard circles. Have the children glue the cardboard circles end to end to make the sections of their caterfeelers. Let them choose construction paper circles for the faces. Use a paper punch to punch two holes at the top of each face. Let the children thread chenille sticks through the holes to make feelers. Secure each feeler with a twist. Let the children decorate the faces with markers. Talk about the different textures.

Math Center

Teacher Talk

We can learn through our senses.

Resources

frozen bread dough; flour; greased cookie sheets; damp towels; butter, honey, or jam; number line

Thaw frozen bread dough before class. Sprinkle a small amount of flour on the table in front of each child. Give the children balls of dough to knead. Have the children shape the dough into numbers. Have a number line for the children to see. Let whatever they shape be their numbers. Place the numbers on a greased cookie sheet. Cover the dough with a damp towel and let it rise in a warm place. Bake for 12 to 15 minutes at 350 degrees until golden brown. Cool and let the children have their numbers for snack with butter, honey, or jam.

Open the Bible to Luke 8:45.

Say: "Then Jesus asked, 'Who touched me?'" (Luke 8:45).

Have the children repeat the Bible verse.

Wonder Time

Bring the socks from the science center to together time. Open each sock and show the children the item inside as they sit down.

Wonder Question: I wonder why God planned for the sense of touch?
Ask: What things did you touch as you worked and played today? What things did you touch that felt soft? hard? rough? smooth?
Read the Bible Verse.
Say: Jesus was a real person. He could feel it when people touched him just as you can. (Have the children gently touch the arm of the person sitting next to them. Talk about how the gentle touch feels.)
Sing: "I'm Thankful," verse 2 *(see page 215)*.
Pray: Thank you, God, for my sense of touch. Amen.

Group Fun

Resources
blindfolds

Tell the children that they will play a touching game for the group activity. This game may be played outside. Have the children stand in a circle. Make as many circles as you have adults. Choose one child to be blindfolded. The adult holds the blindfolded child's hand while the other children hold hands in a circle around the blindfolded child. The adult then, still holding the blindfolded child's hand, leads the whole circle to something that can be touched and stops. The adult places the blindfolded child's hand on the object that is to be touched. The others watch as the child touches an object and tries to guess what the object is. You can lead the children to touch a tree trunk, grass, a bench, and so forth. If the child can't guess, let the children in the circle give hints. Play until each child has a turn. If there is only one adult and more than six or seven children, play the game at different times during the day to give each child a turn without the children getting too bored with the game.

Never have the children touch something that could be harmful or something that could disgust the children. You will lose the children's trust.

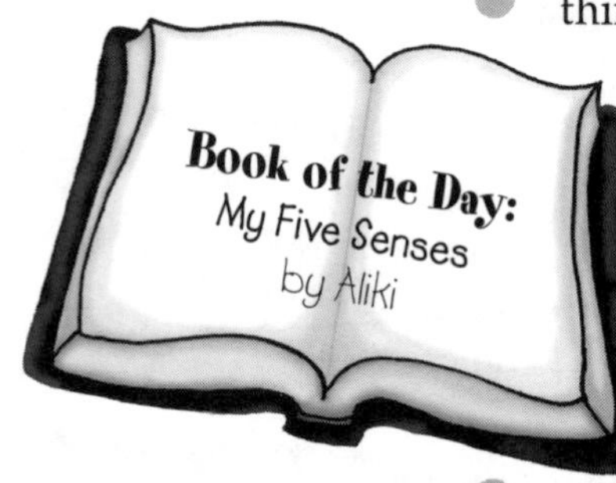

Goodbye Circle

Say: I wonder why God planned for the sense of touch. (Talk about things which children should not touch such as a hot stove, poison ivy, snakes, and so forth.)

Pray: Thank you, God, for my sense of touch. Amen.

Evaluation

Did you discover children who don't like to touch anything messy? Remember this in future planning.

Lesson 27

I Can Hear

Goals:

To help children become aware of their sense of hearing.

To increase the children's hearing skills.

Objectives:

By the end of this session the children will:

Listen to different sounds.

Listen to music.

Make cricket chirpers.

Talk about the importance of hearing.

Faith Connections

Bible verse: Let anyone with ears to hear listen! (Luke 8:8)

Children need times to hear the sounds of nature. They also need time to listen to the quiet around them. Make sure they have a chance to hear all the different sounds of nature today.

Teacher's Prayer

O God, as I listen to the children today, help me to hear not only their words but also their feelings and needs. Help me to truly hear them as Jesus would. Amen.

Teacher Talk:

Thank you, God, for our senses.

God plans for our ears to hear.

Please listen!

Center Time

Encourage the children to use their sense of hearing as they work in the centers today.

As children arrive, tell them what you hear as they walk to the class. You might hear footsteps, a voice, or Mother's keys.

Writing Center

Teacher Talk

God gives us ears to listen with.

Resources

markers, lined chart paper, drawing paper, crayons

Let each child dictate a story about a sound. The sound might have frightened them or reminded them to do something. Write the child's story on lined paper. Give each child a piece of drawing paper. Have the children draw pictures for their stories. Attach the stories and pictures. Display in the classroom.

Math Center

Teacher Talk

We can learn when we listen.

Resources

wooden beads, metal pan, other objects

Let the children count the number of beads you drop into the metal pan. Add other objects and listen for the different sounds.

Building Center

Teacher Talk

We can use our ears to listen.

Resources

bicycle horns, cardboard boxes, ribbons, pretend steering wheels, small radios, blocks

Encourage the children to build roads and pathways for their cars. Make cars from cardboard boxes with the tops and bottoms cut out. Children can step into the cars and hold them as they pretend to drive. Attach ribbon to opposite sides of the boxes to be used like suspenders. (This will allow the children to hold the cars while they drive them.) Attach horns, pretend steering wheels, even small radios. Let the children make car sounds as they pretend to drive.

Science Center

Teacher Talk

God plans for our ears to hear.

Resources

cassette player, ear phones, tape with various sounds

Create an audio cassette with a variety of sounds: music, water dripping, dog barking, baby crying, and so forth. See how many sounds the children can remember at together time.

Worship Center

Teacher Talk

Thank you, God, for our senses.

Resources

glasses of different sizes, water, metal spoon

Fill each of the glasses with a different amount of water. Let the children lightly tap each glass with the metal spoon. Listen for the different sounds. Let the children create a melody.

Pray: Thank you, God, for my ears that hear so many different sounds. Amen.

Cooking Center

Teacher Talk

We like to listen.

Resources

popcorn, popcorn popper, oil, clean sheet

Listen to popcorn pop! Place a clean queen- or king-sized sheet on the floor and put the popper in the center without a lid. Fill the popper as usual. **The children must stand behind the edge of the sheet to keep safe from grease spatters.** Let the corn pop out onto the sheet. Then enjoy it for a snack.

Wonder Time

As children come to the circle, turn on the cassette player again without the earphones. Let the children listen to the sounds *(see science center)* until all have arrived in the circle. Ask the children what sounds they heard.

Wonder Question: I wonder why God planned for us to hear?

Talk about all the wonderful sounds they can hear. Let them tell you some of their favorite sounds.

Sing: "I'm Thankful," verse 3 *(see page 215).*

Play a game. Have the children stand in a circle in an open area of the room. Play "Ring Around the Rosie" with the children. Play the game again, and tell the children to listen carefully as you sing the song. As you sing, change the word *ring* to a different movement word like *hop*. Have the children hop around the circle. Continue playing the game with different movement words.

Read the Bible verse.

Whisper: Be very still. Let's listen to the quiet all around us.

Pray: Thank you, God, for our ears that let us hear your wonderful world. Amen.

Open the Bible to Luke 8:8.

Say: "Let anyone with ears to hear listen!" (Luke 8:8).

Have the children repeat the Bible verse.

Group Fun

Resources

emery boards or sandpaper, pencils, small sticks, metal jar lids, aluminum soda cans

Send the children to the tables where they will make their cricket chirpers. Tell the children that they may make cricket chirpers from a variety of items. Each child can choose items to make the sound of a cricket. Show the children how to rub the emery boards or sandpaper together to make scratching sounds and rap pencils, small sticks, metal jar lids, or aluminum soda cans together to make tapping sounds. Let the children experiment using the items to make their own sounds. Take the children outside. Let them make their cricket sounds. Then put the noise makers down and listen to the sounds. After a few minutes talk about what you hear. Then listen again.

Goodbye Circle

Play a clapping game with the children. Have the children listen carefully as you clap your hands in a rhythmic pattern. Have the children clap their hands in the same pattern. End the game by clapping your hands in applause for your class of good listeners.

Pray: Thank you, God, for our ears that let us hear your wonderful world. Amen.

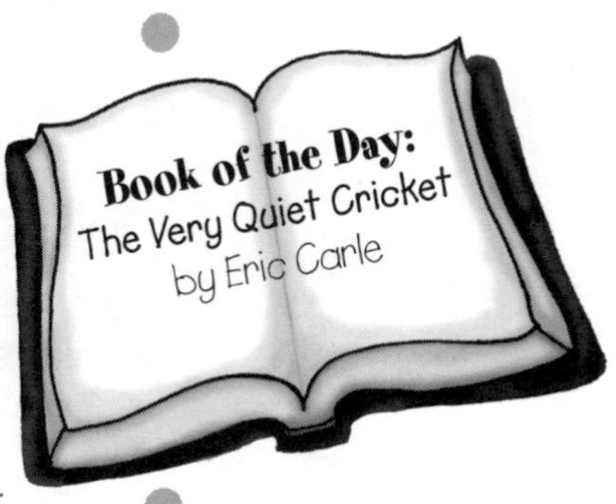

Evaluation

Which children have trouble listening? How can you help?

Lesson 28

I Can See

Teacher Talk:

Thank you, God, for our senses.

God plans for our eyes to see.

Look and see!

Goal:

To help the children explore their sense of sight and enjoy all the beauty around them.

Objectives:

By the end of this session the children will:

Draw rainbows.

Make scratch pictures.

Make cardboard binoculars.

Use their eyes to enjoy the world.

Faith Connections

Bible verse: Come and see what God has done. (Psalm 66:5)

Children help us see the beauty and newness of the world which we often miss. During this session give them opportunities to see interesting and marvelous creations of nature.

Teacher's Prayer

O God, take from my eyes all the preconceived ideas I have about each child and each parent. Help me to see each child with new eyes, the eyes of Jesus, the eyes of love. Amen.

Center Time

Encourage the children to use their sense of sight as they work in the centers today.

As children arrive, have sea shells, rocks, leaves, and other interesting nature items available to see with a magnifying glass.

Writing Center

Teacher Talk

God plans for our eyes to see.

Resources

colored pencils, white paper

Let the children write with colored pencils. Let the children name the different colors they see.

Math Center

Teacher Talk

We can use our eyes to learn.

Resources

coffee filters, craft stems, markers

Show the children how to fold a filter in half to make an umbrella. Let children poke the craft stem through the center of the filter and fold the end down. Talk with the children about rain.

Ask: "What does rain look like? Are raindrops clear? Are they different colors? What happens to the drops when they hit glass on a window?" Let the children dot various colored raindrops on their umbrellas with different colored markers. Help the children count their rain drops.

Worship Center

Teacher Talk

Thank you, God, for our senses.

Resources

large sheets of paper, pencils, crayons, masking tape

Have the children sit cross-legged on the edge of a large sheet of paper. Using a pencil or a crayon to draw arches from one side of the body to the other. When the child stands up, there will be a rainbow shape. Let the children color the rainbow. Use masking tape to hang the rainbows on the wall.

Pray: Thank you, God, for eyes that can see rainbows. Amen.

Home Living Center

Teacher Talk

We use our eyes to help us.

Resources

reading glasses, books, magazines

Add books, magazines, and reading glasses to this center. Talk about all the ways we use our eyes at home.

Building Center

Teacher Talk

God plans for our eyes to see.

Resources

level

Show the children how to use a level. (When the bubble is between the two black lines, the object on which it is resting is level.) Place a block on an angle and show the children where the level's bubble is. Then ask them to check their buildings to see if they are level. They can also check items such as your desk, counter tops, the sink, and so forth.

Art Center

Teacher Talk

Thank you, God, for our senses.

Resources

foam trays, ball point pens, tempera paints, brayer (optional), drawing paper, scissors, paintbrushes

Cut edges from foam meat trays so they are flat on both sides. Let each child draw a design with a ball point pen on the foam tray. Let the children use brayers or paint brushes to cover their designs with tempera paint. Show each child how to put a piece of drawing paper on top of the painted tray to make a print. Remember that writing will come out backwards.

Open the Bible to Psalm 66:5.

Say: "Come and see what God has done" (Psalm 66:5).

Have the children repeat the Bible verse.

Wonder Time

Call the children to together time. Say things like "I see *(child's name)* picking up the blocks. *(Child's name)* come to the circle."

Wonder Question: I wonder why God planned for us to see?
Talk about the things our eyes help us do. (See things in God's world; see to walk; see things that help keep us safe like a sticker that tells us something is poison.)
Sing: "I'm Thankful," verse 1 *(see page 215)*.
Read the Bible verse.
Say: We can use our eyes to see all the beautiful things God has made in our world.

Group Fun

Resources

cardboard tubes, stickers, tape

Tell the children that you are all going on an "I see" walk. The walk may be outside or inside. If you choose to take the children outside, review the rules for your walk.

Let the children make binoculars to take on their "I see" walk. Before class tape two cardboard tubes together for each child. Give each child a pair of tubes. Let the children decorate the tubes with stickers. Show the children how to use the tubes like binoculars.

Take the children on an "I see" walk. This is a wonderful language activity for the children. Start the children on the walk. Stop walking and encourage one child to look through his or her binoculars and say, "I see…" and name something she or he sees. Ask the child questions to give hints about the characteristics of what the child sees such as color, size, movement, and so forth. Let the other children guess what the child is describing. Continue on the walk, stopping along the way until each child has a turn being the one to say, "I see."

Goodbye Circle

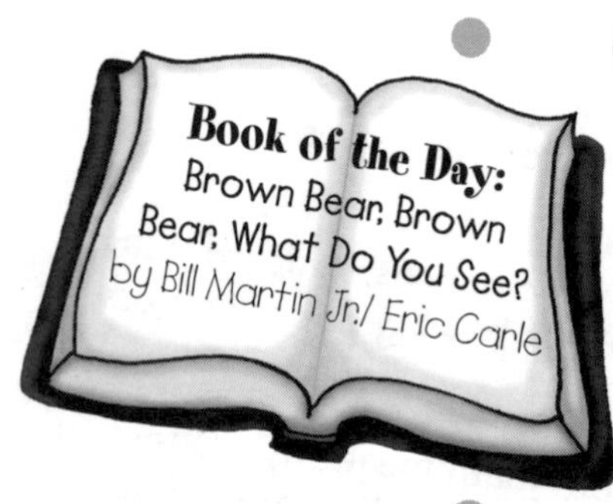

Have the children name something beautiful they saw today. Play a "watch and do" game with the children. Tell the children to use their eyes to watch you and do what you do. Have the children watch you do a motion like bending your arm at the elbow. Encourage the children to copy your motion. After a few moments, change your motion (move your arm up and down without bending your elbow) without saying anything to the children. See how long it takes before the children see you and change their motions to match.

Pray: Thank you, God, for eyes to see and ears to hear and hands to touch. Amen.

Evaluation

Use today's activities to assess each child's language skills. Make notes about children's vocabulary and abilities to communicate for each child's folder.

Lesson 29

I Can Smell

Goal:

To give the children the opportunity to use their sense of smell and to enjoy a variety of aromas.

Objectives: By the end of this session the children will:

Smell a variety of spices and condiments.

Make and play with cinnamon play dough.

Draw with scented markers.

Faith Connections

Bible verse: The blossoms on grapevines smell sweet.

(Song of Solomon 2:13, paraphrased)

Children need to experience the wonders of smell. Often preschoolers shy away from scents which are too potent. Provide simple aromas for children to enjoy.

Teacher's Prayer

God of the ocean, the earth, the desert, fill my nose with your wonders. Help me to breathe your richness in what we do today. Amen.

NOTE: Be aware of children with allergies to scents. Modify your activities for these children.

Teacher Talk:

Thank you, God, for our senses.

God plans for our noses to smell.

How does this smell?

Center Time

Encourage the children to use their sense of smell as they work in the centers today.

> **Before the children arrive,** spray air freshener or use potpourri to create a pleasant smell. If you have children with allergies, use cinnamon sticks.

Writing Center

Teacher Talk

God plans for our noses to smell.

Resources

petals of dried flowers, glue, plain stationery; scented markers

Give the children pieces of plain stationery. Let the children glue dried flowers on the corners and borders of their stationery. Have the children write on the stationery with scented markers.

Worship Center

Teacher Talk

Thank you, God, for our senses.

Resources

a variety of fruits including grapes, large plastic bowl, paper plates, napkins

Place a large plastic bowl full of fruit in the center of the table in the home living area. Provide paper plates and napkins. Let each child have a piece of fruit. Talk about the smell and taste of the different fruits. Say the Bible verse, "The blossoms on grapevines smell sweet" (Song of Solomon 2:13, paraphrased), as the children eat grapes.

Pray: Thank you, God, for my nose. I like to smell different things. Amen.

Math Center

Teacher Talk

How does this smell?

Resources

cinnamon sticks, ten plastic foam cups, marker

Number each of the plastic foam cups 1 through 10. Let the children count out loud as they place a cinnamon stick in each cup. Older children may want to correspond the number of sticks in the cup with the outside number. Younger preschoolers may just want to play with the cinnamon sticks; this is a beginning step to counting. Point out that the cinnamon sticks have a spicy smell.

Art Center

Teacher Talk

How does this smell?

Resources

drawing paper, scented markers

Let the children draw pictures or make colorful designs using the scented markers. Talk about the smell of each marker and the color. With older children you may want to talk about why certain colors are associated with certain smells. For example, cinnamon is brown; cherries are red; oranges are orange.

Science Center

Teacher Talk

God plans for our noses to smell.

Resources

lemon juice, ketchup, mustard, cinnamon, cloves, oranges, grapes

Place each spice, fruit, and condiment in a separate small paper cup. Let the children smell each cup and guess what is making the scent.

Building Center

Teacher Talk

God plans for our noses to smell.

Resources

real trailer tires, trucks, blocks

Let the children roll the tires to various spots and pretend to fix flat tires or use them to "make" a car or truck. Encourage the children to smell the tires. Talk about the smell.

Wonder Time

As children come to together time, place a dab of scented hand lotion in the palm of each child and let the child rub it in. Talk about how it smells.

Wonder Question: I wonder why God planned for a sense of smell?
Let the children tell you all the different smells they experienced this morning.
Ask: Were there any smells which were bad? Why do we need to smell? Smelling helps us know where we are and what is about to happen, like when it is almost supper time. Smelling helps us know what something is, such as an orange or a flower.
Let the children tell you what smells they like the best.
Sing: "I'm Thankful," verse 5 (see page 215).
Read the Bible verse.
Ask: Have you ever smelled grapes?
Say: God plans for us to have noses that can smell the world.
Pray: Thank you, God, for noses to smell. Amen.

Open the Bible to Song of Solomon 2:13.

Say: "The blossoms on grapevines smell sweet" (Song of Solomon 2:13, paraphrased).

Have the children repeat the Bible verse.

Group Fun

Resources
cinnamon play dough, cookie cutters, rolling pins, plastic utensils, pencils, ribbon, scissors

Tell the children that they will need to use their noses for the group activity today.

Bake cinnamon play dough before class. Allow the children to play with the dough. Encourage the children to smell the dough as they enjoy manipulating it. Show the children how to use the cookie cutters to cut shapes from the dough. Use a pencil to make holes in the shapes. Cut ribbons into lengths long enough to fit over the children's heads. Tie the ribbons through the hole in the shapes. When the shapes dry, let the children wear them as necklaces.

Cinnamon Play Dough
2 cups water
2 cups all purpose flour
⅓ cups cooking oil
2 cups salt
4 tablespoons cinnamon
4 tablespoons cream of tartar
2 tablespoons vanilla extract

Mix together all ingredients and cook over medium heat until elastic. Knead the dough on a floured surface until lumps are gone and it has a smooth texture. Be sure to store unused portion in plastic bags and the refrigerator.

Goodbye Circle

Talk with the children about all the senses you have studied. Ask the children to use their noses to discover interesting smells at home tonight. Have the children put their index fingers on their noses.

Pray: Thank you, God, for my nose and the smells it smells. Amen.

Evaluation

Did you discover the wonders of your own nose today? Which children are especially sensitive to smells? Plan a review of all the senses tomorrow as we learn about taste.

Lesson 30

I Can Taste

Teacher Talk:

Thank you, God, for our senses.

God plans for our tongues to taste.

How does this taste?

Goals:

To let the children experience different-tasting foods and know that God planned for the sense of taste.

To review what the children have learned about their senses this week.

Objectives: By the end of this session the children will:

Taste a variety of foods.

Talk about the differences in sweet and sour.

Make toast.

Review the week's lessons.

Faith Connections

Bible verse: O taste and see that the LORD is good.

(Psalm 34:8)

Children need to connect the joy of eating and tasting with God's plan for their wonderful bodies. Help them to see that all of our senses help us to enjoy the earth and keep our bodies healthy.

Teacher's Prayer

Thank you, God, for the wonderful tastes of sweet fruit, salty pretzels, warm bread, and of course—chocolate! You have created so many wonderful things. Help me share the wonder with my children. Amen.

NOTE: Be aware of children with food allergies. Modify your activities for these children.

Center Time

Encourage the children to use their sense of taste as they work in the centers today.

> **As children arrive,** ask parents if there are any food allergies. Use their comments to confirm your records.

Home Living Center

Teacher Talk

God plans for our tongues to taste.

Resources

baby food; plastic spoons; tissues; paper towels; baby plates, spoons, bottles; dolls

Let the children taste baby food in the home living center. Let the children pretend to feed dolls and talk about how the babies like their food. Let the children taste the baby food if they wish by giving them a small amount on a plastic spoon. Throw away the spoons and have tissues ready for spit-outs.

Science Center

Teacher Talk

How does this taste?

Resources

lemon wedges, peppermint candies

Tell the children that you are having a taste test. Give each child a lemon wedge to taste first, then give the child a peppermint candy stick. Tell the children that you will talk more about the taste test in together time.

Worship Center

Teacher Talk

Thank you, God, for our senses.

Resources

chocolate chips, salsa, oyster crackers, dill pickle slices, cooked macaroni, paper plates, plastic spoons

Cut the pickle into small bits. Place each item on a separate plate. Let the children taste each item and decide if it is: sweet, sour, spicy, or bland.

Pray: Thank you, God, for my tongue that can taste so many wonderful things. Amen.

Cooking Center

Teacher Talk

God plans for our tongues to taste.

Resources

3 flavors of jelly, table knives or craft sticks for spreaders, bread, four-slice toaster, adult helper

Let the children make their own toast. Provide a toaster and an adult helper. Let the children toast bread and then use a table knife to cut the bread into halves and fourths. Let the children try different jellies on their toast. Talk about which jellies they like best.

Writing Center

Teacher Talk

How does this taste?

Resources

cassette recorder with microphone, adult helper

Tell the children you want them to record their favorite recipe. Have the children tell their names and then name a food they like. Then prompt the children to tell how the food is made. Have an adult (parent or director) supervise this activity. After class take the cassette home and write out what the children said. The recipes make great gift books for parents.

Block Center

Teacher Talk

Thank you, God, for our senses.

Resources

blocks, plastic food

Have the children create a grocery center from the blocks. Display the food on the shelves. Let the children make their selection, trying to choose from a variety of tastes.

Open the Bible to Psalm 34:8.

Say: "O taste and see that the LORD is good" (Psalm 34:8).

Have the children repeat the Bible verse.

Wonder Time

After cleanup have children gather on the carpet with you.

Wonder Question: I wonder why God planned for us to have a sense of taste?
Talk about foods they enjoyed tasting and foods they did not like.
Say: Our tastes change as we grow. Some things you don't like now you will like when you grow older.
Ask: Who took the taste test with the lemon and peppermint? Which item was sweet? Which item was sour?
Read the Bible verse.
Say: God is good. God plans for food for us to eat and that keeps us strong and healthy.
Review the five senses with the children. Talk about each sense and how it helps us.
Sing: "I'm Thankful," verse 4. Then sing verses 1-5 *(see page 215)*.

Group Fun

Resources

facial features (noses, mouths, eyes, ears) and hands cut from magazines, glue, construction paper

Place the magazine pictures on the table. Let the children create a Five Senses Montage by gluing the different pictures onto their pieces of construction paper. Talk about how each of the parts helps us to learn about God's world.

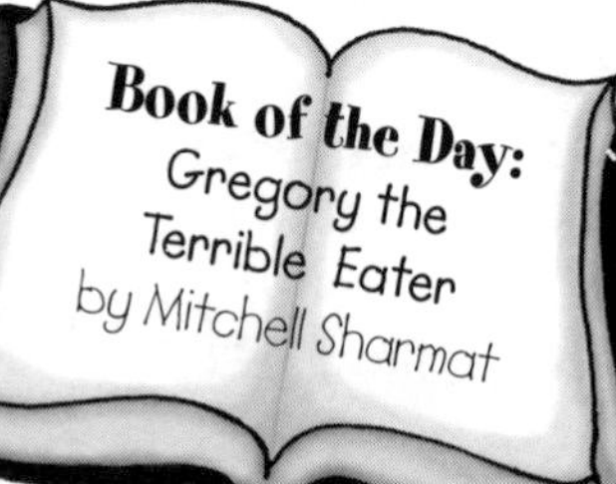

Goodbye Circle

Say a litany prayer together. Tell the children that when you turn your hands palms up, they are to say, "Thank you, God, for my wonderful body."

I have hands to touch things that are soft and smooth or rough and hard.
Thank you, God, for my wonderful body.
I have ears to hear birds sing and voices of those I love.
Thank you, God, for my wonderful body.
I have eyes to see my friends and the world outside.
Thank you, God, for my wonderful body.
I have a nose to smell the rich earth, the flowers, and good things to eat.
Thank you, God, for my wonderful body.
I have a mouth for tasting things that are delicious.
Thank you, God, for my wonderful body. Amen.

Evaluation

As you plan for next week's emphasis on the heart and heart-healthy practices, you may choose to keep some of the centers children have enjoyed this week.

I HAVE A HEART

This week's lessons are included to help very young children learn to care for their hearts. It is important to encourage eating healthy foods, exercising, and not smoking as a way of life.

The American Heart Association has a kit called *Heart Power* for preschools. Most local offices will let you borrow the kit for a refundable deposit. It includes a big book, posters, two stethoscopes, an audio cassette, a video, and a chart showing the heart. The kit sells for $149.00. Call 1-800-AHA-USA1 for more information.

Lesson 31

My Heart Is a Pump

Goal:

To help the children discover that their heart is a muscle that needs care.

Objectives: By the end of this session the children will:

Use different pumps to see how pumps work.

Feel their pulses.

Faith Connections

Bible verse: "I am wonderfully made." (Psalm 139:14, adapted)

Children are fascinated with information about their bodies. Children this age have already been introduced to the heart in connection with emotions. They are ready to discover that God plans for the heart muscle to pump blood through each of their bodies.

Teacher's Prayer

O God, thank you for my wonderful body. Help me learn to treat it with respect. Amen.

Teacher Talk:

God plans for our bodies to grow and move.

God plans for our heart muscles to pump blood through our bodies.

Your body is a wonderful creation.

Center Time

Display pictures of the heart in your center area today. Pictures are available through the American Heart Association.

As children arrive, tell them we are learning about our hearts today and direct them to the centers.

Math Center

Teacher Talk

You are wonderfully made. God made your body with a heart that beats.

Resources

heart picture (*see page 219*), markers, clock or watch with second hand, tape

Photocopy and cut out the heart picture (*see page 219*) for each child. Station a helper in the math center to show each child how to take his or her own pulse. Use your middle and ring fingers. Hold the pads of these fingers side by side just below and to the side of the Adam's apple on the child's neck. Look at a clock or watch with a second hand and count how many beats you feel in 15 seconds. Counting out loud with the child will help the child understand that the heart beats over and over. Multiply the number you get by 4 (or hold fingers in position for a whole minute) to discover the number of beats per minute. Now help the child feel where to take his or her own pulse. Write the child's name and pulse rate on his or her heart picture and display it in the classroom.

Art Center

Teacher Talk

You are wonderfully made.

Resources

eye droppers, food coloring, coffee filters, cups

Place several drops of food coloring in three or four cups (one color to a cup). Show the children how to suck up the colored water with the eye dropper and then squirt it onto the coffee filter. Let them make their own designs. Tell the children that the eye droppers are small pumps. **Ask:** "What is in your body that works like a pump?" *(your heart)*

Worship Center

Teacher Talk

God made your heart to be a muscle.

Resources

mural paper, crayons, heart picture (*see page 219*), masking tape

Let the children play a game like "Pin the Tail on the Donkey." Before class photocopy and cut out the heart picture (*see page 219*). Have one child lie down on a piece of mural paper. Use a crayon to trace around the child's body. Mount the outline on a door or wall. Have the children come one at a time to stand in front of the body outline. Place a loop of tape on the back of the heart picture. **Say:** "God planned for the heart to be a muscle. It is near the center of the chest." Show the children how to place their hands over their hearts. Have each child close his or her eyes or tie a blindfold around each child's head. Let each child try to place the heart in the center of the chest on the body outline.

Pray: Thank you, God, for our hearts that pump our blood and help us live. Amen.

Science Center

Teacher Talk

God plans for your heart to pump blood.

Resources

water table or dishpan partially filled with water, turkey baster, red food coloring

Show the children how to use the turkey baster to draw water in and squirt the water out. For more fun add red food coloring to the water. Help the children squirt the water in a rhythm. Talk about how your heart has a rhythm. **Say:** "The baster is a pump that draws water in and squirts water out just as the heart pumps blood."

Wonder Time

As the children gather together for wonder time, have them tell you what they learned in the centers today.

Wonder Question: I wonder how big our hearts are?

Have each child make a fist.

Say: Your heart is about the size of your fist. My heart is the size of my fist. Your heart grows as your body grows.

Have the children squeeze their fists.

Say: Your heart pumps all the time, squirting blood through your body. When you have been running, your heart beats fast. Show me how your heart pumps if you are running. (Squeeze fist quickly.) When you are sleeping, your heart beats slowly. Show me how your heart pumps when you are sleeping. (Squeeze fist slowly.)

Sing: "I'm Thankful," verse 6 *(see page 215)*.

Read the Bible verse.

Say: God planned for each of our bodies to have a muscle called the heart. Our hearts pump blood through our bodies. Our bodies are wonderful creations.

Pray: Thank you, God, for our wonderful bodies. Thank you for our hearts. Amen.

Open the Bible to Psalm 139:14.

Say: "I am wonderfully made" (Psalm 139:14, adapted).

Have the children repeat the Bible verse.

Group Fun

Resources

fast and slow music, cassette/CD player, scarfs

Say: "Let's exercise our hearts." Move furniture to make an open space in your room. Give the children chiffon or silk scarfs. Play slow music. Let the children dance to the music and move the scarfs. After the children have been dancing for a while, stop the music and let each child feel his or her pulse. Play fast music and let the children dance with their scarfs. Let the children dance for a while, then stop the music and have each child feel his or her pulse. How are their pulses beating now? Did their pulses beat faster after they had been dancing slowly or after they had been dancing fast? Play the slow music again and have the children cool down.

Goodbye Circle

Remind children that the heart is a muscle. Its job is to pump blood through the body.

Pray: Thank you, God, for my beating heart! Amen.

Evaluation

Choose activities to repeat for tomorrow's lesson. Was anything said or done that might have made a child fearful about his or her heart? Be reassuring tomorrow as you help children celebrate their wonderful hearts.

Lesson 32

Listening to My Heart

Teacher Talk:

God plans for each of our bodies to have a muscle called the heart.

God plans for us to have feelings like love. Sometimes we say our feelings are in our hearts.

Your body is a wonderful creation.

Goal:

To help children understand the differences between the real heart that pumps and a valentine-shape heart that we use to talk about feelings like love.

Objectives

By the end of this session children will:

See the difference in their real hearts and valentine hearts.

Make a yarn picture of the heart.

Take their pulses and hear their hearts.

Faith Connections

Bible verse: The LORD looks on the heart. (1 Samuel 16:7)

Children often picture valentine hearts when we talk about our hearts. We reinforce this image when we talk about emotions being "in our hearts." The purpose of these lessons is to help the children begin to understand the difference between valentine hearts and our physical hearts. God also planned for us to have the muscle in the body called a heart that pumps our blood and helps us live.

Teacher's Prayer

O God, you know my heart. Fill me with your love and understanding. Amen.

Center Time

Display pictures of the heart in your center area today. Pictures are available through the American Heart Association.

Science Center

Teacher Talk

God plans for your heart to pump blood.

Resources

picture of heart, veins, and arteries; blue yarn; red yarn; glue; doll outline (*see page 218*); scissors; markers; paper towels; shallow trays; red tempera paint; nonpermanent ink pad

Photocopy the doll (*see page 218*) for each child. Use a marker to place a small dot on each doll on the left side of the breast bone where the heart would be. Cut red and blue yarn into 12-inch lengths. Fold paper towels and place them into a shallow tray. Pour red tempera paint onto the paper towels to make a paint pad. Or use a red nonpermanent ink pad. Display pictures of the heart, veins, and arteries in the center.

Give each child a doll. Have the children make a fist. Show the children how to press the side of their hands onto the paint or ink pad and then over the spot on the doll to make a heart. Remind the children that our hearts are about the size of our fists. Have the children wash their hands.

Let the children glue blue and red yarn on the arms and legs and head of the doll outline to represent veins and arteries. Explain that our hearts pump our blood through our veins and arteries.

Building Center

Teacher Talk

God made your body with a heart that beats.

Resources

stethoscopes, white lab coats or men's shirts, blocks, stuffed animals

Let the children make hospital beds out of blocks for stuffed animal patients. Encourage the children to pretend to be doctors and listen to the patients' hearts with the stethoscopes.

Art Center

Teacher Talk

God plans for your body to have a muscle called the heart. God also plans for you to have feelings like love.

Resources

valentine hearts (*see page 221*), glue, glitter, collage materials, real heart shapes (*see page 219*)

Have valentine-shaped hearts (*see page 221*) and real heart shapes (*see page 219 for a pattern*) cut out of construction paper. Let the children decorate the hearts with collage materials and glitter. Talk about the differences in the two hearts. Tell the children we draw valentine-shaped hearts to show feelings like love. The muscle in our body called the heart looks like the other shape.

Worship Center

Teacher Talk

You are wonderfully made. God made your body with a heart that beats.

Resources

drums, music, cassette/CD player

Let the children listen to the music and try to beat the drums to the same rhythm in the music.

Turn off the music. Feel a child's pulse. Use your middle and ring fingers. Hold the pads of these fingers side by side just below and to the side of the Adam's apple on the child's neck. Count the beats out loud. Have the child beat the drum to the counts.

Say: You are wonderfully made. God made your body with a heart that beats over and over. You can feel the beat through your pulse. You can hear the beat with a stethoscope.

Pray: Thank you, God, for our wonderful bodies. Thank you for our hearts that beat. Amen.

Open the Bible to 1 Samuel 16:7.

Say: "The LORD looks on the heart" (1 Samuel 16:7).

Have the children repeat the Bible verse.

Wonder Time

Use the drum to tell children it is time to clean up. As they gather on the carpet let them clap with the same rhythm you use as you beat the drum.

Wonder Question: I wonder what our hearts sound like?

Say: We each have a heart that beats inside our bodies. When our heart beats, it sounds like lub dub, lub dub.

Beat the drum as you say lub dub, lub dub. Have the children repeat the sounds.

Show pictures of a real heart.

Say: The heart is a muscle that pumps blood through our bodies.

Show the children a valentine heart.

Ask: Have you ever seen this kind of heart? Does it look like the hearts inside our bodies?

Say: This kind of heart is like a valentine heart. It helps us remember feelings like love.

Read the Bible verse.

Say: God plans for each of our bodies to have a muscle we call the heart. God also plans for us to have feelings like love.

Sing: "I'm Thankful," verse 6 *(see page 215)*.

Pray: Thank you, God, for our beating hearts. Thank you for love. Amen.

Group Fun

Resources

yarn, large drinking straws, 2-ounce paper cups, tape, paper punch, scissors, stethoscope

Show the children a real stethoscope. Let the children make pretend stethoscopes. Punch a hole on each side of the cups near the bottom. Cut yarn into 18-inch lengths. Wrap a piece of tape around one end of each length of yarn.

Give the children the drinking straws. Let the children cut the straws into pieces. Show each child how to thread the yarn through one piece of the straw. Tie the end of the yarn (without the tape) around the straw piece to prevent added straw pieces from slipping off the yarn. Let the children string straw pieces onto the yarn until the yarn lengths are half-full. Give each child a cup. Help the children string the cup onto the yarn. Let the children continue to add straw lengths until the yarn is full. Tie the end of the yarn to the yarn already looped about the first straw length. Let the children pretend to listen to each other's hearts.

Goodbye Circle

Show the children a valentine heart and a picture of a real heart. Let the children choose which heart shape is like the real muscle in their bodies.

Pray: Thank you, God, for our beating hearts. Amen.

Evaluation

Did your children begin to understand the difference between the hearts inside their bodies and a valentine heart?

Lesson 33

Heart-Healthy Foods

Goal:

To help the children learn that certain foods help their heart stay healthy.

Objectives:

By the end of this session the children will:

Name heart-healthy foods.

Name foods that are not heart-healthy.

Eat heart-healthy foods.

Faith Connections

Bible verse: God gives you food and fills your hearts with happiness. (Acts 14:17, *Good News Bible*, adapted)

Children need to see that God has planned for them to have healthy bodies, but they must make good choices to keep their bodies healthy. We all need to learn this lesson.

Teacher's Prayer

Help me, O God, to make good choices for the body you have given me, and help me to teach these children to love and care for their hearts. Amen.

Teacher Talk:

God plans for each of our bodies to have a muscle called the heart.

God plans for us to take care of our hearts by eating healthy foods.

Your body is a wonderful creation.

Center Time

Display pictures of the heart in your center area today. Pictures are available through the American Heart Association.

> **As children arrive,** have the children name their favorite foods.

Worship Center

Teacher Talk

God plans for you to take care of your heart by eating healthy foods like fruits.

Resources

apples, knife (for teacher only), napkins, photocopy of food pyramid (see page 224)

Remind the children that God plans for us to eat healthy foods to keep our hearts healthy. Show the children the food pyramid (*see page* 224) .

Show the children an apple. Ask: "What group do apples belong to?" (*fruit*) Cut the apple in half across the core. Show the children the inside of the apple and the star formed by the seeds. **Say:** "God made delicious fruits like apples for us to eat."

Pray: Thank you, God, for foods that are good for us to eat. Amen.

Cut the apples into slices for the children to eat in the center. Or wait to cut the apples for snack time.

Note: Always keep knives out of the children's reach.

Science Center

Teacher Talk

God plans for us to eat healthy foods to help our hearts stay healthy.

Resources

construction paper or paper plates, labels or pictures of foods from the four food groups, glue, food pyramid (*see page* 224)

Provide labels or pictures of foods from the four food groups. Talk with the children about the food pyramid (*see page* 224). Hold up some of the pictures and have the children tell you what group each picture belongs to. Tell the children that they need to eat different kinds of foods from the food pyramid to help their hearts stay healthy. Give each child a piece of construction paper or a paper plate. Have the child choose a picture of a food from each group. Let the children glue the pictures onto their papers.

Math Center

Teacher Talk

God plans for us to take care of our hearts by choosing to eat healthy foods.

Resources

5 -10 separate pictures of healthy foods, 5 - 10 separate pictures of junk food, construction paper or index cards, glue, marker

Precut five to ten pictures of healthy foods and five to ten pictures of junk foods from newspaper ads and magazines. Glue the pictures to construction paper or index cards. On the back of each picture put a J for junk food or an H for healthy food.

Let the children choose from all the pictures the foods they like best. After the children have made the stack of their favorite foods ask them to count how many J's and how many H's they have. Make a list in the math center. Graph the results by drawing one tall bar showing how many J's were chosen by all the class and one bar showing how many H's were chosen by the whole class.

Remind the children that they need to eat foods from the four food groups every day to help their hearts stay healthy. Explain that junk food contains lots of fats and sugars. We should not eat a lot of these kinds of foods to keep our hearts healthy.

Wonder Time

As the children clean up, bring food pictures to wonder time that show food from each of the food groups.

Wonder Question: I wonder what foods we should eat to keep our hearts healthy?

Show the food pictures and the food pyramid *(see page 224).* Hold up each picture and have the children name the group the picture belongs to.

Say: The heart is a muscle and it needs lots of energy from good food. We need to eat different kinds of food from the groups in the food pyramid every day to help keep our hearts healthy.

Play a game. Have the children sit in a circle. Have enough food pictures for every child. Play music. Have the children pass the food pictures around the circle. Stop the music. Have each child hold on to a picture. Let each child show his or her picture. Help the child name the food and the group on the pyramid the picture belongs to.

Sing: "I'm Thankful," verse 6 *(see page 215).*

Read the Bible verse.

Say: God plans for us to have food to make our bodies strong and healthy.

Pray: Thank you, God, for good foods to help make our hearts healthy. Amen.

Open the Bible to Acts 14:17.

Say: "God gives you food and fills your hearts with happiness" (Acts 14:17, *Good News Bible*, adapted).

Have the children repeat the Bible verse.

Group Fun

Resources

two paper plates for each child; red, yellow, or green crayons or markers; paper punch; yarn; apple seeds or black construction paper cut into apple seed shapes; glue; scissors

Remind the children that apples are part of the fruit group in the pyramid. Give each child two paper plates. Show the children how to turn the paper plates so that the bottoms of the plates are facing up. Have each child color the bottoms of both plates the color of his or her favorite kind of apple (red, yellow, or green). Encourage the children to color all over their plates.

Have the children turn the plates so that the uncolored sides face up. Let the children glue apple seeds, or black construction paper cut into the shape of apple seeds, on this side of their plates. Punch a hole in both plates. Stack the two plates together so that the seeds are facing inside. Tie a loop of yarn through the holes to make a hinge for the plates. Show the children how to open their apples and look inside to see the seeds.

Goodbye Circle

Remind the children to ask for healthy snacks to help their hearts stay strong.

Pray: Thank you, God, for good foods to help make our hearts healthy. Amen.

Evaluation

What was the overall reaction to healthy foods? Do you need to emphasize this more? Do you need to send a letter home requesting healthy snacks be sent?

Lesson 34

Heart-Healthy Exercise

Teacher Talk:

God plans for each of our bodies to have a muscle called the heart.

God plans for us to take care of our hearts by moving our bodies.

Your body is a wonderful creation.

Goal:

To help children learn that moving around helps their hearts stay healthy.

Objectives: By the end of this session children will:

Exercise to keep their hearts healthy.

Eat heart-healthy foods.

Talk about their hearts.

Practice gross motor skills.

Faith Connections

Bible verse: A cheerful heart is a good medicine. (Proverbs 17:22)

Even preschoolers need to learn that exercise is good for them. They can move around, play outside, dance, or walk. Help the children see that God gave us whole bodies and that all the parts work together.

Teacher's Prayer

O God, although this class is sometimes very active, I know I need to exercise to keep my heart healthy. Help me to learn this lesson I teach. Amen.

Center Time

Display pictures of the heart in your center area today. Pictures are available through the American Heart Association.

As children arrive, ask each child, "Can you jump for me?" Watch the child jump.

Writing Center

Teacher Talk

God plans for us to take care of our hearts. One way we can care for our hearts is to move our bodies and exercise.

Resources

mural paper, crayons

Place mural paper on the floor. Have the children lie down on either side of the mural paper. Let each child choose a crayon. Tell the children to color on the paper without bending their arms. Show the children how to color with large sweeping arm movements.

Say: Show me how you can move your arms. We need to exercise our arms and our legs and our whole bodies. Exercise is one way we can take care of our hearts.

Art Center

Teacher Talk

God plans for you to take care of your heart by exercising. A good way to exercise is to walk.

Resources

mural paper, tempera paint, bucket of water, towels, large pan

Indoors or outdoors let the children take off their shoes and socks. Have the children roll up their pant legs and step in a flat pan of tempera, then walk across the mural paper. Have a bucket of water at the other end with a towel to step on and a towel to dry their feet with. Hang the mural and label it: Happy Feet—Healthy Heart.

Math Center

Teacher Talk

God plans for us to take care of our hearts.

Resources

number cards or 3-by-5 cards, marker

Use number cards for 1–10, or make number cards by writing the numbers 1–10 on 3-by-5 cards. Place the cards face down on the table. Have each child feel his or her pulse (*see page 104*). Then have the child turn over a number and jump that many times. Have the child feel his or her pulse again.

Worship Center

Teacher Talk

God plans for us to take care of our hearts by exercising and moving our bodies.

Resources

active music, cassette/CD player, drum

Let the children dance to the music. Play the drum and let the children move to different rhythms. Let the children take turns beating the drum and having other children move to the beat.

Have the children wave their arms up in the air to the music or beat of the drum. Have the children lie down on the floor and wave their feet up in the air.

Say: Our bodies are wonderfully made. God plans for our bodies to move. We can walk and run and jump and dance. When we move our bodies, we are exercising. Exercising helps our hearts stay healthy.

Have the children lie down on the floor and take deep breaths to cool down.

Pray: Thank you, God, for our wonderful bodies and all the ways we can move. Amen.

Open the Bible to Proverbs 17:22.

Say: "A cheerful heart is a good medicine" (Proverbs 17:22).

Have the children repeat the Bible verse.

Wonder Time

After the children clean up the centers, have them gather on the carpet and dance to the music. Play a quiet song when you are ready to talk.

Wonder Question: I wonder what we can do to keep our hearts healthy?

Say: We keep our hearts healthy when we choose to eat good foods. We also keep our hearts healthy when we move our bodies or exercise. What are some things we can do to exercise? (walk, run, dance, jump, play)
(Let them tell you what activities are not heart healthy, such as sitting on the sofa watching TV too much, eating junk food, adults smoking.)

Sing: "I'm Thankful," verse 6 *(see page 215)*.

Read the Bible verse.

Say: God plans for us to take care of our hearts. One way we can take care of our hearts is by exercising.

Pray: Thank you, God, for all the ways we can take care of our hearts. Amen.

Group Fun

Resources

doll picture (*see page 218*), crayons or markers, yarn, scissors, glue, jump ropes

Make jump rope pictures. Photocopy the doll (*see page 218*) for each child. Let the children decorate the dolls with crayons or markers. Cut yarn into eight-to-ten-inch lengths. Give each child a length of yarn. Let the child glue the yarn on the picture to make a jump rope for the doll.

Say: God plans for us to take care of our hearts. One way we can take care of our hearts is by exercising. A good exercise for the heart is jumping rope. Let's play with jump ropes.

Show the children how to handle the jump ropes. You may have a jump rope for each child. Or you may use a long jump rope and let two teachers twirl the rope while the children take turns jumping. If you have younger children, place the jump rope on the floor. Let the children take turns jumping over the rope. Count how many times each child jumps.

Goodbye Circle

Play a movement game such as "Simon Says" or the "Hokey Pokey." Remind children to exercise when they get home.

Pray: Thank you, God, for all the ways we can take care of our hearts. Amen.

Evaluation

Talk with coworkers about children's gross motor skills and about any children who need special attention.

Lesson 35

Heart Art

Goal:

To help children review all they have learned about their hearts this week by enjoying various art activities.

Objectives: By the end of this session the children will:

Make three-dimensional hearts.

Create squeeze paintings.

Remember what they have learned about the heart.

Faith Connections

Bible verse: Serve the LORD with all your heart. (1 Samuel 12:20)

Help children recognize that the heart is the core of life for us all. Our hearts must beat in order for us to live. When we serve God with all of our heart, we serve with our whole selves.

Teacher's Prayer

Serving you with all my heart, O God, is a difficult request. I will do my best. Amen.

Teacher Talk:

God plans for each of our bodies to have a muscle called the heart.

God plans for us to take care of our hearts.

Your body is a wonderful creation.

Center Time

Display pictures of the heart in your center area today. Pictures are available through the American Heart Association.

As children arrive, tell them today is heart art day and we are making many things.

Writing Center

Teacher Talk

God plans for us to take care of our hearts. One way we can take care of our hearts is by exercising.

Resources

mural paper, crayons, heart pictures (*see page 219*), glue, markers

Photocopy and cut out a heart picture (*see page 219*) for each child. Roll out a length of mural paper on the floor. Have each child lie down on the mural paper. Have the child show you how he or she moves when riding a bike or running. Tell the child to freeze. Use a crayon to trace around the child with her or his legs in a bike riding or running position. Let the children decorate their outlines with crayons or markers. Give each child a heart picture. Have the children glue the hearts onto their bodies in the middle of their chests. Remind the children that bike riding and running are two ways we can exercise our bodies and help keep our hearts healthy.

Art Center

Teacher Talk

God plans for our bodies to have a muscle called the heart.

Resources

red tissue paper, glue, heart picture (*see page 219*)

Photocopy the heart picture (*see page 219*) for each child. Give each child four pieces of red tissue paper. Show each child how to wad the tissue paper into four balls. Have them glue the balls onto their heart pictures. Tell the children the heart is a muscle with four chambers, or rooms, and the blood is pumped through all four chambers.

Science Center

Teacher Talk

God plans for our hearts to pump blood through our bodies.

Resources

turkey baster, large drawing paper, red tempera paint, plastic container, table covering, smocks

Cover the table and have the children wear paint smocks. Pour tempera paint into a plastic container. Show the children how to suck up paint with the baster and then squirt the paint on to their drawing paper. Remind the children that our hearts pump all the time, squirting blood through our bodies.

Have the children fold over their papers. Show the children how to push on the papers to squeeze paint in all directions. Open the papers and let the paintings dry.

Worship Center

Teacher Talk

God plans for our hearts to pump blood through our bodies.

Resources

plastic baggies, flour, water, drinking straws, tape, red food coloring or tempera paint, table covering

Cover the table. Mix flour and water together until goopy. Add red food coloring or tempera paint. Partially fill a plastic bag with the goop. Place a drinking straw into the bag. Securely tape the bag around the drinking straw. Show the children how to squeeze the bag so that the goop goes up the straw. **Say:** "When we squeeze the bag it makes the goop squirt up the straw just as the heart pumps blood through our bodies."

Pray: Thank you, God, for our hearts that pump blood to help us live. Amen.

Wonder Time

Beat a drum to call the children to wonder time. Remind the children that the heart is a pump and that it beats with a rhythm.

Open the Bible to 1 Samuel 12:20.

Say: "Serve the LORD with all your heart" (1 Samuel 12:20).

Have the children repeat the Bible verse.

Wonder Question: I wonder what we have learned about our hearts?

Say: God made our hearts to be muscles. Our hearts are about the size of our fists. We can hear our hearts beat lub dub, lub dub when we listen with a stethoscope. We can feel our hearts beat when we feel our pulses. We can do many things to take care of our hearts. We can eat healthy foods; we can exercise; and we can choose not to smoke.

Sing: "I'm Thankful," verse 6 *(see page 215)*.

Read the Bible verse.

Say: God plans for us to take care of our hearts. A healthy heart helps our bodies stay healthy.

Pray: Thank you, God, for our hearts. Amen.

Group Fun

Resources

heart picture (*see page 219*), red tempera paint, dish soap, water, spoon, pan, drinking straws, table covering, smocks

Let the children decorate heart pictures with bubble prints. Photocopy the heart picture (*see page 219*) for each child. Cover the table and have the children wear smocks. Put ten spoonfuls of red tempera paint, one spoonful of dish soap, and one spoonful of water in a pan. Mix them together. Give each child a drinking straw. Have the children practice blowing, not sucking, through their straws. Show the children how to place their straws in the bubble mixture and gently blow. If the bubbles are hard to blow, add more water. If the bubbles do not have much color, add more tempera paint.

Have the children blow until the bubbles will rise above the pan. Help each child gently touch his or her heart picture to the bubbles. Lift up the paper to see the print made from the bubbles. Set the pictures aside to dry.

Goodbye Circle

Ask the children what they will do over the weekend that will keep their hearts healthy.

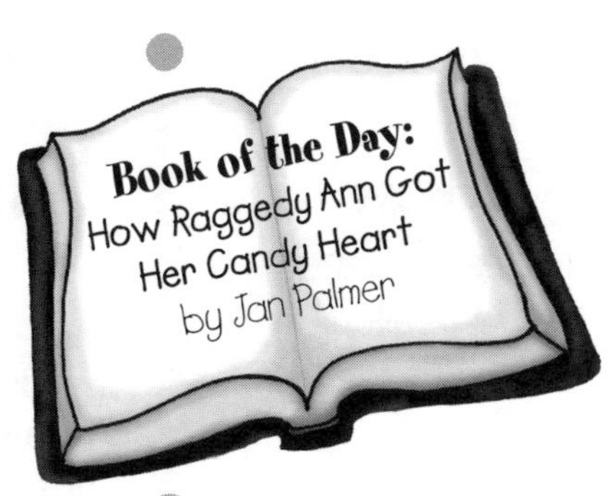

Pray: *(Let each child say a prayer, silently or out loud, about their heart.)*

Evaluation

Remember as you plan future lessons to refer to the importance of good exercise. You may want to send home a letter suggesting ways parents can continue the lessons about the heart.

I CAN CARE

Learning to care is one of the most valuable lessons children can experience. As we care for ourselves and for others we learn how to live in today's world. We learn to respect ourselves and others, a value which is the basis for happy and peaceful living.

This week look for ways for children to show caring. Whether it's cleaning the furniture to care for their building or baking something to show care for a friend, give them opportunities to care.

Lesson 36

Caring for Myself

Teacher Talk:

You're very important to God.

God wants you to take care of yourself.

God loves you and cares about you.

Goal:

To help the children begin to understand the importance of caring for themselves.

Objectives:

By the end of this session the children will:

Learn the correct way to brush their teeth.

Practice washing their hands.

Begin making a caring book.

Faith Connections

Bible verse: God cares about you. (1 Peter 5:7, adapted)

Because God created us and cares about us, we can care about ourselves. This includes helping the children learn the importance of daily health habits like brushing their teeth, washing their hands, and wearing clean clothes.

Teacher's Prayer

I know you care for me, Lord. Help me learn to care for myself. Amen.

Center Time

If you do not have a sink available, prepare one dishpan partially filled with soapy water and one dishpan partially filled with clean water. Have clean towels ready to use.

Science Center

Teacher Talk

God plans for us to take care of our bodies. One way we can take care of our bodies is to brush our teeth.

Resources

Five 1-liter clear plastic soda bottles, large utility brush in shape of a toothbrush, pictures of teeth and children brushing teeth, masking tape or duct tape, heavy scissors

Make big teeth using the bottom halves of plastic soda bottles. Cut off and discard the top half of each soda bottle. Cover the cut edge of the bottom half with masking or duct tape. Turn the bottom halves upside down so that the bottoms are facing you. They will look like big teeth. Use the large utility brush to show the children how to brush each of the teeth. Let the children practice brushing the large teeth.

Ask a local dentist to donate pictures of teeth and children brushing their teeth for you to display. The dentist may also be willing to donate toothbrush and toothpaste samples for the children to take home.

Home Living Center

Teacher Talk

God plans for us to take care of our bodies. One way we can take care of our bodies is to keep cuts and scratches clean.

Resources

red nonpermanent marker, adhesive bandages, sink or dishpan partially filled with water, clean towel

Say: "Let's pretend you have a scratch." Use a red marker to draw a pretend scratch on each child's hand. Show the child how to wash the scratch and dry the area with a clean towel. Put an adhesive bandage over each pretend scratch.

Art Center

Teacher Talk

God plans for us to take care of our bodies. One way we can take care of ourselves is by being careful around cars.

Resources

construction paper, shallow trays, toy cars, tempera paint, table covering, smocks

Cover the table and have the children wear paint smocks. Pour tempera paint into shallow trays. Give each child a piece of construction paper. Show the children how to dip the wheels of the toy cars into the paint and then drive the cars over their papers to make paint tracks. Talk with the children about safety rules around cars and traffic. Remind the children to never run out in front of a car and to hold an adult's hand when crossing the street.

Worship Center

Teacher Talk

God plans for us to take care of ourselves. One way we can take care of our bodies is to wash our hands.

Resources

sink or dishpan, water, soap, towels

Have the children wash their hands. Have the children sing "God Cares" *(see page 212)* or say the alphabet from beginning to end as they wash. **Say**: "This is how long you should take every time you wash your hands."

Say: God plans for us to take care of our bodies. One way we take care of our bodies is by washing our hands. When we wash our hands, we wash off dirt and germs that can make us sick.

Pray: Thank you, God, for all the ways we can take care of ourselves. Amen.

Open the Bible to 1 Peter 5:7.

Say: "God cares about you" (1 Peter 5:7, adapted).

Have the children repeat the Bible verse.

Wonder Time

This is the way
We brush our teeth,
Brush our teeth,
Brush our teeth.
This is the way
We brush our teeth
To take good care of our bodies.

Call the children for wonder time.

Wonder Question: I wonder what we can do to care for our bodies?

Say: We can care for our bodies by brushing our teeth, washing our hands, eating good foods, exercising, and getting enough sleep.

Sing and Move: Have the children stand in a circle. Sing the song "This Is The Way" *(see box at right)* and pretend to brush your teeth as you sing. Add additional verses like "This is the way we wash our hands."

Sing: "God Cares" (see page 212).

Read the Bible verse.

Say: God loves and cares for each one of us. God wants us to take care of ourselves. One way we take care of ourselves is to take care of our bodies.

Pray: Thank you, God, for your love and care. Help us to take care of ourselves. Amen.

Group Fun

Resources

construction paper, cardboard box with sides, marbles, tempera paint, small containers for paint, table covering, paint smocks

Let the children make caring books. They can add pages to their books throughout the week. Cover the table and have the children wear paint smocks. Give each child a piece of construction paper. Have the children place their paper flat in the bottom of the box. Show the children how to dip several marbles in paint, using the same or different colors, and then place the marbles in box. Have the children slant the box from side to side so that the marbles roll and make designs on the paper. Just playing with the marbles this way is fun and children will want to do more than one.

Goodbye Circle

Review with the children some of the ways we can take care of our bodies *(brush our teeth, wash our hands, eat good foods, exercise, get enough sleep).*

Pray: Thank you, God, for your love and care. Help us to take care of ourselves. Amen.

Evaluation

What did the children enjoy today? Are there children who were absent who will need to begin their books tomorrow?

Lesson 37

Caring for My Family

Goal:

To think about ways they can show love and care for their family members.

Objectives: By the end of this session children will:

Name ways their families needs their help.

Name ways they can help in their families.

Make something for their families.

Practice caring for a baby.

Faith Connections

Bible verse: Let love make you serve one another.

(Galatians 5:13, *Good News Bible*)

Children need to know that God cares about their families. Children often expect others to do and care for them. They often need that care. But even young children need to know that they can do things themselves to care for others. They can care for and help their families. Caring for one another is one way that families serve one another with love. Today's lesson will help the children discover different ways they can show care in their families.

Teacher's Prayer

My own family, O God, also needs your love and care. Help me, as I care for these children, to know how to also care for my own family. Amen.

Teacher Talk:

Your family is important to God.

God plans for family members to take care of one another.

God loves your family and cares about your family.

Center Time

Display pictures that show family members playing, eating, and working together.

As children arrive, ask them who brought them to school today.

Art Center

Teacher Talk

God plans for us to show love to the people in our families.

Resources

construction paper, clear self-adhesive paper; marker, star stickers or star cookie cutters, paper towels, shallow trays, tempera paint, table covering, paint smocks

Let the children make "You're a Star" place mats for their families. Cover the table and have the children wear paint smocks. Fold paper towels and place them in the bottom of a shallow tray. Pour tempera paint onto the paper towels to make a paint pad. Give each child a piece of construction paper. If you choose, write the words "You're a Star!" on each paper. Show the children how to press the star cookie cutters onto the paint pad and then onto their papers. Encourage the children to make several prints. Let the paint dry. Or let the children enjoy placing a variety of star stickers on their papers.

Cover the place mats with clear self-adhesive paper. Tell the children that they can take their place mats home for their families. Each day one person in their family can use the place mat and be the "star" of the family for that day.

Worship Center

Teacher Talk

God plans for us to help one another.

Resources

paper, crayons

Give each child a piece of paper. Have the child place a hand on the paper. Use a crayon to trace around the hand. **Say:** "Each of us has hands that we can use to help the people in our families. Let's count how many helping hands you have in your family." Help each child name a person in his or her family. Let the child place two circle stickers or make two marks inside the handprint for the person named. Continue until the child has named each person in her or his family (you may need to help the child remember each person). Then have the child count the number of circle stickers or marks made in the handprint. Write that number of the paper. **Say:** "*(Child's name)* has *(number)* helping hands in his *(or her)* family." Save these pictures to put in their caring books.

Say: God plans for us to help one another.

Pray: Thank you, God, for families that show care by helping. Amen.

Water/Sand Play Center

Teacher Talk

Babies need lots of love and care. God plans for families to take care of babies.

Resources

baby dolls, baby bathtub, washcloths, towels, water, pretend baby food, baby toys

Let the children practice taking care of a baby. Partially fill the baby bathtub with water. Show the children how to gently bathe a baby doll. If someone in your class has a baby brother or sister, ask the parent to bring the baby in and talk about how to care for him or her.

Home Living Center

Teacher Talk

God plans for us to take care of our families. One way we take care of our families is by helping around the house.

Resources

child-size mops, brooms, and vacuums

Encourage children to pretend to help around the house. Talk with the children about the things they can do to help such as picking up their toys, taking out the trash, or sweeping the floor.

Wonder Time

Call the children for wonder time.

Wonder Question: I wonder how we can help the people in our families?

Play "Stand Up, Sit Down." Give the children the following directions. Include statements that will allow every child to stand up at least once.

If you have an older brother or sister, stand up. Sit down.

What can you do to care for older brothers or sisters? *(Share toys, help clean up the toys, ask permission to use their things, and so forth).*

If you have a younger sister or brother, stand up. Sit down.

What can you do to care for younger brothers or sisters? *(Help keep them safe, play with them, not let them put harmful things in their mouths, and so forth.)*

Add other statements about moms, dads, grandmothers, grandfathers, uncles, aunts, stepmothers, stepfathers, and so forth as time and interest allow.

Sing: "Thank You, God, for Loving Me" *(see page 212).*

Read the Bible verse.

Say: When we help each other and take care of each other we are showing love. God plans for family members to take care of each other and to love one another.

Pray: Thank you, God, for our families. Help us to take care of each other. Amen.

Open the Bible to Galatians 5:13.

Say: "Let love make you serve one another" (Galatians 5:13, *Good News Bible*).

Have the children repeat the Bible verse.

Group Fun

Resources

heavy cream (at room temperature), clean marbles, jars with lids

Make butter. Fill a jar half full of the heavy cream that has been warmed to room temperature. Drop in a clean marble. Close the jar tightly and have children take turns shaking the jar for ten to fifteen minutes. You will not hear the marble when the butter is ready. Pour out or drink the buttermilk which is left and press the remaining liquid from the butter. Shape the butter and put it in the refrigerator to use at snack time with bread or crackers.

Or have a jar for each child and let the children take the butter home as a gift to their families. Remind the children that God plans for families to show love and care for one another. One way families care is by cooking food and by eating together.

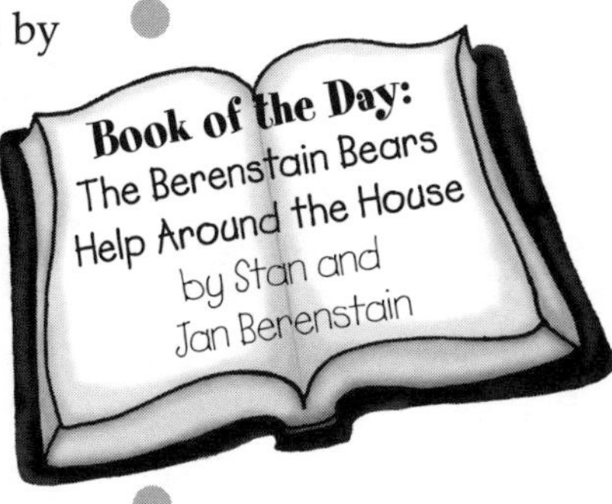

Goodbye Circle

Give each child her or his place mat. Let the children name something they will do to care for their families today.

Pray: Thank you, God, for our families and the ways we take care of one another. Amen.

Evaluation

Do the children show concern about their families? Are there families that demonstrate any needs? Find out how you can connect these families with help.

Lesson 38

Caring for My Friends

Teacher Talk:

You and your friends are important to God.

God wants you to take care of your friends.

God loves you and your friends and cares about you and your friends.

Goal:

To help children understand that to have friends you must be a friend.

Objectives: By the end of this session children will:

Play with their friends.

Talk about how to be a friend.

Make friendship bracelets.

Faith Connections

Bible verse: A friend loves at all times. (Proverbs 17:17)

Preschoolers are moving from being egocentric—seeing the world from just their own perspective—to understanding that others have needs and wants and different points of view. They need to learn that Jesus was a friend to others and wants them to be friendly and care for their friends.

Teacher's Prayer

Help me be a friend, O Lord. I am too busy, I forget, and I let time go by. Help me be a friend. Amen.

Center Time

Plan activities that encourage the children to work and play together during center time today.

As children arrive, tell them their friends are here and ready to play!

Art Center

Teacher Talk

God plans for us to show love and care to our friends.

Resources

construction paper, two precut circles for each child, glue, yarn, crayons or markers

Give each child a piece of construction paper and two paper circles. Have the children glue the circles side-by-side on their construction papers. **Say:** "Let's pretend one of these circles is your face and the other circle is the face of your friend." Let the children make faces on each circle with crayons or markers. They may glue on yarn for hair. Write each child's name under the circle that represents his or her face. Have the child name a friend. Write the friend's name under the second face.

Talk with the children about ways we can take care of our friends like taking turns, sharing toys, and helping each other clean up the room. Save the pictures for their caring books.

Building Center

Teacher Talk

God plans for us to take care of our friends. One way we take care of our friends is by getting along when we work and play together.

Resources

several sheets, blocks, chairs or tables

Let each child choose a friend and work together to make a tent. Help the children listen to each other and share ideas with each other. The children may drape sheets over tables, chairs, or shelves. Be sure that their tents are constructed safely. Let the children enjoy playing together in the tents.

Math Center

Teacher Talk

God plans for us to take care of our friends.

Resources

yarn, beads or drinking straws, scissors, tape

Let the children make friendship bracelets to share. The children may string beads or pieces of drinking straws. Let the children use safety scissors to cut drinking straws into short pieces. Cut yarn into 8-inch lengths. Wrap one end of each yarn length with tape.

Help the children count the number of friends in your class. Then help the children count out the same number of beads or straw pieces. Let each child to use the beads or straw pieces to make two bracelets. Show the children how to string the beads or straw pieces onto the yarn. Help them tie knots in the ends. Encourage each child to give one bracelet to a friend.

Worship Center

Teacher Talk

God plans for us to take care of our friends.

Resources

paper, crayons

Let the children "write" letters or decorate cards for their friends. Encourage the children to deliver the letters or cards to their friends during center time. If you have a child or teacher who is absent due to an illness, let the children make cards for that person.

Say: One way we can take care of our friends is by sending them letters or cards when they are sick or need cheering up.

Pray: Thank you, God, for all the ways we can take care of our friends. Amen.

Open the Bible to Proverbs 17:17.

Say: "A friend loves at all times" (Proverbs 17:17).

Have the children repeat the Bible verse.

Wonder Time

As children clean up, tell them to bring a friend to wonder time.

Wonder Question: I wonder how we care for our friends?

Say: It is important to be a friend to others. When we take turns, help each other clean the room, share toys, smile at each other, make cards or letters for each other, and say things like, "I like you!" we show love and care to our friends in our class.

Take a poll. Say the following statements for the children. If the children think the statement is a good way to care for a friend, have the children stand up. If they think the statement is not a good way to care, have the children stay seated. **Say, "I like you!"** (Stand up.) **Share the toys.** (Stand up.) **Grab a toy away from someone.** (Sit down.) **Smile.** (Stand up.) **Take your turn.** (Stand up.)

Play a game. Choose one child to begin the game. Have the child sit with his or her back to the group. Choose another child to tiptoe up behind the child in the chair and say: "I like you, friend." Then have the child sit back down. Let the child in the chair turn around and try to guess who spoke. Continue the game as the children show interest.

Sing: "Thank you, God, for Loving Me" (see page 212).

Read the Bible verse.

Say: When we show love to one another, we are being good friends.

Pray: Thank you, God, for our friends. Help us to be a good friend to others. Amen.

Group Fun

Resources

ball of yarn

Have the children sit in a circle on the floor. Hold on to one end of the ball of yarn and toss the ball to a child sitting across the circle. **Say:** "Friend (*child's name*), I like you." Have that child hold onto part of the yarn and then toss the ball to another child in the circle. Encourage the child to say the child's name and "I like you." Continue around the circle with each child holding part of the yarn and then tossing the ball to another child. This will make a giant spider web. Let the children admire their giant web. **Say:** "When we say things like 'I like you!' to our friends, we are showing love and care."

Goodbye Circle

Have each child name a friend with whom she or he played today. Help the children remember if they cannot.

Pray: Thank you, God, for our friends. Help us be a good friend to others. Amen.

Evaluation

Are there children in your class who are lacking in social skills and don't make friends easily? Think of ways you can help.

Caring for Animals

Goals:

To help children see animals as part of God's creation.

To help the children learn ways to care for animals.

Objectives: By the end of this session children will:

Practice caring for animals.

Hear a veterinarian talk about caring for animals.

Make dog biscuits.

Construct an animal.

Faith Connections

Bible verse: Then God commanded, "Let the earth produce all kinds of animal life." (Genesis 1:24, Good News Bible)

Children need to know that animals are part of God's plan for our world. They need help in finding ways they can care for animals.

Teacher's Prayer

O God, help me to show these children love and care so that they will know how to love and care for others. Amen.

Teacher Talk:

Animals are important to God.

We can help take care of animals in God's world.

God loves you and cares about you even more than the animals.

Center Time

Invite someone with a child-friendly pet to bring the pet for a visit today.

As children arrive, have them name their favorite animal and then make the sound of that animal.

Home Living Center

Teacher Talk

God plans for us to show love and care to our pets.

Resources

stuffed animals, leashes, collars, pet bowls, small bags of pet food

As children play in the center, include care of pets in their play. Remind them to walk and feed the pets.

Worship Center

Teacher Talk

God plans for us to show love and care to animals.

Resources

paw print stamp, stamps of animals, paper, nonpermanent ink pads

Give each child a piece of paper and let them enjoy stamping with paw print and animal stamps. If you do not have rubber stamps, make paw prints stamps from rubber shoe inserts. Cut a paw print out of of the insert. Glue the insert onto a wooden block

Say: God plans for us to take care of animals.

Pray: Thank you, God, for animals. Help us remember to take care of them. Amen.

Building Center

Teacher Talk

We can help take care of animals.

Resources

smaller wooden blocks, plastic animals, straw or shredded paper

Tell the children that each animal needs a place to live and something to eat. Let them build fences and homes for the animals. You can purchase farm animals or safari animals.

Math Center

Teacher Talk

God made all the animals in God's world.

Resources

large box of animal crackers, plastic bags

Before class, count out 8 to 10 animal crackers and put them in a bag for each child. Tell children to count the number of animals in their bags; then they can eat the crackers.

Cooking Center

Teacher Talk

God plans for us to care for our pets.

Resources

ingredients and items needed for making dog biscuits, plastic bags

Let the children do the measuring, rolling, and cutting to make dog biscuits. After cooking the biscuits, let each child take some home. Be sure to place a label on the baggie that says "Dog Biscuits." As you are making the biscuits, talk about safety with other people's pets. Never touch a dog or cat you do not know. Always ask pet owners if you may pet their dogs or cats. Never let an animal out of its fence. Never tease or throw things at an animal.

Dog Biscuits

½ cup cornmeal
1 ¾ cups whole wheat flour
2 tablespoons garlic powder
2 tablespoons beef stock mix
2 tablespoons bacon bits
2 tablespoons oil
⅔ cup water (may need more or less water)

Mix the ingredients together. Roll out the mixture and cut with cookie cutters or slice into rectangles. Bake at 350 degrees for thirty-five or forty-five minutes. Baste with meat drippings. Store in a plastic bag when cooled.

Wonder Time

Have the children pretend to be animals and hop, crawl, slither, or creep to wonder time.

> Animals Need Love
> words by
> Millie and Wes Goodson
>
> Animals need love and care,
> Love and care, love and care
> If you were my animal
> You would need love and care.

Wonder Question: I wonder what we can do to take care of the animals in God's world?

Say: When we do things like take care of our pets, put out birdseed for wild birds, or leave bread crumbs for ducks, we are taking care of the animal's in God's world.

Introduce the veterinarian or pet visitor. Let the visitor talk to the children about the animal and how to care for it.

Sing: Sing the song "Animals Need Love" to the tune of "Mary Had a Little Lamb."

Read the Bible verse.

Say: God has planned for animals, but they need us to love and care for them. (Ask the children if they have pets and to tell how they care for their pets.)

Pray: Thank you, God, for all the animals. Help us remember to take care of them. Amen.

Remind children that they talked about being friends yesterday and that they must be friends to animals also.

Open the Bible to Genesis 1:24.

Say: "Then God commanded, 'Let the earth produce all kinds of animal life'" (Genesis 1:24, *Good News Bible*).

Have the children repeat the Bible verse.

Group Fun

Resources

small boxes of all sizes, tissue paper rolls, plastic bottle caps, masking tape, glue, tempera paint, paint brushes, camera, indoor film, paper

Let the children construct animals of their own creation. Have them tape boxes, tissue paper rolls, and plastic bottle caps together to make legs, heads, tails, eyes, and so forth. Let them paint their animals any color they like. Get the children to tell about their animals and how they would care for them. Let each child give his or her animal a name. Take a picture of the child with the animal to put in his or her caring book.

Goodbye Circle

Tell the children that if they do not have dogs to give the biscuits to, they can break up the biscuits for the birds and squirrels.

Pray: Thank you, God, for all the animals of the world. Amen.

Evaluation

Was it helpful to have an animal in the class? Sometimes animals are soothing to children; sometimes they create havoc. You may need to invite another furry friend at another time.

Lesson 40

Caring for God's World

Teacher Talk:

The world is very important to God.

God wants you to take care of God's world.

God loves you and cares about you.

You are part of God's world.

Goals:

To help children see the earth as God's creation.

To understand that the earth needs our loving care.

Objectives: By the end of this session the children will:

Make a nature collage.

Create a paper aquarium.

Play with toy animals.

Plant something beautiful

Faith Connections

Bible verse: The earth is the LORD's. (Psalm 24:1)

Many children have very little contact with the earth. Our world is sometimes one of asphalt, concrete, and carpeting. Help the children get close to the earth in this lesson. Hug a tree, touch the earth, and watch the clouds. Help make the children aware of the earth as their home.

Teacher's Prayer

Keep me connected, O God, to your creation. Help me feel your beauty in your earth. Amen.

Center Time

Display pictures that show the beauty to be found in God's world.

As children arrive, send them to the centers for fun.

Worship Center

Teacher Talk

God plans for us to care for the earth.

Resources

items from nature, glue, cardboard, posterboard, or plastic foam trays

Have available moss, small sticks, seeds, needles, small cones, and other nature items for children to make a collage. Use quick drying glue and let the children glue the nature items to cardboard, posterboard, or plastic foam trays.

Pray: Thank you, God, for your beautiful world. Help us to take care of it. Amen.

Math Center

Teacher Talk

God made the stones and rocks on the earth. God plans for us to care for all the earth.

Resources

small stones, play dough

Tell the children to roll out the play dough and push holes in the dough with the stones. Place one stone in each hole and count the stones. Allow the children to experiment with the dough and the stones. They can make a slender roll of dough and line stones up on it. Keep the stones away from the children's mouths, eyes, ears, and noses.

Writing Center

Teacher Talk

God made the trees. God plans for us to care for all the earth.

Resources

construction paper, crayons, paper towels, tempera paint, shallow trays, table covering, smocks, stapler, staples

Have the children make handprint trees. Cover the table and have the children wear paint smocks. Fold paper towels and place them in the bottom of a shallow tray. Pour tempera paint on the paper towels to make a paint pad.

Give each child a piece of paper. Have the child place an arm and hand down on the paper. Trace around the arm and hand with a crayon. This will make the tree trunk and tree branches. Let the children color the tree trunk arms with crayons. Show the children how to press their thumbs onto the paint pad and inside their handprints to make leaves for their trees.

Talk about the trees in your area. Are they beginning to change colors? Do they stay green all year long? Ask the children how we can take care of trees (*give them water, be careful of their branches, and so forth*). Ask the children if they have ever hugged a tree. Set the pictures aside to dry and add them to the caring books. Stack each child's book pages together and staple the pages along the left-hand side.

Art Center

Teacher Talk

The ocean and all the animals in the ocean are part of God's world. We can take care of God's world.

Resources

pictures or stickers of fish, cardboard box lids (*pizza boxes work well*), clear food wrap, construction paper, small sea shells, sand, scissors

Let the children build underwater scenes by gluing items inside cardboard box lids. Older children may cut out fish shapes from construction paper. Younger children may use precut paper fish or fish stickers. Have the children glue or stick the fish onto the box lids. Show the children how to put glue on the box lid and then sprinkle sand on it. You can also sprinkle confetti on lines of glue for an underwater effect. When children have finished, help them cover the surface of their underwater collages with clear, blue, or green food wrap.

Open the Bible to Psalm 24:1.

Say: "The earth is the LORD's" (Psalm 24:1).

Have the children repeat the Bible verse.

Wonder Time

Have the children pretend to be leaves falling from a tree and to let the wind blow them to wonder time.

Wonder Question: I wonder how we can take care of the earth?

Say: God has made a beautiful world for us to live in. Some of the things we can do to take care of the earth are: picking up litter, planting flowers, watering plants and trees, and feeding animals.

Help the children think of other ways they can help to care for God's earth.

Talk with children about the beauty of the earth. Let them tell you where they like to go outside to enjoy the beauty of the earth. Let children show the collages they made. Talk about the items in their pictures and how well God planned for them.

Sing: "Animals Need Love" (*see page 129*). Sing the song again substituting the words "trees and plants" or "birds and fish" for "animals."

Read the Bible verse.

Say: God made everything that lives on the earth. God made all the plants and animals and land and water. God plans for things to grow.

Pray: Thank you, God, for all the earth. Help us to take care of your world. Amen.

Group Fun

Resources

bulbs or a small tree or shrub and gardening tools; or gravel, charcoal, sand, potting soil, small plants, large bowl or fish aquarium, water, spoons

Plant something outside if it is possible. You will need to coordinate this activity with persons responsible for your grounds. You might let the children plant a bulb garden that will come up in spring or a small tree or shrub that the children can care for and watch grow.

If planting inside, let children make a terrarium. Let the children take turns creating layers with the gravel, charcoal, sand, and potting soil in the bottom of the bowl or aquarium. Show the children how to dig holes for the plants and plant them. Lightly water the terrarium.

Goodbye Circle

Name something from God's world such as animals, fish, birds, leaves blowing in the wind, or a flower growing. Let the children pretend to be whatever you name. Remind the children that we need to take care of the earth.

Pray: Thank you, God, for all the earth. Help us to take care of your world. Amen.

Evaluation

Have the children learned a greater appreciation for the earth? Are they answering for themselves? As you plan for next week, remove any items from centers that you do not plan to use again.

Unit 3

My Community

Goals:

1. The children will learn about the people and places in the community.
2. The children will understand that there are people who care about them in their neighborhoods.
3. The children will learn that there are people in their neighborhoods to help them.
4. The children will learn to stay safe in their neighborhoods.

This month we will be learning about the people and places in our community. This unit is meant to help children take pride in their neighborhoods and to feel a part of them.

You will need to gather a variety of materials to help children experience the various community helpers. Ask parents to let you borrow items or ask doctors' offices, police stations, fire stations, and the post office for donations.

Visitors this Month
Doctor, Nurse
Police Officer
Firefighter
Letter Carrier
Teacher

Field Trip Suggestions
Fire Station
Post Office
Library

Bible Stories for this Unit
Matthew 8:5-8, 13 (The Centurion's Servant)
Matthew 8:14-16 (Peter's Mother-in-law)
John 6:1-14 (Jesus Feeds the Five Thousand)
Luke 19:1-10 (Zacchaeus)
1 Corinthians 13 (A Love Letter)

THE HELPERS

Children will enjoy pretending to be various helpers. It is important that they get to do their role playing after they have visited with or learned about the helper. Otherwise, stereotypes of police work or doctors giving shots will predominate their play.

Uniforms, including boots, are easy to find in thrift and second-hand stores. Also ask local community helpers for help in finding second-hand uniforms for the week. Leave role playing equipment out each day this week .

Lesson 41

Doctors & Nurses

Teacher Talk:

God plans for people to help us stay healthy.

God plans for people to help us when we are sick.

God is with us when we are sick and when we are well. God is always with us.

Goal:

To help the children see medical professionals as their friends.

Objectives:

By the end of this session the children will:

Hear the duties of doctors and nurses.

Pretend to be doctors or nurses.

Hear that Jesus healed people.

Faith Connections

Bible verse: Heal the sick. (Matthew 10:8, *Good News Bible*)

Children need to know that Jesus healed people who were sick. They need to see medical professionals as their friends and as people whose job it is to help them. They need to know that when they are sick, God cares about them and will comfort them.

Teacher's Prayer

O God, as I watch the children play today, I will remember that you are the great Healer. Amen.

Center Time

Display props and pictures that show healthcare workers helping others.

As children arrive, ask them to help set up the hospital.

Building Center

Teacher Talk

God plans for people to help us stay healthy and to take care of us when we are sick.

Resources

sheets, gauze bandages, adhesive bandages, scarves for slings, rulers for splints, boxes with cameras taped to them for x-ray machines, white lab coats, stethoscopes, clipboard, paper and pens, cotton swabs

Rearrange the building center to make a hospital. Or let the children use the blocks to make a hospital. Add the props listed under resources for pretend play. Have several lab coats for those pretending to be medical professionals, and have dress-up clothes for those pretending to be sick. If you would rather not let children pretend to be sick—younger children especially have a hard time remembering it is pretend play—provide dolls to be doctored!

Worship Center

Teacher Talk

God is with us when we are sick and when we are well.

Resources

quiet music, cassette/CD player, pillows

Set up an area with pillows for the children to relax and listen to quiet music. Talk with the children about how music can make us feel calm or make us feel excited. Music can even help us feel better when we are sick.

Say: God plans for people to help us when we are sick. God is with us when we are sick. God plans for people to help us grow and stay healthy. God is with us when we are well. God is always with us.

Pray: Thank you, God, for people like doctors and nurses who help us. Amen.

Art Center

Teacher Talk

God plans for people like doctors and nurses to help us when we are sick.

Resources

tongue depressors, small paper plates or construction paper circles, crayons, white tissue paper, markers, glue, yarn

Let the children make doctor dolls. Give each child a small paper plate or a construction paper circle. Help the children tape the tongue depressor or craft stick to the back of the plate or circle. Let the children use markers to draw faces, glue yarn to make hair, and glue white tissue around the depressor to make lab coats.

Math Center

Teacher Talk

God plans for people to help us stay healthy and grow strong.

Resources

growth chart, scale to weigh children, doll pattern (*see page 218*), marker

Photocopy the doll (*see page 218*) for each child. Have an assistant help you weigh and measure the children. Write each child's name and figures on the doll pattern to send home. Write the words "I'm Growing!" across each picture. Plan to keep a set of each child's weight and height for your files.

Note: Center time might be stressful for children who are fearful of doctors, especially if they are undergoing medical treatment. Provide activities, like play dough or puzzles, that allow children to distance themselves from any stress the medical activities may cause.

Open the Bible to Matthew 10:8.

Say: "Heal the sick"

(Matthew 10:8, *Good News Bible*).

Have the children repeat the Bible verse.

Wonder Time

Before the children come to you, you will need to go to those who are pretending to be sick and tap them on their heads. **Say:** "You are better. Center time is over. Put your bandages away until next time." This will help the children make the transition to wonder time.

Wonder Question: I wonder who helps us when we are sick?

Visitor: *(If you have invited a health professional, introduce the visitor to the children.)*

Say: People in our families help us when we are sick. Sometimes we need to have other people help us as well. Sometimes we need help from doctors and nurses.

Let the children tell you what the doctor does when they go for a visit. Let each child have a turn as this is an important topic for preschoolers and some will want to say much about it.

Say: Doctors and nurses also help us when we are not sick. They help our bodies grow strong and healthy.

Sing: "Thank you, God, for Loving Me" *(see page 212).*

Read the Bible verse.

Say: Jesus healed people who were sick and wanted his friends to help people too.

Pray: Thank you, God, for all the people who help us grow strong and healthy and who help us when we are sick. Amen.

Group Fun

Resources

construction paper, adhesive bandages, cotton swabs, pieces of gauze, tongue depressors, glue

Give each child a piece of construction paper. Let the children use things they might see in a doctor's office to make a collage. Have adhesive bandages in a variety of colors and sizes. Let the children enjoy sticking the bandages on their papers and on themselves. Caution the children to keep the tongue depressors out of their mouths.

Goodbye Circle

Remind children that doctors and nurses and other healthcare helpers help us when we are well and when we are sick.

Pray: Thank you, God, for all the people who help us stay well. Amen.

Evaluation

Did the children have fun? Did they learn anything new about medical professionals?

Lesson 42

Police Officers

Goal:

To help the children learn that police officers care about children and families. We can trust them to help us.

Objectives:

By the end of this session the children will:

Meet a friendly police officer.

Make badges.

Talk about rules.

Make seat-belt dolls.

Faith Connections

Bible verse: Jesus said, "Peace be with you." (John 20:19, adapted)

Discipline is from the same root word as disciple—to follow. Children need rules to follow. They need models of quiet voices and kind acts. Help them to know that Jesus was a wonderful person who wanted us to have peace with one another.

Teacher's Prayer

Lord, every day I work here help me to seek peace. Let my words and actions point children to you. Amen.

Teacher Talk:

God plans for people to help keep us safe.

We thank God for police officers and other people who help keep us safe.

Jesus wants us to live together in peace.

Rules help us live together in peace.

Center Time

As children arrive, ask each of them to tell you one of the rules of the class.

Display props and pictures that show police officers helping others.

Building Center

Teacher Talk

God plans for people to help keep us safe.

Resources

dark blue shirt with a silver badge, paper plates, safety cones, blocks, whistles (bring enough for each child to have one)

Use the safety cones or blocks to set up a road. Let one child pretend to be a police officer. Give the other children paper plates. Tell the children that the paper plates are their pretend steering wheels. Have the children hold the paper plates and pretend to drive cars. They must stop when the police officer holds up his or her hand and says, "Stop!" They may go again when the police officer puts down the hand and says, "Go!"

You may wish to create this activity on the playground. Let the children take turns being drivers and police officers.

Remind the children that drivers must follow the rules when they drive in order to keep everyone safe.

Math Center

Teacher Talk

God plans for people like police officers to help us stay safe.

Resources

badge pattern (*see page 221*), scissors, marker or crayon

Make a memory game by photocopying the badge pattern and cutting out twenty badges. Number the badges from 1 to 10 twice. The children can mix up the badges and put them face down on the table. Each child takes a turn turning over two badges and trying to match them.

Art Center

Teacher Talk

God plans for people like police officers to help us follow the rules so that we can stay safe.

Resources

heavy duty aluminum foil, cardboard cut in badge pattern (*see page 221*), tape, safety pins, press on numbers

Photocopy a badge pattern (*see page 221*). Use the pattern to cut a badge out of cardboard for each child. Instruct the children to cover the cardboard with foil. Let them choose three numbers to go on their badges. Tape a safety pin to the back of each badge and help the child put the badge on.

Worship Center

Teacher Talk

We thank God for people who help keep us safe.

Resources

nonpermanent ink pads, paper, colored pencils

Give each child a piece of paper. Show the children how to roll their finger tips on the ink pad and then roll them on the paper to make a finger print. Help each child print each finger of each hand. Place the child's name and date on the paper for parents' future reference.

Say: God has made each one of us special. Everyone has their own fingerprints. No one else in the world can have fingerprints just like yours. You are a special child of God. Police officers use fingerprints to help them find people. God plans for people like police officers to help keep us safe.

Pray: Thank you, God, for people like police officers who help keep us safe. Amen.

Wonder Time

As you call children together, encourage them to follow the clean up rule and put toys away.

Wonder Question: I wonder why we have rules?
Say: Rules help us get along with each other and live with each other peacefully. (Let the children tell you some of the rules in their homes such as *keep feet off the furniture, do not touch the stove, use good manners at the table, and so forth.*)
Ask: What rules should we have in class to work and play together?
Say: Police officers help us follow rules. Their job is to help people remember the rules that help keep us safe. Police officers also help us when we are in trouble.
Visitor: *(If you have invited a police officer, introduce the visitor to the children.)*
Sing: "Thank You, God, for Loving Me" *(see page 212)*.
Read the Bible verse.
Say: God plans for people to help us live together in peace.
Pray: Thank you, God, for the police who help us live together in peace. Amen.

Open the Bible to John 20:19.

Say: "Jesus said, 'Peace be with you'" (John 20:19, adapted).

Have the children repeat the Bible verse.

Group Fun

Resources

doll pattern (*see page 218*), cardboard or posterboard, wide ribbon, self-sticking velcro strips or circles, scissors, crayons or markers, glue

Let the children make seat-belt dolls. Cut cardboard or posterboard into 9-by-12 inch pieces. Before class, cut two slits about two inches long on each side of the boards. The slits need to be at least five inches apart. Cut the ribbon into eight-inch lengths.

Photocopy and cut out a doll (*see page 218*) for each child. Older children may cut out the dolls themselves. Let the children decorate the dolls with crayons or markers. Have the children glue the dolls in the middle of the posterboard. Thread each ribbon through one slit, around the back of the poster board and through the slit on the opposite side. The ends of the ribbon should overlap over the doll's stomach. Let each child stick a velcro strip or circle on each end of the ribbon. Show the children how to fasten and unfasten the seat belt around the doll. Remind the children that it is a rule to wear a seat belt when we are in our cars. This rule helps keep us safe.

Goodbye Circle

Remind the children of the classroom rules. Tell them to ask their parents what the important rules in their home are .

Pray: Thank you, God, for police officers and other people who help keep us safe. Amen.

Evaluation

Did you meet your objectives? Do the children know the rules?

Lesson 43

Firefighters

Teacher Talk:

God plans for people like fire-fighters to help us be safe.

We thank God for firefighters.

Goals:

To help the children learn to trust firefighters.

To help the children know what firefighters do to help their communities.

Objectives: By the end of this session the children will:

Pretend to be firefighters.

Learn to stop, drop, and roll.

Talk about fire safety rules.

Faith Connections

Bible verse: Protect me, O God; I trust in you for safety.

(Psalm 16:1, *Good News Bible*)

Children need to feel safe at home and school. Often just having a fire drill or hearing about a fire causes them to worry about their things and their families. Help the children know that there are many people in their community who will help them if there is a problem. Firefighters put out fires and help keep their neighborhoods safe.

Teacher's Prayer

Help me, O God, in what I say and do today to create a sense of security for my children. Amen.

Center Time

Display props and pictures that show firefighters at work.

Art Center

Teacher Talk

God plans for people to help keep us safe.

Resources

red and yellow finger paint, finger paint paper, table covering, smocks

Cover the table and have the children wear paint smocks. Let the children paint a fire with red and yellow finger paint. Talk about ways to stay safe around fires as the children paint.

Building Center

Teacher Talk

God plans for people like firefighters to help keep us safe.

Resources

toy fire truck, large boots, rubber or plastic raincoats, red construction paper, cardboard box, markers, hose or bucket of water, towels, blocks

Let the children pretend to be firefighters. Have the children build houses with the blocks. Add torn construction paper flames to the block houses. Let the children take turns driving the toy fire truck to the block houses and pretending to put out the fire.

If your setting permits, let the children go outside and use a hose and water. Draw flames on a cardboard box. Let the children put out the pretend flames by spraying the box with water.

Or let the children have a bucket brigade. Have the children stand in a line starting at the box. Partially fill a bucket with water and set it at the opposite end of the line. Shout, "Fire! Fire! Fire!" Have the child next to the bucket pick up the bucket and pass to the next child. Have the children continue passing the bucket so that the last child can pour the water on the box.

Math Center

Teacher Talk

God plans for firefighters and other people to teach us how to be safe from fires.

Resources

smoke detector without batteries, matchbox or matchbook without matches, construction paper flames, unlit candle, tray, towel or cloth

Place all the items on the tray. Talk with the children about each item. **Say:** "The smoke detector reminds us that we need to go out of our houses to the spot where we are to meet our parents. The matchbook reminds us never to play with matches. The flame reminds us to stop, drop, and roll. The candle reminds us to never leave candles burning."

Cover the tray with a towel or cloth. Have the children cover their eyes. Remove one of the items from underneath the cloth and hide it from the children. Have the children open their eyes and try to name which item is missing. Continue as the children show interest.

Worship Center

Teacher Talk

We thank God for firefighters.

Resources

jar with a lid, a small amount of sand, matches (which the teacher keeps)

Put the sand in the jar. Light a match and drop it in the jar. Put the lid on. Show children how the fire goes out when it doesn't have any oxygen.

Say: Firefighters can help us know how to be safe around fires.

Pray: Thank you, God, for firefighters and for ways we can learn to be safe around fire. Amen.

Open the Bible to Psalm 16:1.

Say: "Protect me, O God; I trust in you for safety"
(Psalm 16:1, *Good News Bible*).

Have the children repeat the Bible verse.

Wonder Time

After clean up time bring the experiment from the worship center and repeat it so every child can see it.

Wonder Question: I wonder how fires get started?
Talk about how fires get started.
Say: Never play with matches or fire.
Show the children how to dial 911. Give them several situations in which there might be a fire in the home. For instance, **ask:** "Would you call 911 when there is a fire in the fireplace?" Give some situations where a fire is out of control and they should call 911, and some such as a flame in an outdoor grill when they do not call 911.
Visitor: *(If you have invited a firefighter, introduce the visitor to the children.)*
Sing: "Thank You, God, for Loving Me" *(see page 212).*
Read the Bible verse.
Say: God plans for us to stay safe. Firefighters help us to be safe by making sure that fires are put out or kept under control.
Pray: Thank you, God, for firefighters.

Group Fun

Resources

self-sticking notes, red and yellow crayons; or red construction paper, tape

Teach the children to "stop, drop, and roll." Have the children form a circle. One child will be the fire. Color a self-sticking note bright red and yellow to make a paper flame. Or place a piece of masking tape on a construction paper flame. Give the child the paper flame. Have the remaining children walk in place. Have the fire walk around the circle and place the paper flame on a child in the circle. The child with the flame stops, drops, and rolls. Continue the game until every child has practiced "stop, drop, and roll."

Goodbye Circle

Remind the children of fire safety rules. Ask them to work with their parents to make a plan to keep everyone safe if there is a fire. Practice the plan until everyone knows what to do.

Pray: Thank you, God, for firefighters and all the people in our community who help keep us safe. Amen.

Evaluation

What a busy day! Are there activities children might like to repeat?

Lesson 44

Mail Carriers

Goals:

To help children understand that mail carriers are helpers in our community.

To learn how mail is sent.

Objectives: By the end of this session children will:

Send themselves a letter.

Experiment with glue.

Pretend to be mail carriers.

Faith Connections

Bible verse: Love never ends. (1 Corinthians 13:8)

Tell children that long, long ago people wrote letters and delivered them to their friends and family. We know that a man named Paul wrote many letters to his friends to tell them about Jesus. We can read the letters Paul wrote in our Bible. Paul wrote about love in one of his letters. Paul wrote, "Love never ends."

People who carry letters are helping us to be a community and to keep in touch with each other. Children love mail. Have you sent a card lately?

Teacher's Prayer

O God, keeping in touch is so important to me. Help me find time to write a letter to my friend, to write to parents, and to talk with the children more. Amen.

Teacher Talk:

People in Bible times wrote letters.

We write letters today.

Mail carriers help us send our letters.

We thank God for mail carriers.

Center Time

Before class write or copy a short note for each child. Sign the note and put it in an envelope. Give the children their mail when they arrive for class.

Post Office Center

Teacher Talk

We thank God for the people who help us by delivering the mail.

Resources

American flag, cardboard boxes, table, toy cash register, play money, bags for mail delivery, homemade mailbox, stickers, hand stamp, nonpermanent stamp pad

Create a post office from cardboard boxes. The center can be as small as a cardboard box or as big as half your room with a pretend parking lot, mailboxes, stations for clerks, and so forth. Encourage the children to pretend to buy stamps and send letters and packages.

Let the children take turns being the postmaster. Show them how the postmaster sells stamps to people and sends packages.

Worship Center

Teacher Talk

People in Bible times wrote letters, and we write letters today.

Resources

writing paper, envelopes, pencils, stickers for stamps, heart stickers

Let the children write letters. Remember any pencil marking on paper is a step toward writing letters and numbers. Give the children heart stickers to add to their letters.

Say: Bible people wrote letters and delivered them to their friends and family. We know that a man named Paul wrote many letters to his friends to tell them about Jesus. We can read the letters Paul wrote in our Bible. Paul wrote about love in one of his letters. Paul wrote, "Love never ends" (1 Corinthians 13:8).

Pray: Thank you, God, for letters in the Bible that tell us about love. Amen.

Home Living Center

Teacher Talk

God plans for people to help each other in the community. Mail carriers help us deliver the mail.

Resources

small boxes, brown paper, pens, stickers, masking tape

Let the children pretend to get packages ready to mail to friends and relatives. Cut paper to the size of the boxes to be wrapped before class. Show the children how to wrap the boxes in brown paper. Use masking tape to seal the paper so the packages can be easily unwrapped and used again. When the packages are ready, ask the children to deliver them to the class post office where the letter carriers will deliver them to various members of class.

Science Center

Teacher Talk

God plans for people like mail carriers to help each other in the community.

Resources

glue sticks, school glue, rubber cement, construction paper, envelopes, self-sticking notes, self-adhesive stickers, lick-and-stick stickers, paper scraps

Let the children experiment with glue. Show the children the different types of glue you have provided. Let the children glue paper scraps onto construction paper. Ask the children to decide which glue worked best. Then give the children self-sticking notes, self-adhesive stickers, and lick and stick stickers. Let the children add the stickers to their papers. Have the children decide which stickers worked best. Help the children fold up their papers and put them in envelopes. Show the children how to lick and seal the envelopes. Remind the children that we use glue to make the envelopes stay closed and to keep the postage stamps on our letters.

Wonder Time

Call the children to wonder time.

Wonder Question: I wonder how we get mail?

Show the children some mail you have received. Point out the writing on the front of the envelope: the return address, the address, and the stamp. Tell the children the entire process of sending and receiving a letter from beginning to end.

Visitor: *(If you have invited a mail carrier, introduce the visitor to the children.)*

Sing: "Thank You, God, for Loving Me" *(see page 212).*

Read the Bible verse.

Say: A man named Paul wrote many letters to his friends to tell them about Jesus. We can read the letters Paul wrote in our Bible. Paul wrote about love in one of his letters. Paul wrote, "Love never ends" (1 Corinthians 13:8).

Pray: Thank you, God, for mail carriers who bring us messages from our friends. Amen.

Open the Bible to 1 Corinthians 13:8.

Say: "Love never ends" (1 Corinthians 13:8).

Have the children repeat the Bible verse.

Group Fun

Resources

paper, envelopes, colored pencils, rubber stamps, nonpermanent ink pads, pen, postage stamps, children's addresses, markers

Each child will mail a letter to his or her address. Before class write the Bible verse, "Love never ends" (1 Corinthians 13:8), on a piece of plain paper. Photocopy the verse for each child.

Give each child the Bible verse paper. Let the children decorate the letter with rubber stamps and nonpermanent ink pads, markers, and colored pencils.

After the children have finished their letters, help them fold the letters and put them in envelopes. Have the names and addresses of the children on hand. Let each child watch you address the envelope to the child. Borrow from the office a rubber stamp that has your school address on it. Let the children use that stamp to add the return address to the envelopes. Have stamps available and show the children where to place the stamps on the envelopes.

Walk with the children to a nearby mailbox or to your preschool office. Let the children put their letters into the mailbox or in an office basket for mail pick-up. Or make plans for your school's mail carrier to stop by, meet the children, and take the letters to the post office.

Goodbye Circle

Let the children guess where their letters are at this moment and where they will be in a few days.

Pray: Thank you, God, for mail carriers who bring us messages from our friends. Amen.

Evaluation

Do the children understand a little more about the mail?

Lesson 45

Teachers

Teacher Talk:

Jesus was a special teacher.

Jesus taught us to love each other.

God plans for teachers to love us and help us.

Goal:

For the children to realize that teachers love us and help us.

Objectives: By the end of this session the children will:

Learn about mixing blue and yellow paint together.

Make a big book about Jesus.

Talk about what teachers do.

Faith Connections

Bible verse: Then Jesus went to the villages, teaching the people. (Mark 6:6, adapted)

Tell the children that Jesus was a teacher. He told stories to the people he taught. Many people followed him and did what he said to do. He taught us to love one another and to care for one another.

Teacher's Prayer

O God, help me to learn from you as a teacher. Teach me gentleness and love; teach me the ways of my children. Amen.

Note: Invite a teacher such as a dance instructor, gymnastics coach, art teacher (perhaps a potter), or music teacher to visit with the children today. Ask this person to teach the children a simple movement, craft, or song.

Center Time

Display props and pictures that show different subjects we can learn from teachers.

Math Center

Teacher Talk

God plans for teachers to help us learn things like our letters and numbers.

Resources

two packs of number or letter flash cards

Place two matching sets of ten number or letter flash cards in this center. Let the children match the cards. Encourage the children to use language skills by saying the numbers or letters they match.

Worship Center

Teacher Talk

We thank God for Jesus, a special teacher who taught us about God.

Resources

old Sunday school curriculum pictures, large construction paper or posterboard, glue, paper punch, yarn, crayons or markers

Make a big book about Jesus. Precut pictures of Jesus from old Sunday school curriculum resources. Show the children the pictures. **Say:** "Jesus is a special teacher. He taught us about God and God's love."

Give the children large pieces of construction paper or posterboard. Let the children glue the pictures onto the paper. Make a cover for the book using another piece of construction paper or posterboard. Write, "Our Book About Jesus" on the paper. Let the children work together to decorate the cover with crayons or markers.

Stack the pages together to make a book. Use a paper punch to make holes along the left-hand side of the pages. Tie loops of yarn through the holes to bind the pages together. Look through the big book with the children.

Pray: Thank you, God, for Jesus—a special teacher who taught us about God. Amen.

Art Center

Teacher Talk

God plans for teachers to help us learn things like colors.

Resources

white paper, yellow and blue tempera paint, table covering, smocks

Cover the table and have the children wear paint smocks. Tell the children that when you mix the colors yellow and blue together they make green.

Give each child a piece of white paper. Have each child hold out their hands. Place a dab of blue paint in one hand and a dab of yellow paint in the other hand. Have the children rub their hands together to mix the paint and make the color green. Let the children make green handprints on their papers.

Remind the children how to wash their hands *(see page 119)*.

Science Center

Teacher Talk

God plans for teachers to help us learn new things.

Resources

plastic dinosaurs, modeling clay, small green branches, cardboard box, small pebbles, pictures or books about dinosaurs

Allow the children to create a habitat for dinosaurs. Display books and pictures to give the children ideas. Remind the children that since there are no more dinosaurs in the world we must learn about dinosaurs from our teachers and from books.

Open the Bible to Mark 6:6.

Say: "Then Jesus went to the villages, teaching the people" (Mark 6:6, *Good News Bible*, adapted).

Have the children repeat the Bible verse.

Wonder Time

Call the children individually to wonder time.

Wonder Question: I wonder who the teachers are in our class?
Have the children name the teachers.
Say: Teachers help us learn many things like the names of colors, how to read and write letters and numbers, how to play musical instruments, and even how to wash our hands.
Visitor: *(If you have invited a teacher, introduce the visitor to the children.)*
Say: Teachers also teach us songs to sing.
Sing: "Clap, Clap" *(see page 211).*
Read the Bible verse.
Say: Jesus was a special teacher. He taught us about God.
Pray: Thank you, God, for all teachers who help us learn many things. Amen.

Group Fun

Resources

none

Say: "Teachers help us learn many things. Some teachers teach others American Sign Language. Sign language is a way to talk that uses your hands."

Teach the children the chorus of "Jesus Loves Me" in American Sign Language.

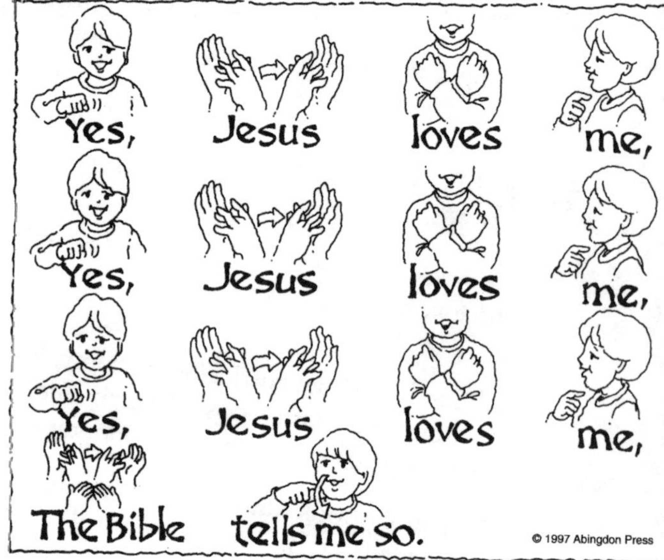

Jesus - Touch the middle finger of the right hand to the palm of the left hand. Reverse.

Loves - Cross hands at wrist and press over heart.

Me - Point the index finger of your right hand toward your chest.

Goodbye Circle

Review with the children all the community helpers they have learned about this week.

Pray: Thank you, God, for all teachers who help us learn many things. Amen.

Evaluation

Did any of the children's ideas of teachers teach you?

THE BUILDINGS

This week we will be learning about the different buildings in our community. Enjoy building with blocks or hammers and wood. If you have a parent or carpenter available, ask them to come and help the children make things.

Display photographs of various buildings in your immediate vicinity. Take photographs and use them in wonder time to encourage the children to recognize places in their community. Ask parents to take pictures of their homes and the places in which they work. Make a display of these pictures.

Lesson 46

My Home

Goal:

To help the children see their homes as part of the larger community.

Objectives:

By the end of this lesson the children will:

Build houses.

Begin learning their addresses and phone numbers.

Talk about neighborhoods.

Teacher Talk:

Thank you, God, for our homes.

God plans for us to have a safe place to live.

Faith Connections

Bible verse: People will build houses and get to live in them.

(Isaiah 65:21, *Good News Bible*)

God plans for each child to have shelter. Be sensitive to the types of living quarters the children in your class have. Whether children are living in shelters, mobile homes, apartments, or houses, include their dwelling places as you talk about homes.

Teacher's Prayer

I am thankful for the place where I live. Help me to know those around me. Amen.

Center Time

As children arrive, tell them we are making houses today.

Display pictures and photographs of different kinds of houses.

Building Center

Teacher Talk

God plans for us to have homes to live in.

Resources

paper grocery bags, newspapers, tempera paints and paintbrushes or markers (optional)

Let the children make paper bag blocks. Show the children how to crumple newspapers and stuff them into grocery bags. When a bag is stuffed, turn another bag upside down over the top of the stuffed bag to make a paper block. Make a few blocks ahead of time. Let the children create more blocks and build with them.

The center can continue all week as children make more blocks each day and build libraries, churches, and so forth with them. They may paint the blocks if you wish or use markers to draw windows and doors.

Home Living Center

Teacher Talk

Telephones help us talk to family and friends. We need to know our telephone numbers.

Resources

toy telephones, posterboard telephones, crayons or markers

Split the home living center into two homes. Encourage the children to visit their "neighbors" in the next home. They can call their neighbors on the phone, take their neighbors food, or visit with their neighbors.

Have a telephone cut out of posterboard for each child. Write the child's phone number on it. Let the children decorate their telephones. Help the children learn their phone numbers. When a child learns his or her phone number, let the child take the posterboard telephone home.

Math Center

Teacher Talk

Each house has an address. We need to know our addresses.

Resources

sandpaper, scissors, crayons, plain paper, blocks with numbers on them

Put out blocks with numbers on them. Help the children manipulate the blocks to show their house numbers.

Before class cut sets of numbers from sandpaper. Give the children plain paper. Help the children choose the numbers that make up their house numbers. Let the children trace around the sandpaper numbers or rub over the sandpaper numbers to write their addresses. Display the children's house numbers in your room.

Worship Center

Teacher Talk

God plans for us to have homes to live in.

Resources

building blocks

Let the children build houses using the building blocks. Encourage the children to make several houses and set them up in a neighborhood.

Say: Some people live in houses. Some people live in apartment buildings. Some people live in mobile homes. *(Say examples that include all your children)*. God plans for us to have homes to live in.

Pray: Thank you, God, for our homes and our neighborhoods. Amen.

Wonder Time

After the children clean up, call them to you and talk about what they did in each center.

Wonder Question: I wonder where you live?
Say: If you live in a house, clap your hands. If you live in an apartment, stomp your feet. If you live in a mobile home, pat your head. If you live in a shelter, tap your elbow.
Have each child's address available.
Say: If you live on (*name of street*), stand up.
Continue until you have named each child's street. Have everyone sit down.
Say: All our homes together make a neighborhood. If you live in (name of city), stand up. (Have everyone sit down.) If you live in (name of state), stand up. (Have everyone sit down.) If you live in (name of country), stand up. (Have everyone sit down.) If you live in the world, stand up!
Sing: "God Cares" (*see page 212*).
Read the Bible verse.
Say: God plans for each one of us to have a place to live.
Pray: Thank you, God, for the places where we live and for our neighborhoods. Amen.

Open the Bible to Isaiah 65:21.

Say: "People will build houses and get to live in them" (Isaiah 65:21, *Good News Bible*).

Have the children repeat the Bible verse.

Group Fun

Resources
lunch-size paper bags, crayons or markers, construction paper, mural paper, masking tape, colored tape, glue

Let the children make houses out of small paper bags. Give each child a bag. Turn the bag upside down so the bottom of the bag is the roof of the house. Let the children decorate their bags with crayons and markers. Or let the children glue on construction paper shapes to make doors and windows on their houses. Mount mural paper onto the wall. Help the children tape their houses to the mural paper. Make roads with colored tape or draw them on the mural to connect the houses and to make a neighborhood.

Goodbye Circle

Tell the children to look at their neighborhoods on the way home.

Pray: Thank you, God, for the places where we live and for our neighborhoods. Amen.

Evaluation

Did everyone get to make a home? Do you need to talk more about different types of homes?

Lesson 47

My School

Teacher Talk:

Thank you, God, for our schools.

Thank you for our teachers and friends at school.

We come to school to learn and to play with our friends.

Goals:

To help the children learn more about their school.

To help the children learn that their school is part of a neighborhood.

Objectives:

By the end of this lesson the children will:

Tour the school building.

Measure their classroom.

Help their school.

Faith Connections

Bible verse: Jesus grew both in body and in wisdom.

(Luke 2:52, *Good News Bible*)

Tell the children that Jesus went to synagogue school to learn. He probably wrote in the sand or on a clay tablet.

Children need to know that God wants them to stretch their minds and to learn all they can.

Teacher's Prayer

Help me, O God, to bring your loving spirit into our class. Help me to help the children grow. Amen.

Center Time

Make construction paper footprints and tape them on the floor from the entryway to your classroom.

As children arrive, ask the children if they followed the footprints.

Worship Center

Teacher Talk

We thank God for our room and our school.

Resources

drawing of your classroom, tape measures, pencils, happy face stickers, items such as blocks, crayons

Make a simple drawing of your classroom. Photocopy the drawing for each child. Let the children measure the classroom. Have each child start on one side of the room. Let the child count how many steps it takes to walk to the other side of the room. Expect the children to get different numbers. Help them write their measurements on their drawings, then color the drawings of their room. Let the children experiment with measuring using different objects such as blocks. How many blocks does it take to go across the room?

Say: "We have a room in our school where we come to learn and play with friends. There is something missing on the map of our room. Can you guess what it is? You! You are an important part of our school. Let's add you to our map." Give each child a happy face sticker. Let the children add the stickers to their maps.

Pray: Thank you, God, for our room and for our school. Thank you for all our friends at school. Amen.

Building Center

Teacher Talk

We have school where we come to learn and play with friends.

Resources

blocks

Let the children build a school with the blocks. Help them think about all the parts of your school.

Art Center

Teacher Talk

Our school is in a building. We have our own classroom in our school.

Resources

plain paper, tape, crayons with papers removed

Lightly tape a piece of plain paper on the wall for each child. If possible, find an area of your classroom wall that is textured (cement block or brick). Or take the children outside and tape the paper to an outside wall or sidewalk. Let the children rub over their papers with crayons (with papers removed).

If your school building has a cornerstone, let the children take turns making rubbings of the cornerstone.

Cleaning Center

Teacher Talk

We can help take care of our room and our school.

Resources

shaving cream, smocks, paper towels, dust cloth, sponges, blocks, dishpan partially filled with water and soap, dishpan partially filled with water, towels

Tell the children that one way they can help take care or their room is by cleaning. Squirt shaving cream on a table. Let the children wear smocks and enjoy fingerpainting with the shaving cream. Then let the children help wipe the shaving cream off the table with damp sponges and paper towels. Let other children dust the chairs and book shelves with a dust cloth. Or set up a block washing center with one dishpan of soapy water, one dishpan of rinse water, and towels.

Open the Bible to Luke 2:52.

Say: "Jesus grew both in body and in wisdom" (Luke 2:52, *Good News Bible*).

Have the children repeat the Bible verse.

Wonder Time

When the room is clean, call the children to the carpet and thank them for cleaning up the school.

Wonder Question: I wonder what we call the place where we go to learn and play with our friends?

Say: Our school is called (*name of school*). In our school we have a classroom. Our classroom is a place where (*name each child*) comes to learn and play with friends.

Sing: "I Want a Friend" (*see page 211*). Stand in a circle and do the suggested actions.

Read Bible verse.

Say: Jesus went to school. Jesus learned many things at his school just as you are learning many things at your school.

Pray: Thank you, God, for our school and for all our friends. Amen.

Group Fun

Resources

adult helpers

Prepare the children for their walk around the school building. If there are any special features such as stained glass windows, steps out front, statues, a garden, or a cross, point these features out to the children. If possible, let the children touch the special features to help them remember them.

Stop and look around the neighborhood. Point out the other buildings that are in the neighborhood.

When you get back to your class, talk about what you saw. Let the children remember and act out their walk. **Ask:** "What is the first thing we did when we went on our walk?" (*Opened the classroom door, lined up at the door.*) Let's pretend to open the door. (Act out opening the door.) What happened next? (*We walked down the hall, walked outside, and so forth.*) Let's pretend to walk outside. (Walk in place.) What happened next? (*We walked up some steps; we saw a bird; we went around the block.*) Let's pretend we are the bird. (Flap your arms.) Let's pretend . . .

Continue to remember the walk and act it out.

Goodbye Circle

Remind the children to look at their school building as they go home and to find something they didn't see before. Ask each child to bring a favorite book to class tomorrow; you may need to send a note home to tell parents.

Pray: Thank you, God, for our school and for all our friends. Amen.

Evaluation

Did the children have fun? Are there ways you can include care of your class and school building in your regular routine?

Lesson 48

The Library

Goals:

To help the children see the library as a part of the neighborhood.

To help the children discover how the library helps people.

Objectives: By the end of this session children will:

Make bookmarks.

Read library books.

Make a bookworm.

Faith Connections

Bible verse: Jesus stood up to read. (Luke 4:16, adapted)

There is a warmth and an intimacy in reading out loud to children. You and the child are experiencing the story together. Books stimulate children's imaginations and teach them about worlds far away. Children need to see the Bible as the special book that tells us stories about Jesus and God's love.

Help young children know that the Bible is a storybook that tells us about God's love for everyone. It also tells about people who lived in Bible times. Hold the Bible each time you tell a Bible story or say a Bible verse. Remind the children that the verse comes from the Bible.

Teacher's Prayer

O God, help me take more time to read, to stretch my mind, and to learn new things. Amen.

Teacher Talk:

A library is a place that has many books for us to read and enjoy.

Books help us learn many things.

The Bible is the special book that tells us about God and Jesus.

Center Time

Plan a special book center for today or add something special such as pillows and blankets to your existing book center.

As children arrive, have the children show you any books they brought today.

Book Center

Teacher Talk

Books help us learn many things.

Resources

books, blankets, sleeping bags, pillows, stuffed animals that are characters from favorite books, posters, fabric strips, banners, tent

Add decorations to the book center to make it extra special for today's lesson. Add blankets, sleeping bags, and pillows. Include stuffed characters from favorite books.

Display reading posters (check your local library, Scholastic, or NAEYC). Make a canopy out of strips of cloth, or hang banners. Put up a tent and let the children look at books in the tent.

Let the children take their favorite books to the center to read and to share with their friends.

Math Center

Teacher Talk

Books can help us learn about things we need to know, such as words and numbers.

Resources

construction paper, stapler, staples, plain paper, marker, stickers

Let the children make number books. Make a blank book for each child by stapling five pages of plain paper together with a construction paper cover. Use a marker to write a number 1 on the first page, number 2 on the second page, and so forth up to the number 5.

Give each child a book. Help the child read the number on each page and then place the same number of stickers on that page.

Building Center

Teacher Talk

A library is a place that has many books for us to read and enjoy.

Resources

paper bags, newspapers, photography of the local library, books

Use the paper bag blocks (*see page 150*) to build a library. Help the children think about the library in their community, or place a photograph of it in the center. After they have finished their building, let them take books into the center and read them.

Art Center

Teacher Talk

Books help us use our imaginations.

Resources

construction paper, scissors, rubber stamps, nonpermanent ink pads

Make bookmarks. Cut construction paper into two-inch strips. Give each child a strip and two rubber stamps. Let the child use the rubber stamps to make a pattern on the strip.

Worship Center

Teacher Talk

The Bible is the special book that tells us about God and Jesus.

Resources

a variety of Bibles

Let the children look at different Bibles. Include Bible storybooks. **Say:** "Although the Bibles look different, each one contains the same stories. The Bible is the special storybook that teaches us about Jesus and God."

Pray: Thank you, God, for books. Thank you for the special book, the Bible. Amen.

Wonder Time

Have the children bring their special books and join you for wonder time.

Turn the Pages

The Bible is a special book.
Turn the pages, take a look.
Hear the stories that are there.
Learn about God's love and care.
The Bible is a special book.
Turn the pages, take a look.

Words: Daphna Flegal

Wonder Question: I wonder what we would find at a library?

Say: A library is a place where we can go to read and enjoy books. It is an important building in our community.

Let each child tell the name of the book he or she brought. Tell the children they will have more time during the day to share their books with their friends.

Read the Bible verse.

Say: The Bible tells us about Jesus and about God.

Show the children the Bible. Tell them there are stories in the Bible, which people have been reading for thousands of years.

Sing: "Turn the Pages" to the tune of "Twinkle, Twinkle, Little Star" *(see box)*.

Pray: Thank you, God, for stories and books and libraries. Amen.

Open the Bible to Luke 4:16.

Say: "Jesus stood up to read" (Luke 4:16, adapted).

Have the children repeat the Bible verse.

Group Fun

Resources

lunch-size paper bags in different colors, stapler, staples, construction paper, crayons or markers, newspaper, glue, scissors

Have the children make a book worm to put in the book center. Give each child a lunch-size paper bag. Let the children decorate their bags with crayons or markers. Show the children how to crumple newspaper and stuff it inside their bags. Bring the top edges together and fold down about one inch. Staple two or three times across the edge. When each child has finished his or her bag, select one bag to be the book worm's head. Glue on construction paper eyes. Then staple the rest of the bags (the top of the first bag to the bottom of the next bag) together, forming one very long book worm. Place the book worm in a place of honor in the book center.

Goodbye Time

Thank the children for bringing their books to share with the class.

Pray: Thank you, God, for stories and books and libraries. Amen.

Evaluation

Are books used in your classroom? Make sure you have a basket of books available every day in your class. Encourage parents to come and read to your class. Take children to the library, and change the choice of books often.

Lesson 49

Churches

Teacher Talk:

The church is a special place we go to worship and learn about God.

We have churches in our neighborhood.

Thank you, God, for churches.

Goals:

To make the children aware of the churches in their neighborhoods.

To help the children learn that people go to church to worship, pray, and learn about God.

Objectives: By the end of this lesson the children will:

Make illuminated letters.

Talk about why we have churches.

Make stained-glass windows.

Build a church.

Faith Connections

Bible verse: On this rock I will build my church. (Matthew 16:18)

Preschoolers think so concretely they often misinterpret phrases such as, "This is the house of God." The first person they see at church who is old or who has a beard, they think must be God. Help the children understand that we can't see God, but we know God is with us. People build buildings called churches. Churches are special places where we can come together to pray and worship God. There are different churches because people believe different things about God and Jesus.

Teacher's Prayer

Dear God, I ask your blessings on the churches around the world. Help each church welcome the children in your name. Amen.

Center Time

Display pictures of churches, church bulletins, and a church pictorial directory for today's lesson.

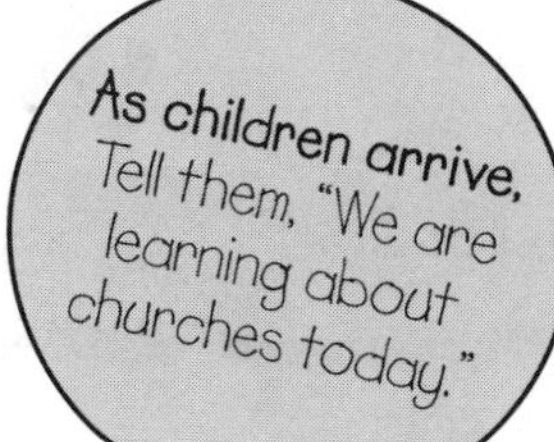

Writing Center

Teacher Talk
The Bible is the special storybook of the church.

Resources
Bible, paper, colored markers, gold markers

Find a Bible or another book from your church or library that has illuminated letters. Illuminated letters are letters that have artwork incorporated into the letters themselves. Hundreds of years ago monks drew these letters when they copied verses from the Bible.

Before class draw the first letter in each child's name on a piece of paper. Place the papers on the table. Help the child find the paper with her or his first initial on it. Show the children the books or Bibles you have provided with illuminated letters. **Say:** "A long time ago people wrote the Bible by hand and made beautiful letters called illuminated letters in special places in the Bible."

Let the children use markers to illuminate (or decorate) their first initials.

Math Center

Teacher Talk
Books help us learn many things.

Resources
shoebox, gingerbread cookie cutter, plain paper, craft sticks, glue, safety scissors

Before class glue two craft sticks together to make a cross. Glue the cross to one end of the shoebox, so that when the box is sitting flat, the cross is standing up. Trace the outline of the cookie cutter many times to fill a page of plain paper; then make copies of the paper so each child will have a page of people.

Let the children cut out people to put in the church. If they haven't developed cutting skills yet, have some people shapes already cut out. Have the children count the people as they put them in the shoebox church.

Home Living Center

Teacher Talk
We go to church to worship God.

Resources
dress-up clothes, high heels, Bibles

Place clothes that people might wear to a church service in your area in the center. Since some churches are more casual than others, place blue jeans along with other dress-up clothes. Encourage the children to pretend to get ready for church.

Block Center

Teacher Talk
We have many churches in our neighborhood. Our school is in a church.

Resources
brown paper grocery bags, masking tape, construction paper or cellophane, scissors

Before class cut construction paper or cellophane into stained glass window shapes. Let the children build a church with the paper bag blocks (*see page 150*) and tape the "windows" to the church.

Worship Center

Teacher Talk
Thank you, God, for churches.

Resources
clear self-adhesive paper, tissue paper

Let the children make stained-glass windows. Cut clear self-adhesive paper into 9-by-12-inch sheets. Remove the backing and lightly tape the sheets to the wall, sticky side out. Provide different colors of tissue paper or cellophane. Let the children tear the colored paper into smaller pieces and stick them onto the self-adhesive paper.

Pray: Thank you, God, for churches. Amen.

Open the Bible to Matthew 16: 18.

Say: "On this rock I will build my church" (Matthew 16:18).

Have the children repeat the Bible verse.

Wonder Time

After cleanup time call the children to you by playing organ music. Ask the children if they have ever heard music like this in church.

Wonder Question: I wonder why people go to church?
Say: People go to church to pray and worship God. They go to church to see their friends. God wants us to help others, so some churches have more than a place for worship. Some have playgrounds and meeting rooms and kitchens.
Sing: "Go to Church" to the tune of "This Is the Way" (see box).
Read the Bible verse.
Say: The church is a special place to worship and learn about God.
Pray: Thank you, God, for churches. Amen.

Go to Church
This is the way we
Go to church,
Go to church,
Go to church.
This is the way we
Go to church,
Step, step, step.
(Walk in place.)

This is the way we
Pray at church,
Pray at church,
Pray at church.
This is the way we
Pray at church,
Thank you, God.
(Fold hands in prayer.)
words: Daphna Flegal

Group Time

Resources
adult helpers, organist

Tour the church building in which you have preschool. Or make arrangements to tour a church nearby. Make sure that the lights have been turned on before you go on your tour. If the church has an organist, make arrangements for the person to meet you and to play for the children. Tell the children ahead of time if the organ, piano, or pulpit is off limits. End your tour in the sanctuary of the church. Sit in the pews and talk with the children about the things they see in the church.

Sit quietly for a minute or two and tell the children that although they can't see God in this church, they can feel good inside and know that God is with them. They can see the beauty of the church and think of God. They can see people helping others and know that God's love is to share.

Pray: Thank you, God, for churches. Amen.

Goodbye Time

Tell the children to look around the neighborhood for churches.

Pray: Thank you, God, for churches. Amen.

Evaluation

Did the children understand why we have churches? Is there more you need to do to clear up any misunderstandings about church? Bring in objects from last week's lessons and this week's lessons to talk about the whole neighborhood.

Lesson 50

My Community

Goal:

To help children see that the helpers and buildings they have studied are all part of a larger community.

Objectives: By the end of this session the children will:

Make community buildings.

Talk about the people in the community.

Have a parade to celebrate their community.

Sing about their community.

Faith Connections

Bible verse: Love your neighbor as you love yourself.

(Mark 12:31, *Good News Bible*)

Children need to see the people in their community as persons who can help them. They need to know that God planned for people to live together and to be helpful to each other.

Teacher's Prayer

O God, help me to show love to all the people in my community. Help me to love my neighbor. Amen.

Teacher Talk:

Jesus told us to love our neighbor as we love ourselves.

We thank God for all the people in our community who help us.

We are part of our neighborhoods and our community.

We can be good neighbors and show love to others.

Center Time

As children arrive, have them name a community helper or a building in the community.

Display pictures of buildings and people from the unit on the community.

Building Center

Teacher Talk

Our community has many buildings.

Resources

paper bags, newspaper, masking tape

There should be enough paper bag blocks (*see page 150*) now to build several buildings. Combine those with your regular blocks and ask the children to make a whole community.

Home Living Center

Teacher Talk

Our community has many helpers.

Resources

items from previous home living centers

Include dress-up clothes and other items in the center that you have used over the past two weeks and that the children have enjoyed.

Art Center

Teacher Talk

Let's have a parade to celebrate the people in our community who help us.

Resources

boxes, rope or string, construction paper, glue, crayons or markers, tempera paint, newspapers, brushes, smocks, tape, scissors

Let the children make floats for a community parade. Before class attach a piece of rope or string to each box to make a handle. The children will use the string to pull the boxes in their parade.

Cover the work area with newspapers. Show the children the boxes. Let the children decorate the boxes with markers and crayons, by gluing on construction paper scraps, or by painting with tempera paint. Have the children wear smocks if you choose to paint.

Writing Center

Teacher Talk

We can celebrate all the buildings and places that are in our community.

Resources

posterboard or mural paper, pictures of buildings, glue, marker

Let the children make a banner for the parade. Precut pictures of buildings from magazines. If possible, include pictures of schools and libraries. Write, "Thank you, *(name of your school or city)*" across a piece of posterboard or mural paper. Let the children glue the pictures on to the posterboard or paper. Tell the children that today you will have a parade to celebrate your community.

Worship Center

Teacher Talk

We can thank God for the many people in our community who help us.

Resources

heart pattern *(see page 221)*, paper plates, crayons or markers, craft sticks, tongue depressors, paint stirrers, or paper towel tubes, crepe paper streamers, glue; tape

Use the heart pattern (*see page 221*) to draw hearts in the center of paper plates. Give each child a paper plate. Let the children decorate the hearts with crayons or markers. Let the children glue crepe paper streamers along the edges of the paper plates. Help each child tape a stick onto the back of the paper plate.

Say: Our Bible verse today says, "Love your neighbor as you love yourself" (Mark 12:31, *Good News Bible*). Our hearts can remind us to love the people in our neighborhoods and community.

Pray: Thank you, God, for all the people in our community who help us. Amen.

Wonder Time

As children gather after cleanup time, talk with them about all the different activities in the room.

Wonder Question: I wonder if we can name the people in our community who help us?
Help the children remember the people and buildings that make up a community.
Say: There are many people in our community who help us. We have learned about doctors and nurses, police officers, firefighters, mail carriers, and teachers. There are many places in our community where we can go to learn and play. There are homes, schools, libraries, and churches.
Sing: "I Want a Friend" (*see page 211*).
Read the Bible verse.
Ask: What are some ways we can show love to our neighbors?
What are some ways we can show love for ourselves?
Pray: *(Go around the circle and let each child name one thing in the community for which he or she is thankful. Remember to tell the children they can say the prayer in their minds or out loud.)*

Open the Bible to Mark 12:31.

Say: "Love your neighbor as you love yourself" (Mark 12:31, *Good News Bible*).

Have the children repeat the Bible verse.

Group Fun

Resources
parade floats, banner, heart streamers, tricycles, dress-up clothes, cassette/CD player, parade music, adult help

Have a parade to celebrate your community. Walk with the children around the block or just around the playground. Let two children carry the banner and lead the parade. Let other children pull the box floats. Still others can wave the heart streamers. Others can dress up as doctors and nurses, mail carriers, police officers, or firefighters using the items from the home living center. If you have tricycles available, let some of the children ride them in the parade. Carry a portable cassette/CD player and play parade music. Always have adult help and follow safety rules when walking with the children.

Goodbye Circle

Have the children put away all the props from the parade. Thank the children for following safety rules.

Say: We have some important people from our community with us right now. Can you guess who they are? You!

Pray: Thank you, God, for all the people in our community who help us. Thank you for *(name each child and teacher)*. Amen.

Evaluation

Do the children understand the concept of community? Begin planning for next week. Think about the kinds of activities the children enjoyed this week and include them in your future planning.

THE FOOD

This week children will learn about the different places in the community that provide food for the family. Help them remember the differences in healthy foods and junk food from the "heart-healthy" lessons. Children are sometimes surprised to learn that people grow the crops that eventually end up on their tables. They often think that their food comes from the store, not the farm.

This week's lessons invite the children to pretend to grow crops, sell them, and cook them. Field trips could be taken any day to places where food is grown, processed, or sold.

Lesson 51

The Farm

Teacher Talk:

God plans for us to have good food to eat.

Farmers grow the food that we eat.

We thank God for all the people who help us have good food to eat.

Goal:

For children to learn how food is grown on the farm and taken to market.

Objectives: By the end of this session the children will:

Make fruit and vegetable puppets.

Talk about the food grown on farms.

Faith Connections

Bible verse: What a rich harvest God's goodness provides!

(Psalm 65:11, *Good News Bible*, adapted)

Many children have never seen a farm or a live farm animal. They need to learn that God planned for food for us to eat. The farmer is also a community helper who cares for crops so that we can have food to eat.

Teacher's Prayer

O God, thank you for all the people who work that I may eat. Amen.

NOTE: Be aware of children with food allergies. Modify your activities for these children.

Center Time

Cut off the tops of carrots and place them in a shallow dish of water. Set the tops in a sunny spot and watch them sprout.

As children arrive, ask them where they get the food they eat.

Math Center

Teacher Talk

God plans for farmers to grow food like carrots.

Resources

paper carrots of different sizes

Before class, cut out carrots of different sizes from construction paper. Encourage the children to put the carrots in order, shortest to tallest. It is all right if they want to play with the carrots and make designs with them as well. (This is the beginning of learning sequences.)

Science Center

Teacher Talk

God plans for us to take care of the land. Farmers take care of the land so that they can grow food.

Resources

rectangular plastic container, sand and dirt, water, table covering, twigs, measuring cup, spoons

Cover the table. Show the children how to pack dirt and sand firmly in one end of a plastic container. Help the children make the soil slope down to what is soon to become a river. Encourage the children to pretend it is a farmer's field. Let the children use small twigs to make rows in the dirt for crops. Stick in a few twigs to be trees.

Have the children take turns making it rain on the field by slowly pouring water from a measuring cup over the dirt. As it rains, the water runs off the ground. The topsoil that is on the field will wash away too. Tell the children that this is called *erosion*. Plants need soil, water, and light to grow. When the soil is washed away, plants cannot grow. Farmers work in their fields to stop the soil from going into the rivers so their plants will grow.

Building Center

Teacher Talk

God plans for farmers to grow food. After the farmers pick the food, the food is taken to sell at a market.

Resources

flannelboard with felt crops, trucks, baskets

Cut fruits and vegetables from felt. Place a flannelboard near this center. Let the children pretend that the flannel board is a field of crops. Place the fruits and vegetables on the field. Let the children pick the crops, load them onto trucks, and take the crops to market.

Worship Center

Teacher Talk

God plans good food to grow.

Resources

fruit shapes (*see page 222*) cut from construction paper, crayons or markers, precut facial features, glue, tape, craft sticks, "God Plans for Many Growing Things" (*see page 213*)

Before class, cut fruit and vegetable shapes out of construction paper. Let each child choose a shape to make a puppet. Let the children add faces with crayons or markers. Or precut facial features and let the children glue them onto the shapes. Help each child glue or tape a craft stick onto the back of his or her shape to a make puppet.

Have the children hold their puppets and crouch down on the floor. Sing the song "God Plans for Many Growing Things" (*see page 213*). Have the children gradually stand up and hold their puppets above their heads.

Pray: Thank you, God, for the good food that grows for us to eat. Amen.

Open the Bible to Psalm 65:11.

Say: "What a rich harvest God's goodness provides!" (Psalm 65:11, *Good News Bible*, adapted).

Have the children repeat the Bible verse.

Wonder Time

After cleanup time call the children together. Talk about the activities in each center.

Wonder Question: I wonder where the food we eat comes from?

Say: Farmers grow food for us. First the farmer sows the seeds. (*Have the children pretend to plant seeds.*) Next the farmer cares for the crops and harvests them when they are full grown. (*Have the children pretend to pick crops and put them in baskets.*) Then trucks take the crops to market. (*Have the children pretend to drive trucks.*) Then parents buy the food and put it in the cabinet or refrigerator. (*Pretend to put food up on shelves.*) Finally, families prepare the food and eat it. (*Pretend to eat.*)

Sing and play "The Farmer in the Dell."

Read the Bible verse.

Say: God planned for food to come from the earth. Rain and sun help the food grow, and the farmer takes care of the crops and harvests them.

Pray: Thank you, God, for our food. Thank you for all the people who help us have food to eat. Amen.

Group Fun

Resources

seed packets, lettuce, cherry tomatoes, carrots, cucumbers, celery, salad dressings, carrot peelers, serrated plastic knife, dishpan of water, paper towels, large salad bowl, hand-washing supplies, bowls, plastic forks

Make and enjoy a salad with the children. Divide your class into as many groups as there are adults to supervise. Show the children the vegetables. If possible, have seed packets to match the vegetables. Hold up a seed packet and let the children find the matching vegetables on the table.

Have the children wash their hands. Show the children how to wash the vegetables. Let some peel carrots—be sure the child peeling carrots stands the carrot on end and puts one hand at the top of the carrot. The other hand strokes downward to peel the carrot. Let the children use serrated plastic knives to cut the celery and cucumbers.

As children prepare the vegetables, have them put them in a large salad bowl and toss the vegetables. Eat the salad at lunchtime or for a snack. Say a thank-you prayer.

Goodbye Circle

Have the children tell you something they learned about farmers today. Send field trip notices home if you are planning a trip Thursday or Friday.

Pray: Thank you, God, for the good food that grows for us to eat. Amen.

Evaluation

Do you think the children are beginning to understand where food comes from?

Lesson 52

The Dairy

Goal:

To help children understand that milk comes from cows and is good for us.

Objectives: By the end of this session children will:

Drink milk or milk substitutes.

Mix powdered milk.

Pretend to milk a cow.

Make ice cream.

Faith Connections

Bible verse: Abraham took some cream, some milk, and the meat, and set the food before the men.

(Genesis 18:8, *Good News Bible*, adapted)

Milk, yogurt, and cheese are part of the food pyramid. Children need to see that milk comes from cows before we buy it at the grocery store. Cows are wonderful animals planned by God. They give us a nourishing food—milk.

Teacher's Prayer

O God, thank you for milk, which nourishes us and keeps us healthy. Amen.

NOTE: Be aware of children with food allergies. Modify your activities for these children.

Note: Prepare a note tonight to send home to parents tomorrow asking them to send canned goods with their child.

Teacher Talk:

God planned for cows to give us milk.

Dairy farmers take care of cows and sell the milk at the market.

We thank God for good foods like milk, yogurt, and cheese.

Center Time

Place toy plastic cows in the centers for today. Or use the cow pattern (*see page 220*) to make cows out of posterboard.

As children arrive, ask parents if their child can have milk and milk products.

Math Center

Teacher Talk

God plans for farmers to take care of the cows that give us milk. These farmers are called dairy farmers.

Resources

large piece of white felt, black felt, cow pattern (*see page 220*), scissors

Before class photocopy and cut out the cow pattern (*see page 220*). Use the pattern to cut the shape of a cow from the white felt. Cut facial features and lots of spots out of black felt. Let the children give Bessie the cow her spots. They can put the felt spots wherever they wish on the cow and then count them. They will also need to put on Bessie's eyes and nose. Make a cow for each child in this center.

Art Center

Teacher Talk

The milk we drink comes from cows.

Resources

white construction paper, black tempera paint, plastic container, spoons, table covering, smocks

Cover the table and have the children wear paint smocks. Pour black tempera paint into plastic containers. **Say:** "The milk we drink comes from cows. Sometimes the milk cows we see have black and white spots. Let's paint milk cow spots."

Give each child a piece of white construction paper. Show the children how to fold the papers in half and then open them again. Let the children spoon a small amount of black tempera paint on the fold line. Have the children refold the paper. Show each child how to press the paper from the fold out to the edges of the paper. Let the children open their papers to see their milk cow spot.

Worship Center

Teacher Talk

We thank God for milk.

Resources

powdered milk, cold water, spoons, cups, cold milk (optional: chocolate drink mix)

Let the children pour a cup of water, measure teaspoons of powdered milk into the cup of water, stir, and drink. Talk about how the milk is dried and then dissolves in the water to become a liquid again. After the children have made their cups of milk, you may wish to let each child put in a spoonful of chocolate drink mix to give it flavor. Have cold milk available for the children to try after they have tasted the powdered milk. Ask them to tell you which milk they liked best.

Say: God plans for good food for us to eat and drink. Milk and other foods like cheese and yogurt are part of the food pyramid. They are part of the dairy group. We should eat two to three servings of dairy products each day.

Pray: Thank you, God, for milk and cheese and yogurt. Amen.

Water Play Center

Teacher Talk

Dairy farmers take care of the cows that give us milk.

Resources

clothesline, disposable plastic gloves, buckets, stools, pin, water

Plan for this center to be outside. Put up a clothesline about three feet from the ground. Fill a disposable plastic glove with water. Securely attach the glove to the clothesline with the fingers pointing down. Place a plastic bucket and stool under the glove. Use a pin to poke several small holes in the fingers of the glove. Show the children how to squeeze the fingers with a downward motion to squirt the water into the bucket.

Wonder Time

After cleanup time call the children to wonder time.

Wonder Question: I wonder where milk and yogurt and cheese come from?

Say: God planned for cows to give us milk. The dairy farmer takes care of the cows and sells the milk to a dairy. The dairy makes the milk into cheese and yogurt and ice cream. The dairy also makes the milk safe for us to drink.

Say: Foods like milk and cheese and yogurt are called dairy foods. I will name a food. If it is a dairy food, I want you to moo like a cow. If it is not a dairy food, stay quiet.

Name some foods (cottage cheese, strawberry yogurt, carrots, American cheese, chocolate milk, cream cheese, tomatoes, whipped cream, mozzarella cheese, ice cream) and have the children moo when you name a dairy product.

Sing: "I'm Thankful," verse 7 (*see page 215*).

Read the Bible verse.

Say: Abraham was a man in Bible times. He had milk and cheese to eat and drink just like we do today. Milk is a special drink God planned for us. It is good, and it keeps us healthy. It has calcium in it, and calcium makes strong bones and strong teeth.

Pray: Thank you, God, for milk that keeps us strong and healthy. Amen.

Open the Bible to Genesis 18:8.

Say: "Abraham took some cream, some milk, and the meat, and set the food before the men."
(Genesis 18:8, *Good News Bible*, adapted)

Have the children repeat the Bible verse.

Group Fun

Resources

for each bag: 1 cup milk, 1 tablespoon sugar, 1 teaspoon vanilla, ice, gallon-size resealable plastic bag, quart-size resealable plastic bag, salt

Let the children make ice cream in a bag. Pour milk, sugar, and vanilla in a quart-size resealable bag. Seal the bag securely. Fill the gallon-size resealable plastic bag with ice. Place six tablespoons of salt on top of the ice. Place the quart-size bag inside the gallon-size bag and seal the gallon-size bag securely. Let the children take turns shaking the bag for about four to five minutes until the ingredients become thick like ice cream. Remove the ice cream from the quart-size bag and eat immediately.

Goodbye Circle

Ask the children which milk product they like the best. Let them play with the felt cows as they wait for their parents.

Pray: Thank you, God, for milk. Thank you for all the people who help us have good food to eat. Amen.

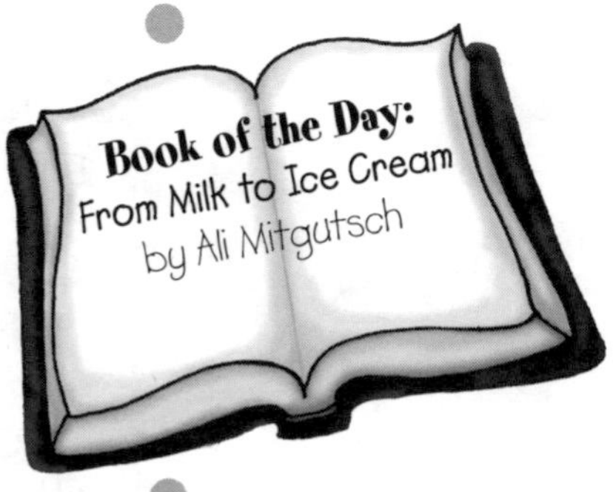

Evaluation

Do the children know milk comes from cows? Are there ways you can use milk and milk products in future lessons?

Lesson 53

The Bakery

Teacher Talk:

God planned for everyone to have good food to eat.

Farmers grow the grain that is made into breads and cereals.

We thank God for good foods like bread and cereal.

Goal:

To help the children learn that bakery products come from grains that are grown by farmers.

Objectives: By the end of this session the children will:

Make bread.

Paint with wheat.

Grind grain into flour.

Taste different kinds of breads.

Faith Connections

Bible verse: Go, eat your bread with enjoyment.

(Ecclesiastes 9:7)

Again, your children may have no experience with how grains are grown. For many of us bread comes from the bakery, not the wheat field. Help your children relate the products they eat, like bread and cereal, to the various grains grown on a farm. God planned for grains that can be made into good food. We thank God for the bounty of the earth.

Teacher's Prayer

O Lord, when I eat my bread, when I bake for my family, I am aware of your plan for my good life. Thank you. Amen.

NOTE: Be aware of children with food allergies. Modify your activities for these children.

Center Time

Have a sheath of wheat to show the children and display pictures of corn, wheat, or barley growing.

As children arrive, have a loaf of bread in a basket. Let each child pinch off a small piece of bread to taste.

Worship Center

Teacher Talk

God plans for food.

Resources

none

Say the following action poem with the children as today's worship center prayer.

God Plans for Food

God gives the sun,
(Make circle with hands for sun.)
rain,
(Wiggle fingers for rain.)
and soil,
(Point to the ground for soil.)
To help seeds grow into wheat.
(Make fist, open slowly, and point fingers up.)
From wheat we grind the flour
(Make grinding or pounding motion.)
To bake bread we like to eat.
(Rub stomach.)
Thank you, God, for food.
(Fold hands in prayer.)

Written by Jean Whicker

Art Center

Teacher Talk

Farmers grow the grain that is made into breads and cereals we find at the store.

Resources

decorative stalks of wheat, construction paper, tempera paint, shallow trays, table covering, smocks

Cover the table and have the children wear paint smocks. Pour tempera paint into shallow containers. Give each child a piece of construction paper. Provide decorative stalks of wheat (found in craft stores). Show the children how to use the stalks like paint brushes.

Science Center

Teacher Talk

God plans for food like grains to grow. Bakers use the grain to make breads and cereals.

Resources

table covering; wooden cutting board, rounded rock, wheat, corn; or oat cereal squares, resealable plastic bags

Cover the table. Place the cutting board on the table. Spread a few wheat kernels or corn kernels on the board. Show the children how to grind the wheat with a rock.

If you choose not to grind grain, provide oat cereal squares. Show the children how to put a few squares in a plastic bag and crush the oats between their fingers to make oat flour. Tell the children that the farmers grow the grain and pick it. Then the grain is taken to a mill, a place where the grain is crushed up into flour. The flour is used to make the breads and cereals we eat.

Home Living Center

Teacher Talk

God plans for everyone to have food to eat.

Resources

different types of bread, bowl of cooked rice, napkins, paper plates, spoons

Let the children taste different types of fresh bread. Include breads from countries around the world, such as French bread, tortillas, pita bread, Hawaiian bread, and German rye bread. Add a bowl of cooked rice.

Open the Bible to Ecclesiastes 9:7.

Say: "Go, eat your bread with enjoyment" (Ecclesiastes 9:7).

Have the children repeat the Bible verse.

Wonder Time

After cleanup time, talk with the children about their center activities.

Wonder Question: I wonder how the bread we buy in the grocery store is made?
Show the children pictures of grains such as wheat. Let the children who ground up the grains show the flour they made. Tell the children that there are big machines that grind wheat and oats into flour.
Sing: "I'm Thankful," verse 7 (*see page 215*).
Read the Bible verse.
Say: God planned for people to have good food to enjoy.
Pray: Thank you, God, for grains that are made into breads and cereals. Amen.

Group Fun

Resources

muffin mix, ingredients needed for mix, large resealable plastic bag, cupcake papers, muffin pan, spoon, loaf of store-bought bread, cereal box, oatmeal box

Let the children make muffins. Use a resealable plastic bag instead of a mixing bowl. Add the ingredients as indicated on the muffin mix. Securely seal the bag. Let the children take turns squishing and shaking the bag to mix the ingredients together. Have the children line a muffin pan with cupcake papers. Spoon the batter into the muffin pan. Bake according to the directions.

Show the children the loaf of bread, cereal box, and oatmeal box. Tell the children that all these foods are made from grain. Farmers grow the grain that we make into breads and cereals. Let the children eat the muffins at snack time.

Goodbye Circle

Ask the children to see if they can find something in their dinner tonight that is made from grains. Do the action rhyme "God Plans for Food" (*see page 171*) again.

Pray: Thank you, God, for grains that are made into breads and cereals. Amen.

Evaluation

There are so many different items your class can enjoy that are made from grains. Be sure in the future to point out to them a grain item you serve for a snack. Send home a note asking the children to bring canned goods for the community food bank.

Lesson 54

The Grocery

Goal:

To help the children understand that items from the farm are taken by truck to the grocery store and that is where their parents buy food to eat.

Objectives: By the end of this session the children will:

Play grocery store.

Place items in grocery carts.

Sort food items.

Decorate boxes for food for the food bank.

Faith Connections

Bible verse: God, our God, has blessed us. (Psalm 67:6)

Food is a blessing from God. Help the children understand that God plans for everyone to have food to eat. Young children have probably had experiences with a grocery store. Help them understand there are many people in the community who help get the food to the grocery store. Children also need to know that there are people who do not have much money to buy food and that God wants us to help those who have no food.

Teacher's Prayer

Dear God, thank you that our food is so plentiful. It is amazing to walk into the grocery store and see all the choices we have. Help me to remember to share this bounty with others. Amen.

NOTE: Be aware of children with food allergies. Modify your activities for these children.

Teacher Talk:

God planned for everyone to have good food to eat.

Many people help get the food to the grocery store.

We can share food with those who do not have enough money to buy food.

Center Time

Set up a pretend grocery store for center time. Use play foods or ask parents to save clean empty food boxes.

As children arrive, ask them to put their canned goods on the table.

Worship Center

Teacher Talk

We can share food with people who do not have enough money to buy food.

Resources

donated items, cardboard boxes, wrapping paper, glue, scissors, pictures of food

Let the children organize the donated items by different categories. They may choose to put all fruits together and all vegetables together. Or they may choose to put the food in groups by the color of the labels or in order by size. Halfway through center time ask the children at the center to help you wrap the food boxes. They can measure the paper, cut it, and glue it to the outside of the box. You may wish for them to glue pictures of food on the outside of the boxes.

Say: God plans for everyone to have food to eat. We can share food with people who do not have enough money to buy food.

Pray: Thank you, God, for all the people who help us have good food to eat. Help us remember to share food with others. Amen.

Home Living Center

Teacher Talk

We can buy many different kinds of food at the grocery store.

Resources

magazine pictures of food, grocery cart pattern (*see page 223*), glue, scissors, construction paper

Photocopy the grocery cart (*see page 223*) for each child. Cut out the cart for younger children. Let older children cut out the cart themselves. Show the children how to glue the cart onto a piece of construction paper, leaving the top of the cart unglued. Let the children cut or tear food pictures out of magazines and put them in their carts.

Building Center

Teacher Talk

Farmers grow the grain that is made into breads and cereals we find at the store.

Resources

food product packages, cereal boxes, canned goods, drink bottles, empty milk containers, empty ice cream containers, play money, toy trucks, grocery bags, child-size grocery carts

Turn the building center into a pretend grocery store. If you do not have child-sized shopping carts, give the children grocery bags in which to put their purchases. Have toy trucks for the children to pretend to be the truck drivers that deliver the food to the grocery store. Let the children take turns so that some of them run the store and take money, while others drive the trucks or buy groceries.

Writing Center

Teacher Talk

Many people help get the food to the grocery store so that we can buy good food to eat.

Resources

paper; pencils; nonpermanent ink pads; rubber stamps of foods, or foam trays and wood blocks; or food advertisements and glue; scissors (teacher use only)

Cut paper in half lengthwise to make shopping lists. **Say:** "Let's pretend we need to go to the grocery store. Before we go, we will make a shopping list. What do you need to put on your list?" Have the children pretend to write their lists. Have rubber stamps of different foods and let the children stamp pictures on their papers. Or cut simple food shapes out of foam trays. Glue the shapes onto small wood blocks. Let the children use the shapes like rubber stamps. Or cut food advertisements from the newspaper. Let the children glue the ads onto their lists.

Wonder Time

Encourage the children to clean up their centers and come to the circle. Ask them what groceries they bought today.

Wonder Question: I wonder what foods we can buy at the grocery store?

Let the children name different foods. Talk with them about the groceries that their parents buy. See if they can tell you where the fruits and vegetables come from.

Sing: "I'm Thankful," verse 7 (*see page 215*).

Repeat the action rhyme from yesterday with the children (*see page 171*).

Read the Bible verse.

Say: Food is a blessing from God. God plans for everyone to have good food to eat.

Pray: Thank you, God, for good food to eat. Amen.

Talk with the children about those who do not have enough food to eat. Tell how the community helps them. Thank them for bringing food for others to eat. Show them the food boxes they have made and tell them where you will be taking them.

Open the Bible to Psalm 67:6.

Say: "God, our God, has blessed us" (Psalm 67:6).

Have the children repeat the Bible verse.

Group Fun

Resources

small empty food boxes, berry baskets, egg cartons, foam trays, construction paper, tempera paint, shallow trays, brushes, table covering, smocks

Cover the table and have the children wear paint smocks. Pour tempera paint into shallow trays. Give each child a piece of construction paper. Let the children make prints with items they would find at a grocery store. Show the children how to dip things such as small empty food boxes or berry baskets into the paint and then press them onto their papers. Let the children brush paint onto the bottoms of foam trays or egg cartons. Then show the children how to press paper on top of the painted bottoms to make prints. Set the papers aside to dry.

Goodbye Circle

Help the children review the lessons for this week. Talk about the whole process of food being grown by the farmer, taken to market, and being bought and prepared by their parents.

Pray: Thank you, God, for good food to eat. Amen.

Evaluation

What has worked well in this lesson? What activities could work better under different circumstances? Begin your plans for the next week's lessons.

Lesson 55

Restaurants

Teacher Talk:

God planned for everyone to have good food to eat.

Many people help us have food to eat when we go to restaurants.

Goals:

To help the children understand that restaurants are another place we can go to for food.

To help the children discover that many people get food at restaurants.

Objectives: By the end of this session the children will:

Play restaurant.

Eat green eggs and ham.

Make fast-food puppets.

Faith Connections

Bible verse: O taste and see that the LORD is good.

(Psalm 34:8)

Eating out is a way of life for many people. Even young children have many experiences in eating out, especially at fast-food restaurants. Help your children see that we can appreciate and be thankful for all the people who work so that we may eat good food. These include people who work on farms, as truck drivers, at dairies and bakeries, at grocery stores, and at restaurants.

Teacher's Prayer

Dear God, thank you for the many ways we are able to get food. Help us appreciate all the people who work so that we may eat the food you provide. Amen.

NOTE: Be aware of children with food allergies. Modify your activities for these children.

Center Time

Have the book, *Green Eggs and Ham*, by Dr. Seuss, in the book center today.

As children arrive, ask them if they have ever had green eggs and ham.

Art Center

Teacher Talk

We can remember to eat healthy foods.

Resources

fast-food restaurant sandwich boxes; tempera paint; paintbrushes; plastic paint containers; construction paper circles, circle stickers, or large wiggly eyes; glue; table covering; smocks; scissors (teacher use only)

Let the children make fast-food puppets. Ask fast-food restaurants to donate clean sandwich containers. Carefully cut a hole in the back of each lid and a second hole near the back of the bottom. Cover the table and have the children wear smocks. Give each child a container. Let the children paint the containers with tempera paint. After the paint dries, let the children add faces to their puppets. The children might glue on construction paper circles, stick on circle stickers, or glue on large wiggly eyes. Show the children how to put their index fingers through the holes at the top and their thumbs through the holes at the bottom. When the children move their fingers and thumbs up and down, the puppets will talk.

Talk with the children about fast-food restaurants. Have the children tell you what their favorite restaurant is. Tell the children that it is fun to eat at fast-food restaurants, but we need to eat healthy foods most of the time.

Home Living Center

Teacher Talk

We can say thank you to the people who help us at restaurants.

Resources

pretend food, aprons, menus, trays, pretend money

Let the children act out eating at a restaurant. One child may be the host or hostess. Another child can clean the table, and another one can take the money for the meal. Have an apron for the waiter or waitress to wear.

Encourage the children to take their turn ordering from the menu. Stress the importance of saying *please* and *thank you* as the children order.

Writing Center

Teacher Talk

Many people help when we eat at restaurants.

Resources

paper; green crayons; large construction paper, wallpaper or construction paper scraps, glue, marker

Write the word *Menu* at the top of a plain piece of paper. Photocopy the paper for each child. Give each child the page with the word *Menu* written on it. Let the children color the menu page with green crayons. Give each child a large piece of construction paper. Let the children decorate one side of the construction paper by gluing on wallpaper or construction paper scraps. Show the children how to fold the paper in half like a menu cover. Let the children glue the menu pages into the covers.

Say: Green eggs and ham is the special on today's menu.

Worship Center

Teacher Talk

Many people help us when we eat at restaurants.

Resources

mural paper, glue, restaurant advertisements

Cut restaurant advertisements from newspapers. Let the children make a montage of advertisements on mural paper.

Say: Many people help us when we eat at restaurants.

Pray: Thank you, God, for all the people who help us have food to eat. Amen.

Open the Bible to Psalm 34:8.

Say: "O taste and see that the LORD is good" (Psalm 34:8).

Have the children repeat the Bible verse.

Wonder Time

Encourage the children to clean up their centers and come to the circle.

Wonder Question: I wonder how we get foods at restaurants?

Say: Many people help us get the food we eat at restaurants. Can you think of who grows the food we eat at restaurants? (*farmers*) Who brings the food to the restaurants? (*truck drivers*) Who serves us the food at restaurants? (*waiters and waitresses*) Who cooks the food at restaurants? (*the cook, the chef*) Who cleans the tables and dishes at restaurants? (*bus boy, dishwasher, janitor*) I'm thankful for the many people who help us have food to eat.

Sing: "I'm Thankful," verse 7 (*see page 215*)

Read the Bible verse.

Say: We can thank God for all the good food we have to eat.

Pray: Thank you, God, for good food to eat. Amen.

Group Fun

Resources

eggs, sliced honey ham, spatulas, electric skillets, forks, napkins, plates, cups, milk, large measuring cups, spoons, green food coloring, spray cooking oil

Divide the class into groups, as many as you have adults to help. For each group you will need eggs, sliced ham, a spatula, and an electric skillet. You will also need forks, plates, napkins, and cups of milk for each child. Let the children break the eggs into large measuring cups. Help them remove any shells with spoons. Let them put several drops of green food coloring into the eggs and stir the eggs. Tell the children the skillet is hot. Have the children stand back from the skillet. Spray cooking oil in the electric skillet and cook the eggs. Cook the ham after you have emptied the pan of eggs. Give each child a serving of green eggs and ham. Sit down with them and enjoy! Thank God for good food to eat—even green eggs and ham.

Goodbye Circle

Help the children review the lessons for this week. Talk about the whole process of food being grown by the farmer, taken to market, and being bought and prepared by their parents or people at restaurants.

Pray: Thank you, God, for good food to eat. Amen.

Evaluation

What has worked well in this lesson? What activities could work better under different circumstances? Begin your plans for next week's lessons.

I'm Thankful

Goal:

1. The children will think of the wonderful gifts God has given us.
2. The children will give thanks for their families, for the animals in God's world, for day and night, and for the seasons.
3. The children will have opportunities to say thank-you prayers.
4. The children will discover that God is dependable and that God is always with us.

Children need to learn and say simple prayers, especially thank-you prayers. They need to experience awe and wonder at God's world. These lessons on "I'm Thankful" will offer children opportunities to experience feelings of thanksgiving.

This unit thanks God for day and night and for the seasons. The cycle of the seasons can be a hard concept for young children to understand. They have not lived long enough to realize that the seasons return year after year. They view time in segments, rather than as an orderly progression of events. Teach your children that there is beauty in all of God's seasons. Help them discover that through day and night and all the seasons that God is dependable and that God is always with us.

Bible Stories for this Unit:
Genesis 1
Genesis 8:20-22
Ecclesiastes 3:1-11

I'M THANKFUL

This week we will be helping the children think about the wonderful gifts God has given us. Our families, the animals, night and day, and the seasons are just a few of those gifts. If there are particular blessings you would like the children to remember, add them to the lessons this week or substitute your lessons for those printed here.

This is a good time to help the children learn to feel comfortable talking to God. Prayers of thanks can be a word or a song. Even silent motions can become prayers.

Lesson 56

My Family

Teacher Talk:

God plans for families to love and care for us.

The people in our families do many things.

We thank God for our families.

Goal:

For children to think about the things that family members do and to be thankful for them.

Objectives: By the end of this session the children will:

Cut and paste pictures of family members.

Make papier-mâché horns of plenty for their families.

Thank God for their families.

Faith Connections

Bible verse: O give thanks to the LORD. (Psalm 105:1)

Most children know they love their family members, but many children have little idea what family members do all day. Encourage children to talk with their parents to find out what they do. Help them give thanks for the things they do not even know about.

Teacher's Prayer

For every family in my class I give thanks to you, O God. Amen.

Center Time

Have a picture of a cornucopia displayed in your classroom today.

As children arrive, thank their parents for bringing them to school.

Writing Center

Teacher Talk

We can say thank you to our families.

Resources

thank-you notes, envelopes, pencils, colored pencils

Purchase thank-you notes that have "thank you" written on the front and are blank inside. Tell the children that they can send a thank-you note to their parents. Help the children think of things to put in their notes. They may want to say thank you for my breakfast, thank you for reading to me, and so forth. Let the children draw pictures or tell a teacher what to write. Let the children put their cards in envelopes. Write the children's names on the envelopes, and have them take the envelopes home to their parents. Continue this activity throughout this week, letting the children write thank-you cards to friends and relatives.

Cooking Center

Teacher Talk

We thank God for our families.

Resources

cornucopia pattern (*see page 223*), Bugles snack chips, soft cream cheese, raisins or small fruit-shaped candy, resealable plastic bags

Show the children a picture of a cornucopia, or horn of plenty *(see page 223)*. **Say:** "Some families use cornucopias as decorations at Thanksgiving time to remember all the things for which they are thankful. We are thankful for our families. Let's make Thanksgiving treats for our families that look like cornucopias."

Give each child a Bugles snack chip. Show the children how to scoop cream cheese into the chips. Let the children place raisins or small fruit-shaped candy in the cream cheese. Let each child make several for their families. Place the finished cornucopias in plastic bags to take home. Of course the children will want to eat some of them right now.

Home Living Center

Teacher Talk

The people in our families do many things.

Resources

dress-up clothes, briefcases, adult-size shoes, play car or tricycle

Let the children pretend to be a family. If you have a play car or a tricycle, park it in front of the home living center. Let the children use the car or tricycle to pretend to go to work or school.

Ask the children to name something that their mothers or fathers do well. Be sure to discuss stereotypes, as children often like to put their fathers at work and their mothers in the kitchen. Help them think about all the places their parents work.

Worship Center

Teacher Talk

We thank God for our families.

Resources

magazines, scissors, mural paper, glue, cornucopia pattern (*see page 223*), marker

Photocopy and cut out the cornucopia *(see page 223)*. Glue the cutout on mural paper. Write, "Thank You, God, for Families" across the mural. Precut pictures of people, or let the children cut pictures of people out of magazines. Have pictures of different ages and ethnic groups available. Let the children choose pictures that represent their families and glue them onto the mural to fill the cornucopia.

Say: God planned for us to have families that love and care for us.

Pray: Thank you, God, for our families. Amen.

Open the Bible to Psalm 105:1.

Say: "O give thanks to the LORD" (Psalm 105:1).

Have the children repeat the Bible verse.

Wonder Time

Call the children to wonder time.

Wonder Question: *I wonder what the people in our family do to work and play?*
Let the children tell you about their families.
Say: *God plans for families to love and care for us. We thank God for our families.*
Read the Bible verse.
Sing: *"Clap, Clap" (see page 211).*
Pray: *Thank You, God, for our families. Amen.*

Group Fun

Resources

picture of a cornucopia *(see page 223)*, 9-ounce unwaxed paper cups, strips of newspaper, liquid starch, brushes, plastic containers, table covering, smocks, hand-washing supplies

Show the children a picture of a cornucopia, or horn of plenty (*see page 223*). **Say:** "Some families use cornucopias, or horns of plenty, as decorations at Thanksgiving time to remember all the things for which they are thankful. We are thankful for our families. Let's make cornucopias for our families."

Cover the table and have the children wear smocks. Pour liquid starch into plastic containers. Tear newspapers into 2-inch strips. Give each child a large unwaxed paper cup. Instruct the children to smash the ends of large paper cups until they are flat and pointed. Have them put their fists into the opening of the cups to make them round and open.

Have the children paint liquid starch on the cups and then wrap strips of newspaper all over the cups in different directions. The paper will stick to the cups because of the liquid starch. After the cups are covered in newspaper strips, have the children paint all over the cups with the liquid starch and smooth out the rough places with their hands. While the cups are wet, they can squeeze the cups and shape them. Have the children wash their hands.

The papier-mâché will take about two days to dry. Let the children paint the cornucopias. Show them how to put fruits and vegetables in the cornucopias to make decorations.

Goodbye Circle

Have the children name people in their families for whom they are thankful.

Pray: *Thank you, God, for all our families. Amen.*

Evaluation

Did the children have enough time to complete their activities? Did everyone participate in together time? Think of ways to encourage quieter children to become involved verbally.

Lesson 57

Animals

Teacher Talk:

God made all the animals.

Everything God created is good.

We thank God for animals.

Goal:

For children to remember the animals they have studied and to discover other animals and give thanks for them.

Objectives: By the end of this session the children will:

Make animal masks.

Paint with feathers.

Play a fishing game.

Draw animal habitats.

Faith Connections

Bible verse: For everything created by God is good.

(1 Timothy 4:4)

Children need opportunities to learn about animals of the world. They need to know that God planned for all creatures. You can help them by showing pictures and videos of animals that are not familiar in your area.

Teacher's Prayer

There are so many creatures of the earth, O God. Help me to know them and to find ways to care for them. Amen.

Center Time

As children arrive, put a sticker of an animal on the child's hand or clothing. Say: "We thank God for animals."

Have pictures of animals displayed in your center area.

Writing Center

Teacher Talk

We thank God for animals.

Resources

rubber stamps of different animals, nonpermanent ink pads, paper, markers, pictures of animals and their habitats

Give the children plain paper and let them experiment with the rubber stamps. When they have learned the technique, tell them to print as many animals as they wish. Show the children pictures of animals and their habitats. Encourage the children to use markers to add to their pictures. They can draw the places where the animals live or food for the animals.

Building Center

Teacher Talk

God made all the animals.

Resources

blocks, plastic wild animals

Encourage the children to build a zoo. They can make cages for the animals or build pastures in which the animals can roam. Talk about the different animals we can see in the zoo. Remind the children that God made all kinds of animals.

Math Center

Teacher Talk

God made all kinds of animals. God made animals that live in water like fish.

Resources

dowel or paper towel tube, string, magnet, paper clips, fish shapes

Play a fishing game. Make a fishing pole by tying about three feet of string around a dowel or paper towel tube. Tie a magnet onto the end of the string. Cut fish shapes out of construction paper. Place a paper clip onto the nose of each fish. Show the children how to use the magnet fishing pole to catch the fish. Have each child count how many fish he or she catches. Ask the children to name other animals that live in water (crabs, sea horses, whales, and so forth).

Art Center

Teacher Talk

God made all the animals. God made animals that fly.

Resources

construction paper, feathers, tempera paint, shallow trays, table covering, smocks

Cover the table and have the children wear smocks. Pour tempera paint into shallow trays. Show the children the feathers. Ask the children to name animals that have feathers (ducks, chickens, birds, turkeys, and so forth). Show the children how to use the feathers like brushes to paint on their papers. Have the children name other animals that fly (butterflies, bumblebees, ladybugs, fireflies, and so forth).

Worship Center

Teacher Talk

We thank God for all the animals.

Resources

play dough

Encourage the children to make all kinds of animals using the play dough. Snakes are especially popular play dough creations. Talk with the children about all kinds of animals. Remind the children that all the animals God made are good—even snakes!

Pray: Thank you, God, for all the animals you have made. Amen.

Wonder Time

Call the children to wonder time one at a time. Ask each child to move like an animal. Say things like, "*(Child's name)*, hop like a rabbit to wonder time," or "*(Child's name)*, slither like a snake to wonder time."

Wonder Question: I wonder how many animals God made?
Say: God made all the animals. Let's name as many animals as we can.
Let the children name as many animals as they remember.
Play a motion game. Let each child act out an animal with motions and sound. Let the others guess what animal she or he is pretending to be.
Read the Bible verse.
Say: All the animals God created are good. We thank God for animals.
Sing: "Clap, Clap" (*see page 211*).
Pray: Thank you, God, for all the animals of the earth. Amen.

Open the Bible to 1 Timothy 4:4.

Say: "For everything created by God is good" (1 Timothy 4:4).

Have the children repeat the Bible verse.

Group Fun

Resources

pictures of animals, heavy colored paper plates, paper punch, yarn, markers, construction paper, glue, feathers, fabric and collage scraps, tissue paper, curved fingernail scissors

Let the children make animal masks. Before class, cut enough paper plates in half so that each child can have one half. Use curved fingernail scissors to cut eyes in each mask. Punch a hole just above the straight cut on both sides. You may wish to knot a piece of yarn in each side so the child can tie the mask on. Another option is to buy elastic and tie one piece to each mask to hold it on.

Encourage the children to look at the pictures of the animals and choose which animals they want for their masks. Some children will think of their own animals, and that is fine.

Let the children glue scraps, yarn, feathers, and construction paper or art tissue on their masks to create their animals. Write the children's names on the backs of their masks. Have the children tell you the names of their animals. Ask them where the animals live. Do they swim in the water? Do they fly in the air? Do they live in trees? Encourage the children to wear their masks and to make the sounds of their animals.

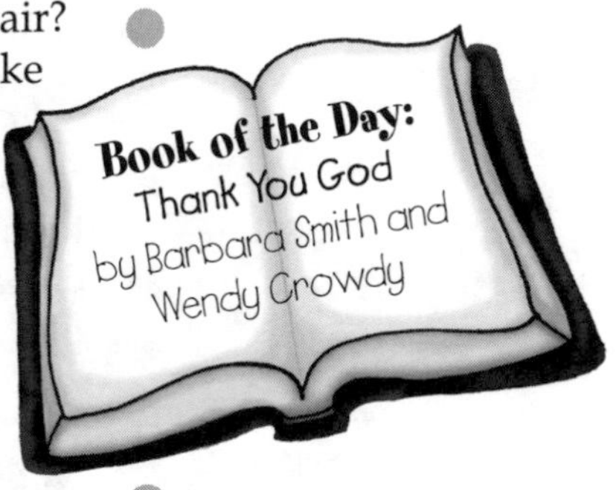

Goodbye Circle

Remind the children that God planned for all the animals of the earth.

Pray: Thank you, God, for all the animals of the earth. Amen.

Evaluation

Was anyone scared today? If so, be sure to show the child who is behind each mask.

Lesson 58

The Day

Teacher Talk:

God plans for day and night.

The sun shines during the day.

We thank God for the day.

Goals:

To help the children think about the joys of the day.

To give the children opportunities to express their thanks for the day.

Objectives:

By the end of this lesson the children will:

Make suns.

Discover why we do not see the moon and stars during the day.

Say prayers of thanks for the day.

Talk about the things we do during the day.

Faith Connections

Bible verse: God called the light Day. (Genesis 1:5)

Children need to know God as Creator. God planned the sun and moon and stars that we see in the sky each day and night. Knowing this helps the children to think of God when they see God's creation. Talk with the children about the day and about God's plan for us to enjoy the day, to make new discoveries, to play and have fun, and to care for others.

Teacher's Prayer

Thank you, God, for each new day. Open my eyes so that I may see the beauty that surrounds me. Amen.

Center Time

As children arrive, say: "I'm glad you're here on this sunny (or rainy or windy) day!

Have a globe and a flashlight. Let the children shine the flashlight onto the globe as if it were light from the sun.

Art Center

Teacher Talk

God made the sun that shines during the day. We thank God for the day.

Resources

paper bowls, gold or yellow tempera paint, gold or yellow construction paper, brushes, tape or glue, scissors (teacher use only), yarn, paper punch, table covering, smocks, marker

Cover the table and have the children wear smocks. Cut gold or yellow construction paper into two-inch strips. Provide gold or yellow tempera paint and brushes. Give each child two paper bowls. Put the child's name on the inside of each bowl. Have the children turn the bowls upside down and paint the bottoms of both bowls.

Give each child several construction paper strips. Show the children how to curl sunbeams by holding the strips by each end and pulling the strips across the straight edge of a table several times.

When the bowls are dry, have the children glue or tape the strips to the edges of one of their bowls. Help each child glue the edges of their two bowls together. Use a paper punch to make a hole in the top of the bowls. Tie yarn through the hole to make a hanger. Hang the suns to shine in your room.

Home Living Center

Teacher Talk

We thank God for each new day.

Resources

alarm clock, cereal boxes, lunch boxes, large pajamas, large nightgowns, sheets

Tell the children that we are pretending it is morning in the house and time to get up. Help them think of all the things they need to do to get ready for school and to start the new day.

Science Center

Teacher Talk

God made the sun that shines during the day. We thank God for the day.

Resources

sun-sensitive paper or dark-colored construction paper, miscellaneous objects

Let the children experiment with sun prints. Purchase sun-sensitive paper available from craft stores and follow the directions for making sun prints. Or give each child a piece of dark-colored construction paper. Have the children place the paper in direct sunlight. Let the children arrange objects on their papers. These might be crayons, blocks, leaves, and so forth. Leave the papers for several hours. Then have the children remove the items from their papers to see the sun prints.

Worship Center

Teacher Talk

God made the sun that shines during the day. We thank God for the day.

Resources

blankets, flashlight, table

Cover the table with a blanket. Bring a flashlight and have the children sit with you under the table. Lift the sides of the blanket so that it is light under the table. Turn on the flashlight.

Ask: "Can you see the flashlight very well?"

Pull down the blankets to make it dark under the table. Turn on the flashlight again.

Ask: "What happens to the light from the flashlight when it is dark? Is the light easier to see?"

Say: God made the sun that shines during the day. When the sun is shining brightly we cannot see the light from the moon and stars. When it is night, and the sun is not shining, we can see the light from the moon and stars.

Pray: Thank you, God, for the sun that shines on our days. Amen.

Open the Bible to Genesis 1:5.

Say: "God called the light Day" (Genesis 1:5).

Have the children repeat the Bible verse.

Wonder Time

Call the children to wonder time. Have a flash-light ready to use.

> The Sun and the Moon
> by Bette Saunders
>
> God planned the sun
> to make the day,
> *(Hold your arms in a circle above your head.)*
> And we go out to
> work and play.
> *(March in place.)*
> Then when the sun
> goes out of sight,
> *(Bring arms behind back.)*
> God planned the moon
> to make the night.
> *(Hold your arms in a circle above your head.)*
>
>

Wonder Question: I wonder why we don't see the moon and stars when it is day?

Say: God planned for the sun to light the day. When the sun is shining brightly, we cannot see the light from moon and stars. When it is night, and the sun is not shining, we can see the light from the moon and stars.

Say the action poem, "The Sun and the Moon" (*see box*).

Sing: "Clap, Clap" (*see page 211*).

Read the Bible verse.

Talk with the children about God's plan for day and night.

Say: God plans the day with light for us to see and the night with dark for us to rest.

Let the children tell you what they like to do when it is light and a new day.

Pray: Thank you, God, for each new day. Thank you for time to (*include things the children mentioned*). Amen.

Group Fun

Resources

construction paper, yellow tempera paint, plastic containers, cotton swabs, spoons, table covering, smocks

Let the children make sun pictures. Cover the table and have the children wear smocks. Give each child a piece of construction paper. Spoon a glob of yellow paint in the center of the paper. Show the children how to use cotton swabs to move the paint out from the center and make the sun's rays.

Say: God made the sun that shines during the day. What are some things we do during the day? *(wake up, eat breakfast and lunch, come to school, play)*

Goodbye Circle

Tell the children that the day is half over and there is still sunlight left for them. Ask them what they are going to do with the rest of their day.

Pray: Thank you, God, for the sun that shines on our busy days. Amen.

Evaluation

Today was a new day in your classroom. What went well? What would you change?

Lesson 59

The Night

Goals:

To help the children understand God's plan for the night.

To help the children find joy in the night.

Objectives: By the end of this session the children will:

Create fuzzy yarn moons.

Talk about happy things in the night.

Make crayon wash pictures.

Count stars.

Faith Connections

Bible verse: The darkness God called Night.

(Genesis 1:5, adapted)

Children need to know that they are surrounded by love at night. The love of their parents and the safety of their homes give them a small idea of the love of God. Nighttime is often a scary time for preschoolers. The monsters they imagine are real to them. Help them to see that there is always night and there is always day and while they are sleeping they are still loved.

Teacher's Prayer

Help me to find joy in the night. Help me to consider the heavens and know that you are there. Amen.

Teacher Talk:

God plans for day and night.

The moon and stars shine during the night.

We thank God for the night.

Center Time

Display pictures of the moon and stars. Hang glow-in-the dark stars or stars cut from aluminum foil from the ceiling.

Writing Center

Teacher Talk

We thank God for the night.

Resources

white construction paper, white crayons, thin black tempera paint, brushes, plastic containers, table covering, smocks

Cover the table and have the children wear smocks. Thin black tempera paint with water to make a wash. Pour the wash into plastic containers.

Give each child a piece of white construction paper and a white crayon. Show the children how to make heavy marks on their papers with the crayons. Let the children make stars, circles, or scribble marks to represent stars on their papers. Show the children how to brush the tempera wash completely over their papers. Their stars will shine through the wash.

Art Center

Teacher Talk

We thank God for each new day.

Resources

white yarn or pompons, glue, paper or plastic bowls, markers, scissors (teacher use only)

Let each child make a fuzzy moon. Show the children how to cut yarn into short pieces (about ¼-inches long). For younger children plan to cut the yarn before class. Or provide small white pompons.

Give each child a paper or plastic bowl. Show the children how to turn the bowls upside down on their papers and then draw around them to make moon shapes. Have the children fill the inside of their moons by gluing on yarn fuzzies or pompons. Show the children how to work inside the moon circles a little at a time.

Math Center

Teacher Talk

God plans for the stars to shine at night.

Resources

star stickers or glow-in-the-dark star stickers, black construction paper, marker

Let the children count the stars in the night sky. Give each child a piece of black construction paper. Have the children put star stickers all over the pages. When they have finished, help them count the stars. Write the number of stars on the back of each child's picture.

Home Living Center

Teacher Talk

God plans for the night as a time for us to sleep and rest.

Resources

night clothes, books, dolls

Tell the children it is nighttime. Have them pretend that it is time for bed. Instruct them to put the babies to bed and read them a story.

Worship Center

Teacher Talk

We thank God for night.

Resources

flashlight, blanket, aluminum foil, pin, table

Cover a flashlight with aluminum foil. Use a pin to poke holes in the foil. Cover a table with a blanket. Bring the flashlight and invite the children to join you under the table. Turn on the flashlight and enjoy looking at the starry sky. Let the children take turns with the flashlight.

Say: God plans for it to be dark at night. God is with us during the day when it is light, and God is with us during the night when it is dark. God is always with us.

Pray: Thank you, God, for the night. Amen.

Wonder Time

Call the children together and talk about the fun they had in the dark. Let them show what they made in the different centers.

Wonder Question: I wonder what happens while we are sleeping at night?

Say: God plans for people and animals to have a time of sleep and rest. Many people and animals sleep at night. But some people, like doctors and nurses, work at night. Some animals, like owls, sleep during the day and stay awake at night. God is with the people who sleep at night and the people who work at night. God is always with us.

Say the action poem, "The Sun and the Moon" (*see page 188*).

Sing: "Clap, Clap" (*see page 211*).

Read the Bible verse.

Talk with the children about God's plan for day and night.

Say: God plans the day with light for us to see and the night with dark for us to rest.

Ask: What do you think is beautiful about the night?

Say: When we see the stars and the moon, we can remember God is with us. When we see moonlight shining on the trees and through the window, we can remember that God is with us.

Pray: Thank you, God, for the night, when we can sleep and when we can watch the moon and stars. Amen.

Open the Bible to Genesis 1:5.

Say: "The darkness God called Night" (Genesis 1:5, adapted).

Have the children repeat the Bible verse.

Group Fun

Resources

dessert-size paper plates, yarn, feathers, beads, glue, paper punch, scissors

Tell the children that Native Americans make dream catchers to hang where they are sleeping.

Cut yarn into 18-inch lengths. Give each child a small dessert-size paper plate. Let the children glue yarn in the middle of their paper plates. Use a paper punch to make holes around the edges of the paper plates. Show the children how to thread yarn lengths through the holes. Tie one length of yarn into a loop to make a hanger for the dream catcher. The children may string beads or feathers onto the yarn ends.

Goodbye Circle

Remind the children that God is with us when we are awake and when we are sleeping.

Pray: Thank you, God, for the night. Amen.

Evaluation

Did you hear any fears of the dark expressed? Think of ways you can help the children find joy in the night.

Lesson 60

The Four Seasons

Teacher Talk:

God plans for the seasons.

The winter season follows the fall season.

We thank God for the seasons.

Goals:

To help the children know there are four seasons.

To help the children learn the differences in the seasons.

Objectives: By the end of this session the children will:

Make sand pictures.

Match the seasons with clothing.

Pretend to be squirrels and find nuts.

Thank God for the seasons.

Faith Connections

Bible verse: God changes the times and the seasons.

(Daniel 2:21, adapted)

Children need to feel there is consistency in the world. It has to make sense to them. Help them see that when God created the world, the changing cycles of the year were part of God's plan. Encourage the children to see that each season brings its special joys and beauty.

Teacher's Prayer

You are always there, O Lord. Summer, winter, spring, and fall, I see you in the changes of the earth. Pull me toward your love so that as I see the changing seasons, I see you. In Jesus' name, Amen.

Center Time

Display pictures that show the four seasons.

> **As children arrive,** say: "We are in the season called fall."

Science Center

Teacher Talk
We thank God for summer.

Resources
dishpan, colored or plain sand, umbrella, glue, construction paper, shallow trays or box lids, beach towel, sign reading "SUMMER"

Place a sign in the center that reads, "SUMMER." Encourage the children to pretend it is summer.

Give each child a piece of paper. Let the children make designs on their papers with the glue. Place each paper into a shallow tray or box lid. Show the children how to sprinkle sand over the glue. Shake the excess sand off into the tray or lid. Pour the excess sand into a trash container. Set the pictures aside to dry.

Tell the children to pretend they are at the beach. Place a beach towel on the floor, with an umbrella at the top of the towel, for an area where the children can rest after or before their work. Add a beach chair and a dishpan partially filled with sand. Have the children take off their shoes and socks and take turns sitting on the chair with their feet in the dishpan.

Art Center

Teacher Talk
We thank God for spring.

Resources
sign reading "SPRING," construction paper, wall paper, scissors, paper towels, shallow trays, tempera paint, glue, bucket or water, towels, table covering, smocks

Place a sign in this center that reads, "SPRING." Before class cut out vase shapes from construction paper or wallpaper. Cover the table and have the children wear smocks. Fold paper towels and place them in shallow trays. Pour tempera paint onto the paper towels to make paint pads.

Give each child a piece of construction paper and a paper vase. Have the children glue their vases at the bottom of their papers. Show the children how to press their hands on paint pads and then onto their papers to make handprints coming out of the vases. Their handprints are spring flowers. Have several colors of paint available for the children to make different colored handprints that become different colored flowers. Children can dip their hands in the water to rinse off and begin a new color.

Building Center

Teacher Talk
We thank God for fall.

Resources
blocks, nuts, old newspapers, sign reading "FALL"

Place a sign in the center that reads, "FALL." Before class, stand the blocks up like trees. Hide nuts in, around, and under the blocks. Tell the children to pretend that they are squirrels in a forest. First they must make nests. Show the children how to tear old newspapers into strips and pile into nests. Then let the children find some nuts and take them to their nests. Each child may share a nest with one other "squirrel."

Worship Center

Teacher Talk
We thank God for winter.

Resources
heavy jackets, boots, gloves, scarves, sign reading "WINTER"

Place a sign in the center that reads, "WINTER." Tell the children to pretend it is winter in a place where the weather gets cold. Let the children try on the winter clothes.

Say: God planned all four seasons: fall, winter, spring, and summer.

Pray: Thank you, God, for the seasons. Amen.

Open the Bible to Daniel 2:21.

Say: "God changes the times and the seasons" (Daniel 2:21, adapted).

Have the children repeat the Bible verse.

Wonder Time

Tell the children that you are the cold winter wind. Go around the room and blow the children to wonder time.

Wonder Question: We are in the season called fall. I wonder what season comes next?
Say: God plans for each season. Winter always comes after fall. We are now in the fall season, and we are getting ready for winter to come.
Name all four seasons.
Ask: What do we do in winter? In spring? In summer? In fall?
Read the Bible verse.
Say: God plans for all four seasons. We know when each season is coming, and each season comes each year. We can thank God for the seasons.
Sing: "Clap, Clap" (*see page 211*).
Pray: Thank you, God, for winter, spring, summer, and fall. Amen.

Group Fun

Resources
none

Have the children move to an open area of the room.

Say: God made the seasons. God made summer. Let's make the summer sun. (*Make a circle above your head.*) God made fall. Let's make leaves blowing in the wind. (*Sweep arms around body.*) God made winter. In some places the air turns cold in winter. (*Hug yourself as if you are cold.*) God made spring. Let's make spring rain. (*Hold your hands above your head and wiggle your fingers as you lower them to waist level.*) Listen as I say the name of one of the seasons. When I say the name, quickly make the motion that goes with the season.

Say the name of each season and have the children do the corresponding motion. Mix up the order of how you name the seasons. Say the names faster and faster.

Goodbye Circle

Tell the children you are glad they know about God's plan for seasons. Let the children listen to a tape of Easter songs, and laugh with them because it is not time for Easter!

Pray: Thank you, God, for winter, spring, summer, and fall. Amen.

Evaluation

Was today too confusing? How would you plan it differently?

Seasonal Holidays

Goals:

1. The children will celebrate the holidays that happen during the fall season.
2. The children will discover the beauty in God's plan for the fall season and will celebrate harvest time.
3. The children will have the opportunity to celebrate Halloween safely and without fear.
4. The children will be introduced to the biblical celebration of Thanksgiving.
5. The children will celebrate Thanksgiving with their class friends.

Children enjoy holidays. The lessons for this seasonal unit are designed to give the children opportunities to celebrate the holidays that happen during the fall season. These lessons are not meant to be used consecutively. Each lesson can be used at the appropriate time in your school's calendar. Simply use one of these lessons instead of one of the regular lessons. Or choose activities from these lessons and add them to the regular lessons.

Some Christian preschools do not celebrate Halloween. Others celebrate the holiday but de-emphasize the scary parts of Halloween. A lesson on Halloween is included in this unit so that you can help your children celebrate this holiday safely. If you choose not to deal with Halloween, you may still want to look at the lesson and choose the activities that deal with the celebration of the harvest.

Bible Stories for this Unit:
Genesis 8:20-22
Ecclesiastes 3:1-11
Leviticus 23:33-36, 39-43

Seasonal Lesson 61

The Fall Season

Teacher Talk:

God plans for the seasons.

It is now the season called fall.

In the fall we harvest fruits and vegetables.

We thank God for the fall season.

Goal:

To help children understand that fall is a time of preparation for winter and a celebration of the harvest.

Objectives: By the end of this session the children will:

Make applesauce.

Make leaf prints.

Discover some of the fruits and vegetables that are harvested in the fall.

Thank God for the fall season.

Faith Connections

Bible verse: For everything there is a season.

(Ecclesiastes 3:1)

How comforting it is for children to know that everything has a purpose, a time, and a season. Preschoolers think that way anyway. There is a time for bed and a time for lunch and a plan for all that happens. Help them see that our earth moves as God planned it. The days get cooler, the seeds that were planted in the spring have grown, and their fruits and vegetables are ready to be picked. God created a wonderful world!

Teacher's Prayer

I need consistency too, O Lord. Sometimes I can't see a plan. Sometimes I want the time to be now. Give me patience and a heart to see life through your eyes in your time. Amen.

Center Time

Display pictures of fruits and vegetables that are harvested in the fall.

As children arrive, tell them it is getting cooler; the fall season must be here.

Worship Center

Teacher Talk

We thank God for fall.

Resources

tape, scissors, different kinds of gourds, knife, paper bag or box, magnifying glass (optional)

Cut a hole in a paper bag or box that is big enough for the children's hands to easily fit through from the side. Place a gourd in the bag or box. Fold down the top of the bag; tape it shut or close the lid of the box.

Let each child reach into the bag or box and feel the gourd. Encourage the children to guess what they are feeling. Show the children the gourd. Let the children examine the gourd with a magnifying glass. If you have a variety of gourds, let the children compare them.

Ask the children to guess what is inside the gourds. Cut open a gourd and encourage the children to examine the inside.

Say: God plans for the seasons. It is now the season called fall. In the fall we pick different kinds of fruits and vegetables such as apples and pumpkins. We call the time in the fall when we pick fruits and vegetables *harvest time*. Gourds grow on vines, like pumpkins do. They are often used for decorations in the fall and at Thanksgiving time.

Pray: Thank you, God, for the fall and for all the wonderful fruits and vegetables that grow in the fall. Amen.

Math Center

Teacher Talk

Fall is harvest time. We pick fruits and vegetables and nuts.

Resources

a variety of nuts (still in shells) in a basket, acorns, egg cartons, marker

Number each egg compartment before class. Children may count how many nuts it takes to fill the egg crates, or they may separate nuts into groups by color, by size, or by kind of nut. Check by the center often to talk with the children about categories and numbers of nuts. Tell the children not to eat the nuts.

Art Center

Teacher Talk

God plans for the seasons. It is the season called fall.

Resources

different colors of tempera paint, plastic containers, brushes, leaves, tape, plain paper, table covering, smocks

Cover the table and have the children wear smocks. Help each child tape a leaf to the table with the vein side up. Instruct the children to use brushes to paint the leaves. Then help each child take a piece of plain paper and place the paper on top of the leaf. Show the children how to rub gently over the paper. Lift the paper to see the leaf print. Allow the children to make several prints.

Home Living Center

Teacher Talk

We thank God for the apples that are picked in the fall.

Resources

cooked apples, potato masher, cinnamon, brown sugar, bowl, spoon, paper cups, spoons, napkins

Before class wash, peel, core, and slice apples. Stew the apples in a small amount of water on low heat until they are tender. Cool.

Show the children how to use the potato masher to mash the cooked apples in a plastic bowl. Add sugar and cinnamon to taste. Let the children stir. Spoon the applesauce into small paper cups to serve.

Open the Bible to Ecclesiastes 3:1.

Say: "For everything there is a season" (Ecclesiastes 3:1).

Have the children repeat the Bible verse.

Wonder Time

After cleanup time talk with the children about their center time activities. Show them pictures of the vegetables and fruits which are being harvested now that it is fall; it is now time to prepare for winter.

Wonder Question: I wonder what happens during the fall season?

Talk with the children about the fall season. Help them see that this is a time of preparation. Animals gather food to last through the winter. Farmers harvest the crops before cold weather comes. Children go back to school, and as it gets cooler, they begin to wear warmer clothes. In cooler climates the trees change colors and leaves fall off the trees. In warmer climates the water begins to get colder and the air is cooler.

Play a movement game. Have the children pretend to harvest fall fruits and vegetables.

Say: Let's go pick apples. *(Walk in place.)* The apples are way up high in the tree. *(Point up.)* I know, we'll climb a ladder. *(Pretend to climb.)* Pick the apples. *(Reach up and pretend to pick apples.)* Now climb back down. *(Pretend to climb down the ladder.)* The apples look good. *(Pretend to polish an apple.)* Let's eat! *(Pretend to eat.)*

Read the Bible verse.

Say: God plans for each season. It is now the season called fall.

Pray: Thank you, God, for the fall season. Amen.

Sing: "Clap, Clap" *(see page 211).*

Group Fun

Resources

lunch-size paper bags, newspapers, green yarn, orange and green tempera paint, paintbrushes, table covering, smocks, tape

Let the children make a pumpkin patch. Cover the table and have the children wear smocks. Give each child a lunch-size paper bag. Show the children how to crumple sheets of old newspapers and stuff the paper inside their bags. Help each child twist the top of the paper bag. Wrap the twist with tape.

Let the children paint the bottom part of their bags (below the twist) orange to make pumpkins. Let them paint the top part of their bags green (above the twist) to make the stems. Let the paint dry.

Have the children arrange their pumpkins on the floor in one corner of your room. Tie all the pumpkins together with green yarn. Remind the children that God plans for fall. In the fall we harvest fruits and vegetables like pumpkins.

Goodbye Circle

Ask the children to name some things they like about fall.

Pray: Thank you, God, for fall. Amen.

Evaluation

Can you think of other ways children can experience fall? If there is either a farm or a farmers' market nearby, make plans for a field trip.

Seasonal Lesson 62

Halloween

Goal:

To help children celebrate Halloween safely and without fear.

Objectives: By the end of this session the children will:

Decorate pumpkins.

Play with costumes.

Talk about Halloween.

Learn Halloween safety rules.

Faith Connections

Bible verse: I trust in God and am not afraid.

(Psalm 56:4, *Good News Bible*)

Children enjoy holidays, especially when treats are involved. However, Halloween can be a difficult holiday for preschoolers. They often have difficulty knowing the difference between what is real and what is not, because they are concrete thinkers. Although they love to dress up, scary costumes and masks can frighten young children. They think you become what you have on.

Christian preschools that do not believe in celebrating Halloween can emphasize the fall season and its beauty. Other Christian preschools can celebrate Halloween but de-emphasize the scary parts.

If you are meeting in a church, remember that children connect the building and what happens there with God and God's love. This is one reason why haunted houses and scary stories are not recommended for preschool classes.

Teacher's Prayer

Help me, O God, to bring joy to my children today. Make me aware of their fears and help me to help them feel safe and warm in your love. Amen.

Teacher Talk:

We thank God for fun times in the fall.

It is all right to be afraid.

We can trust God.

God is always with us.

Center Time

If you plan to have a Halloween party, the centers can serve as party activities.

As children arrive, tell them they can decorate pumpkins today.

Science Center

Teacher Talk

We thank God for fun times in the fall.

Resources

table covering, smocks, red fingerpaint, yellow fingerpaint, fingerpaint paper

Cover the table and have the children wear paint smocks. Give each child a piece of fingerpaint paper. Place a glob of red fingerpaint and a glob of yellow fingerpaint on the paper. Let the children mix the colors together to make orange.

Home Living Center

Teacher Talk

At Halloween we play dress-up.

Resources

costumes without masks

Instruct the children to pretend it is Halloween night and other children are coming for trick-or-treats. Let them pretend to be homeowners and trick-or-treaters. Remind the children that sometimes Halloween costumes are scary, but we can remember that there is a real person wearing the costume.

Worship Center

Teacher Talk

We can trust God. God is always with us.

Resources

mirrors, cornstarch, cotton balls, shallow containers

Place mirrors in the center. Pour a small amount of cornstarch in a shallow container. Give each child a cotton ball. Show the children how to dip the cotton balls in the cornstarch and then brush cornstarch on their faces like makeup.

Say: Sometimes at Halloween we see people with masks covering their faces or with makeup on their faces. Sometimes these people seem scary. We can remember that they are just people dressing up and pretending. We can also remember that God is always with us. God is with us when we are happy and having fun; God is with us when we are afraid.

Pray: Thank you, God, for fun times. Amen.

Art Center

Teacher Talk

Halloween happens in the fall.

Resources

old newspapers, orange tempera paint, sponges or Halloween cookie cutters, shallow trays, table covering, smocks, scissors

Cover the table and have the children wear smocks. Pour orange tempera paint into shallow trays. Cut newspaper into rectangles for each child. Show the children how to dip sponges or Halloween cookie cutters into the paint and then press them onto the newspaper.

Writing Center

Teacher Talk

We thank God for fall.

Resources

white construction paper, orange tempera paint, paper towels, shallow trays, green markers, table covering, smocks

Let the children make a thumbprint pumpkin patch. Cover the table and have the children wear smocks. Fold paper towels and place them in the bottom of shallow trays. Pour orange tempera paint on the paper towels to make a paint pad. Give each child a piece of white construction paper. Show the children how to press their thumbs onto the paint pad and then onto their papers. Let the children make several prints. Let the paint dry.

Let the children use green markers to add leaves, stems, and vines to their thumbprint pumpkins.

Wonder Time

Call the children together to talk about Halloween.

Wonder Question: I wonder how we can have a safe Halloween?

Say: There are some important rules to help us have a safe Halloween.

Talk about safety rules.

Say: Sometimes Halloween can be scary. What makes you afraid?

Talk about the things that scare the children.

Remind the children that people are playing dress-up at Halloween. There are real people behind the masks and makeup.

Ask: What can you do when you are afraid?

Say: When you are afraid, you can go to an adult you trust.

Sing: "God Cares" (*see page 212*).

Read the Bible verse.

Say: Sometimes Halloween can be scary. It is all right to be afraid. When we are afraid we can trust God and remember that God is with us.

Pray: Thank you, God, for fun times like Halloween. Amen.

Halloween Safety Rules

- Always stay with a responsible person. Who would be a responsible person? *(mom or dad, older sister or brother, aunt, grandparent, adult friend)*
- Carry a lighted flashlight.
- Wear something that shows up in the dark on your costume like glow-in-the-dark tape.
- Use safety rules when you cross the street. What are the safety rules about crossing the street? *(Look both ways; cross at the corners; hold hands with an adult.)*
- Do not go inside anyone's home when you are trick-or-treating.
- Don't eat any candy until your mom or dad (or caretaker) looks at it.

Open the Bible to Psalm 56:4.

Say: "I trust in God and am not afraid" (Psalm 56:4, *Good News Bible*).

Have the children repeat the Bible verse.

Group Fun

Resources

small pumpkins for each child, markers, table covering, smocks

Cover the table and have the children wear paint smocks. Give each child a small pumpkin. Pie pumpkins are a good size for preschoolers. Let the children use markers to decorate their pumpkins however they wish.

Goodbye Circle

Remind the children of the Halloween safety rules.

Pray: Thank you, God, for fun times like Halloween. Amen.

Evaluation

Was it a fun day? Did the children have any mistaken ideas about Halloween?

Seasonal Lesson 63

Bible-Times Thanksgiving

Teacher Talk:

Bible people had a special celebration to give thanks to God.

Bible people thanked God for the harvest.

Bible people thanked God for God's love and care.

We thank God for good food to eat.

We thank God for God's care.

Goal:

To help preschoolers learn more about the biblical celebration of giving thanks to God.

Objectives:

By the end of this session the children will:

Make torn-paper fruit montages.

Build a Bible-times booth.

Weave mats.

Faith Connections

Bible verse: O give thanks to the LORD.
1 Chronicles 16:34

Children love traditions. They are beginning to recognize the traditions they share with their families and friends. Thanksgiving is one of those traditional times. The purpose of today's lesson is to add the biblical heritage to our celebration of Thanksgiving.

Bible people celebrated the harvest festival, Sukkot, in the fall. During this festival the people made temporary booths called sukkots, and lived in them. The booths were decorated with branches and fruit to thank God for the harvest. The sukkots served as a reminder of God's care for the people during the time they wandered in the wilderness after escaping from slavery in Egypt. Sukkot is still very much a part of Jewish culture today.

Teacher's Prayer

Like Bible people so long ago, we give you thanks, O Lord. Amen.

Center Time

Display pictures of Bible-times booths. Check your church's Sunday school resources or your local library to find these pictures.

As children arrive, say: "Today we will have a Bible times festival to say thank you to God."

Building Center

Teacher Talk

Bible-times people had a special harvest festival.

Resources

appliance box, knife, paper strips, glue, tape, paper fruit

Before class cut out one side and the top of a large appliance box. The box should now have three sides and no roof.

Place the box in the building center. Let the children make paper chains to hang across the top of the booth. The children may hang paper fruit from the art center or tape leaves to the booth. Encourage the children to sit inside the booth and look up to the sky.

Say: Bible-times people had a special festival in the fall to thank God for the harvest. Families at this time would make booths from palm and willow branches. They would live in the booths during the festival.

Worship Center

Teacher Talk

We thank God for food and for God's care.

Resources

shoeboxes; scissors; tempera paint; paintbrushes; shallow trays; glue; sticks, twigs, and leaves; table covering; smocks

Build shoebox booths with the children. Before class cut a portion of the bottom out of each shoebox to make the roof of the booth. Cut a door in one side.

Cover the table and have the children wear smocks. Let the children paint their shoebox booths with tempera paint. Let the children glue on craft sticks, twigs, and leaves when the boxes are dry.

Say: Bible-times people made booths to live in for their special harvest festival. At this celebration Bible people gave thanks to God for food and for God's care.

Pray: Thank you, God, for good food. Thank you for your care. Amen.

Science Center

Teacher Talk

We thank God for leaves and for things that grow in the fall.

Resources

palm branch or willow branch, magnifying glasses

Provide a palm branch or willow branch for the children to examine. If these trees do not grow in your area, talk with a florist. Or find pictures of these branches in the encyclopedia or from library books. Remind the children that Bible times people used palm branches and willow branches to make booths for their fall festival.

Art Center

Teacher Talk

We thank God for food and for God's care.

Resources

fruit patterns (*see page 222*), construction paper, glue, construction paper or tissue paper scraps, yarn, scissors, paper punch

Make fruit montages. Before class photocopy the fruit patterns (*see page 222*). Use the fruit patterns to cut fruit shapes out of construction paper.

Let each child choose a fruit shape. Provide scraps of tissue paper or construction paper. Show the children how to tear the paper scraps into smaller pieces and then glue the pieces onto their fruit. Use a paper punch to punch a hole in the top of each fruit shape. Tie a loop of yarn through the hole to make a hanger. Hang the fruit from the booth (see building center) or from the ceiling.

Talk with the children about the kinds of fruits and vegetables we pick in the fall. Tell the children that Bible-times people thanked God for the fruit and vegetables that were picked in the fall, just as we do today.

Wonder Time

Open the Bible to 1 Chronicles 16:34.

Say: "O give thanks to the LORD." (1 Chronicles 16:34).

Have the children repeat the Bible verse.

Call the children to wonder time.

Wonder Question: I wonder what the word *harvest* means?

Say: Harvest time is when the foods that grow in the farmers' fields are ready to be picked and taken to the market. The harvest is the food that the farmers grow and that we all eat.

Sing: "Clap, Clap" *(see page 211).*

Read the Bible verse.

Say: Bible-times people gave thanks to God for the harvest and for God's care. We can give thanks to God today.

Have each child name a fruit or vegetable.

Pray: Thank you, God, for good food to eat. Thank you for *(fruits or vegetables children named).* Amen.

Group Fun

Resources

construction paper, fabric strips, colored construction paper strips, scissors

Let the children make woven Bible times mats. Before class cut a mat for each child. Fold a piece of construction paper in half and cut from the fold toward the edges in 1½-inch strips. Do not cut all the way to the edges. The borders will help hold the weaving together. Cut colored construction paper and fabric into 1½-inch strips about 9 inches long.

Give each child a pre-cut mat. Show the children how to weave the strips over and under the cuts in the construction paper mat. Don't be too anxious if the children do not follow the over and under pattern; the mat will turn out just fine anyway!

Tell the children that people in Bible times wove mats to sit on and to sleep on.

Goodbye Circle

Let the children sit on their mats for the goodbye circle.

Pray: Thank you, God, for good food to eat. Thank you for your care. Amen.

Evaluation

Did the children enjoy making the large booth for the class? Did the children have opportunities to give thanks to God?

Seasonal Lesson 64

Thanksgiving

Goal:

To give the children opportunities to express their thanks to God.

Objectives:

By the end of this session the children will:

Make nature centerpieces.

Make a Thanksgiving quilt.

Create autumn colors with melted crayons.

Eat a meal together.

Faith Connections

Bible verse: God has set the right time for everything.

(Ecclesiastes 3:11, *Good News Bible*, adapted)

This lesson on Thanksgiving focuses on giving thanks to God, not on the pilgrims. There are many resources available if you wish to add the story of pilgrims to today's activities. We all need to express thanks to God every day. This lesson will help your children understand Thanksgiving as a special time to give thanks to God.

Often the Thanksgiving holiday is filled with long journeys and family members the children don't know very well. Yet the excitement of doing something with their families fills a children's hearts. Let the children talk about special plans, and give them an opportunity to make say thank you to God.

Teacher's Prayer

I am so thankful, God, for the gifts you have given me. My life and the lives of each child in my care bring me joy. For your graciousness, your strength, your patience with me, I am joyful. Amen.

Teacher Talk:

Thanksgiving is a special time when we give thanks to God.

We thank God for good food to eat.

We thank God for our families.

We thank God for our friends.

We thank God for fall.

Center Time

Plan a Thanksgiving celebration for your class. Provide materials for a centerpiece, a tablecloth, napkins, plates, cups, food, and invitations.

As children arrive, tell them you are thankful they came.

Worship Center

Teacher Talk

We thank God for families, friends, and food.

Resources

posterboard, colored tape, oil pastel crayons, scissors

Let the children make a Thanksgiving quilt. Before class cut posterboard into 8″ x 6″ pieces so that each child has at least four pieces.

Give each child the four pieces of posterboard. Help the children tape the posterboard pieces side-by-side. Flip the pieces over after taping and also tape the joints on the back side. Talk with the children about things for which they are thankful. Let the children use oil pastel crayons to draw the things they named on their posterboard quilts. Display the quilts around the room.

Say: Thanksgiving is a special time when we say thank you to God for family, for friends, and for good food.

Pray: Thank you, God, for all the good things you have given us like family, friends, and good food. Thank you for *(name some of the things the children drew on their quilts)*. Amen.

Math Center

Teacher Talk

Thanksgiving is a special time to give thanks to God.

Resources

play dough or clay, different-colored feathers

Make three or four balls from play dough or clay. Instruct the children to separate colored feathers by size or color. Have the children stick feathers in the clay as they group them. When they finish, ask them to count how many of each color they have, then remove all the feathers so another child can play the game.

Art Center

Teacher Talk

Thanksgiving is a special time to give thanks to God.

Resources

warming tray, plain paper, large crayons, construction paper, glue, children's winter gloves, adult help

Let the children make place mats for the Thanksgiving celebration. Show the children how to use a warming tray to make melted crayon pictures. Plug in the warming tray in a safe area of the room and arrange for adult supervision. Choose large crayons in fall colors to use in this center today.

Have each child wear gloves to protect their hands. Place a piece of plain paper on the tray. Show each child how to slowly move the crayons across the page.

Let each child choose a piece of construction paper in a fall color. Have the children glue their melted crayon pictures onto the construction paper to complete their place mats.

Science Center

Teacher Talk

We thank God for God's beautiful world.

Resources

small paper plates; glue; nature items such as pine cones, acorns, and dried flowers

Let the children make centerpieces for the Thanksgiving celebration. Show the children the nature items. Give each child a small paper plate. Let the children glue the nature items onto the paper plates in any way they wish. Remind the children that we are thankful for God's beautiful world.

Wonder Time

Call the children to wonder time.

Wonder Question: I wonder why we have a holiday like Thanksgiving?

Say: Thanksgiving is a special time when we say thank you to God. Let's think of some things for which we are thankful.

Sing: "I Am Thankful" to the tune of "London Bridge." (See box.) Let each child name an item to go in the song.

I Am Thankful

I am thankful for my
__________,
For my ________,
For my ________.
I am thankful for my__________.
Thank you, God!

God is very good to me,
Good to me,
Good to me.
God is very good to me.
Thank you, God!

Read the Bible verse.

Open the Bible to Ecclesiastes 3:11.

Say: "God has set the right time for everything" (Ecclesiastes 3:11, *Good News Bible*, adapted).

Have the children repeat the Bible verse.

Say: God has planned the right time for everything. We say thank you to God every day, not just at Thanksgiving. Thanksgiving is a *special* time to say thank you to God.

Sing: "Clap, Clap" *(see page 211)*.

Pray: Thank you, God, for family and friends and good food. Thank you for *(name each child and teacher)*. Amen.

Group Fun

Resources

plates, tableware, cups, tablecloth, centerpieces, place mats, lunches or food for Thanksgiving dinner

Ask the children to prepare the tables for a real Thanksgiving meal at school. Have the children help you cover the tables with tablecloths and put their placemats around the tables. Have the children place the centerpieces they made on the table. Let the children completely prepare the table for the meal.

Show the children how to set a table with plates, tableware, and cups. If the children bring their own lunches, they can eat them at the meal. Otherwise you can prepare a real Thanksgiving dinner with turkey and dressing, or you can provide foods like baby carrot sticks, applesauce, and turkey luncheon meat. Say a thank-you prayer and enjoy your Thanksgiving meal.

Goodbye Circle

Let the children sit on their mats (*see page 204*) for the goodbye circle.

Pray: Thank you, God, for family and friends and good food. Amen.

Evaluation

Was every child involved in the activities today? Say a prayer of thanks for each child.

Seasonal Lesson 65

Getting Ready for Winter

Teacher Talk:

God plans for winter to follow fall.

We thank God for winter.

In some places the air turns cold in winter.

Goal:

The children will begin to think about winter and ways it is different from the other seasons.

Objectives:

By the end of this session the children will:

Make snowflakes.

Create weavings.

Make winter collages.

Paint with ice.

Faith Connections:

Bible Verse: There will always be cold and heat, summer and winter, day and night.

(Genesis 8:22, *Good News Bible*)

As each season changes, remind the children of God's plan for the seasons. Help them see that all creatures need to keep warm and to have food for winter. Discover with the children the changes in the appearance of the outdoors, like grass that has turned brown and trees without leaves.

Teacher's Prayer

Help me to find the joy in winter, O God. Help me learn to rest and wait for your plans to unfold. In Jesus' name, Amen.

Center Time

Display pictures that show winter scenes. Add warm dress-up clothes like coats and mittens to the home living center.

As children arrive, ask them if they have ever painted with ice.

Science Center

Teacher Talk

We thank God for winter.

Resources

different-colored yarn, small tree twigs with several branches on them, clay or play dough, scissors

Tell the children they are going to make tree weavings. Give each child a small ball of play dough and a twig. Show the children how to stick their branches in the play dough to make a stand-up tree.

Say: In the fall season the leaves on some trees die and fall to the ground. In winter the branches stay bare. In spring new leaves grow on the trees. In summer the leaves are green. We are in the winter season. During winter in colder climates trees do not have any leaves.

Give each child lengths of different-colored yarn. Show the children how to weave the yarn up and down, around, and in and out of the branches on the tree.

Math Center

Teacher Talk

God plans for winter to follow fall.

Resources

scissors, coffee filters, yarn

Let the children cut snowflakes. Give each child a coffee filter. Show the children how to fold the coffee filters in half. Then have the children fold the filters in half again. Let the children cut little pieces out of the folded edges. Unfold the coffee filters to see the snowflakes.

Children will want to do this several times or cut more and more from their first snowflakes. This practice is fun and helps them gain skill and muscle control. Help the children tie yarn through the snowflake holes and hang the snowflakes around the room.

Art Center

Teacher Talk

In some places the air turns cold in winter.

Resources

bowl of ice cubes, powdered tempera, construction paper, table covering, smocks

Cover the table and have the children wear smocks. Give each child a piece of construction paper. Instruct the children to sprinkle powdered tempera on their papers. Show the children how to take an ice cube and rub it around the paper in the powdered paint. The ice should melt and make a painting. Talk with the children about what makes ice and why it melts.

Home Living Center

Teacher Talk

We thank God for winter.

Resources

warm coats and jackets, boots, gloves, mugs, warming tray hot chocolate mix, marshmallows,

Before class make some hot chocolate. Put mugs on the warming tray and serve children as they play in the center. Tell them to pretend it is winter and to go out and play.

Worship Center

Teacher Talk

We thank God for winter.

Resources

black, gray, or dark blue construction paper; cotton balls; Christmas tree icicles; winter pictures cut from magazines; white foam peanuts; glue

Let the children make winter collages. Give the children construction paper. Let the children glue the collage materials onto their papers.

Say: God plans for winter to follow fall.

Pray: Thank you, God, for winter. Amen.

Open the Bible to Genesis 8:22.

Say: "There will always be cold and heat, summer and winter, day and night" (Genesis 8:22, *Good News Bible*).

Have the children repeat the Bible verse.

Wonder Time

Call the children to wonder time.

Wonder Question: I wonder what happens when it is winter?
Say: God plans for winter to follow fall. When it is winter, the air turns colder. In some places there is ice and snow.
Ask: How do we get ready for winter? (*We wear warmer clothes like coats and hats and mittens. We bring the plants inside. We use snow shovels and snow blowers. Note: Change this to talk about what happens in your area.*)
Ask: How do animals get ready for winter? (*They store food; they fly to the south; or they go to sleep.*)
Sing: "Clap, Clap" (*see page 211*).
Read the Bible verse:
Say: God plans for winter to follow fall.
Pray: Thank you, God, for winter. Amen.

Group Fun

Resources

inexpensive paper plates, cassette/CD player, music

Let the children enjoy playing pretend winter games. Have the children move to an open area of the room. Give each child two inexpensive paper plates. Have the children put the paper plates on the rug and then stand on them. Encourage the children to skate around the room by sliding their feet. Play music and let the children pretend to ice skate. Have the children pretend to skate (only on the rug, for safety reasons).

Have the children lie down on the floor and pretend to make snow angels.

Let the children play freeze tag. Choose one child to be "winter." Have the remaining children pretend to be water and move around the room. Winter will try to freeze the water. When winter tags a child, the child must freeze or be very still. Let the children take turns being winter.

Remind the children that God plans for winter to follow fall. In some places winter is cold and there is snow.

Goodbye Circle

Remind the children that winter is coming soon and that they will need heavier coats. Gather up items to take home.

Pray: Thank you, God, for winter. Amen.

Evaluation

Did the children associate the activities with wintertime? How could this lesson have worked better in your class?

I Want a Friend

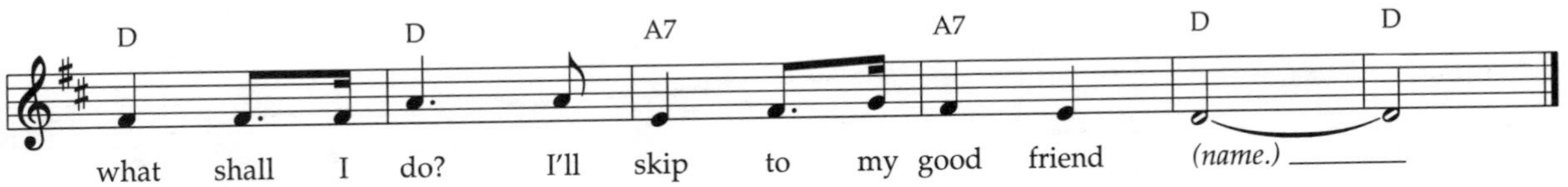

WORDS and MUSIC: Traditional

Clap, Clap

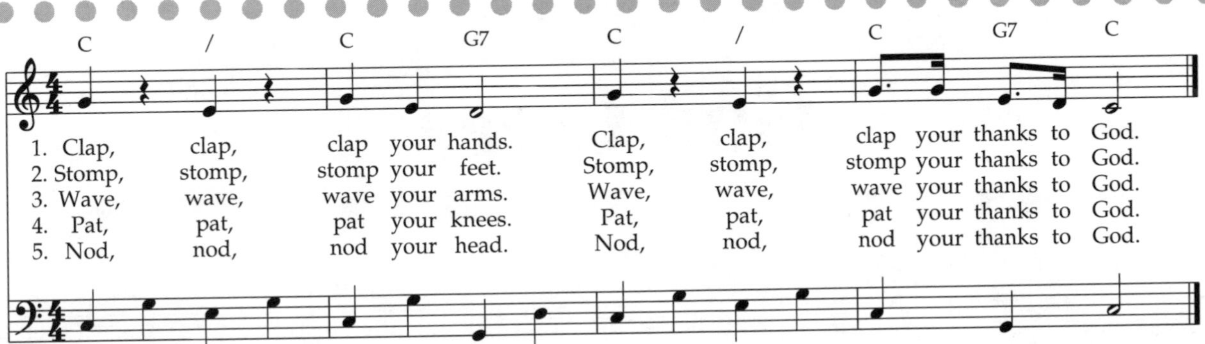

WORDS: Psalm 47:1, adapted; sts. 2-5 by Daphna Flegal
MUSIC: Cecilia Williams

Will You Be a Friend of Mine?

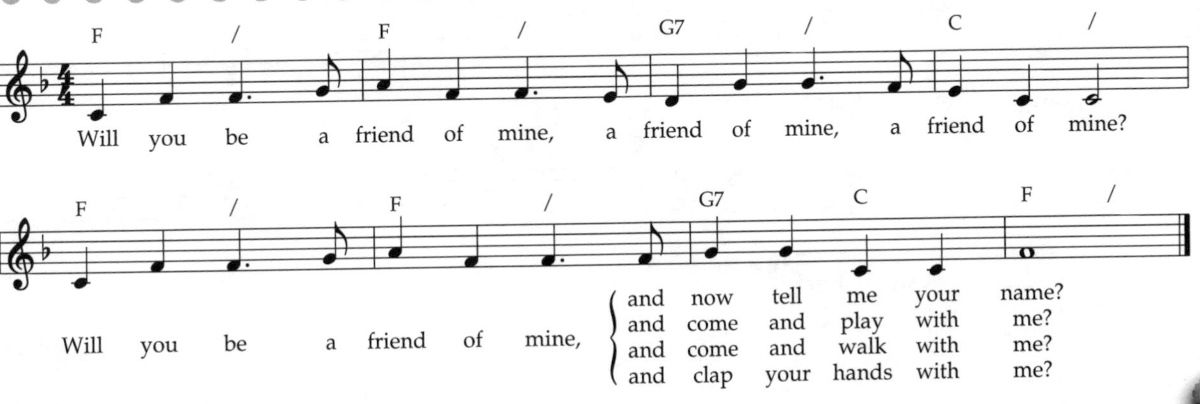

WORDS: Emma Jane White
MUSIC: Traditional

Thank You, God, for Loving Me

WORDS: Elaine Ward
MUSIC: "Rocking," V. Earle Copes

God Cares

WORDS: Lois H. Young
MUSIC: Lois H. Young; arr. by Carol M. Frazier

Faces

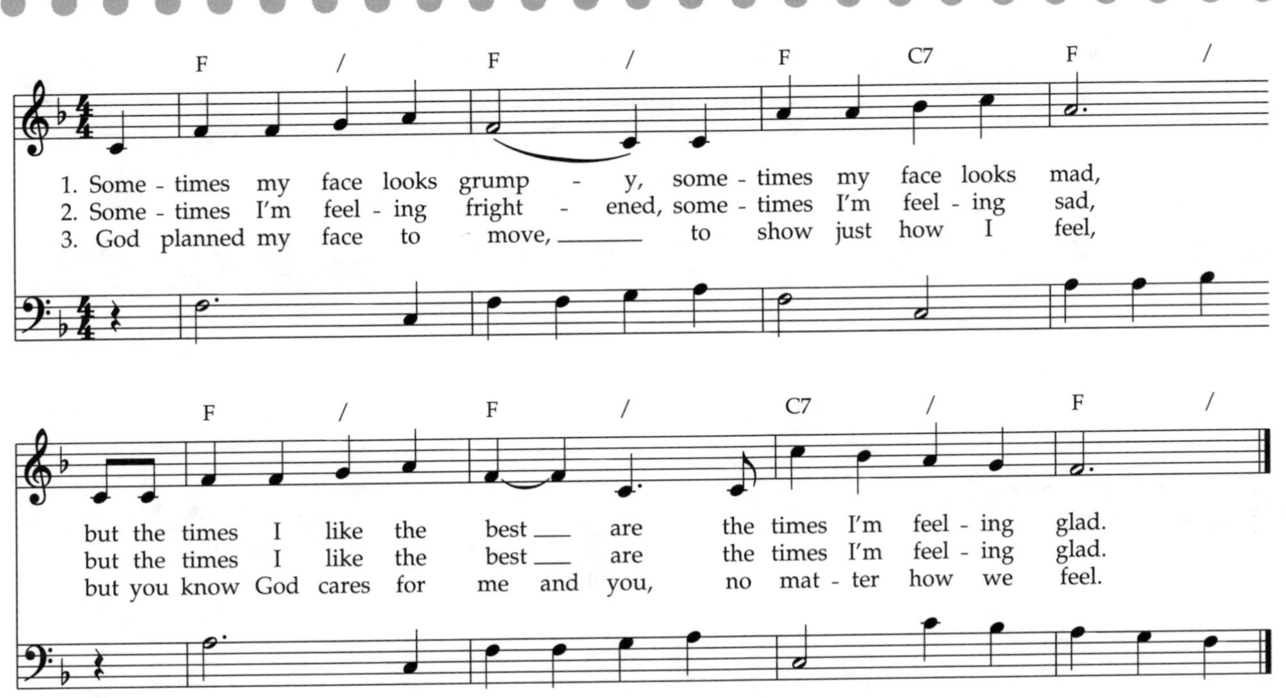

WORDS and MUSIC: Pat Clinger

God Plans for Many Growing Things

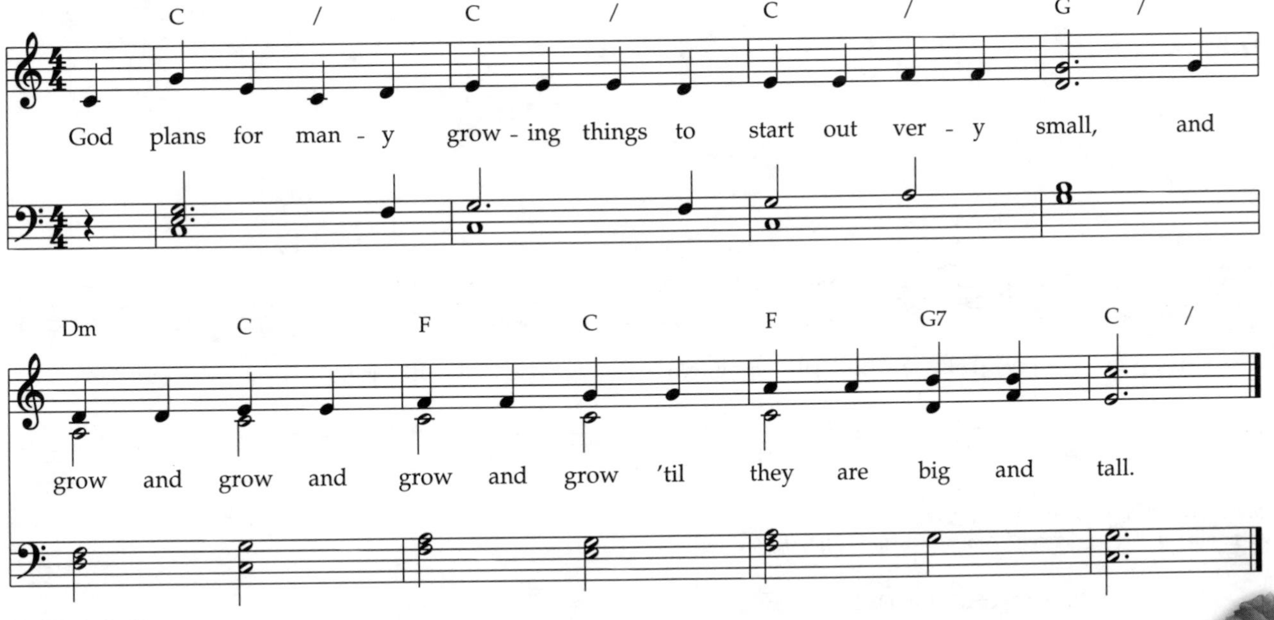

WORDS: Jo Risser
MUSIC: Jane Bledsoe; arr. by Nylea L. Butler-Moore

Just the Way I Am

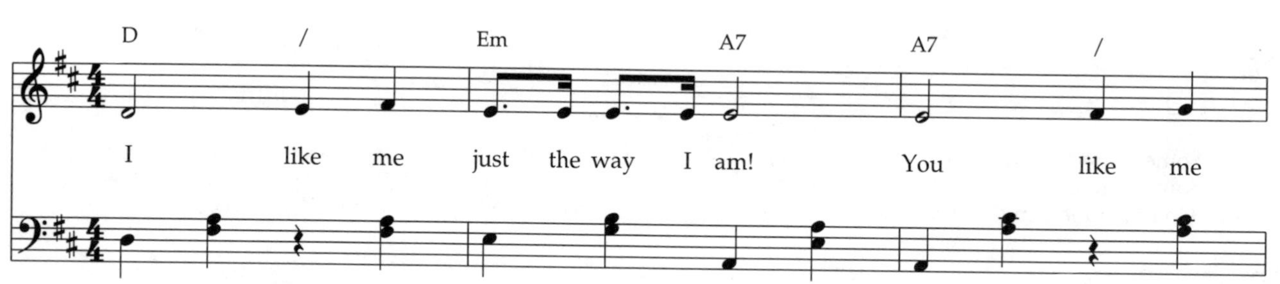

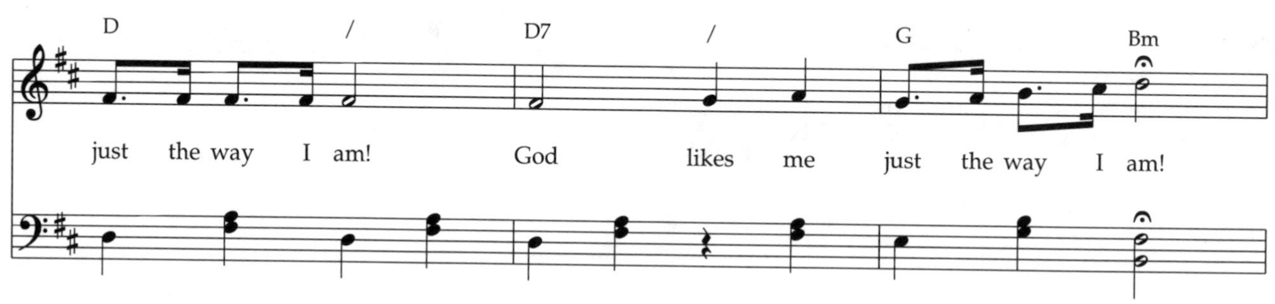

Song can end here if desired.
Variation: In place of "Amen," you might sing "I like me."

WORDS and MUSIC: Pamela L. Hughes

I'm Thankful

WORDS: Sts. 1-4, Evelyn M. Andre; st. 5, Nylea L. Butler-Moore; sts. 6-7 Daphna Flegal
MUSIC: Traditional; arr. by Nylea L. Butler-Moore

Week of ______________________ **Theme** ______________________

Weekly Notes		Bible Verse/Book	Art	Math/Writing
Observations:	MONDAY			
	TUESDAY			
Learning Centers:	WEDNESDAY			
Evaluations:	THURSDAY			
	FRIDAY			

Science/Cooking	Building/Home Living	Music/Movement	Additional Centers

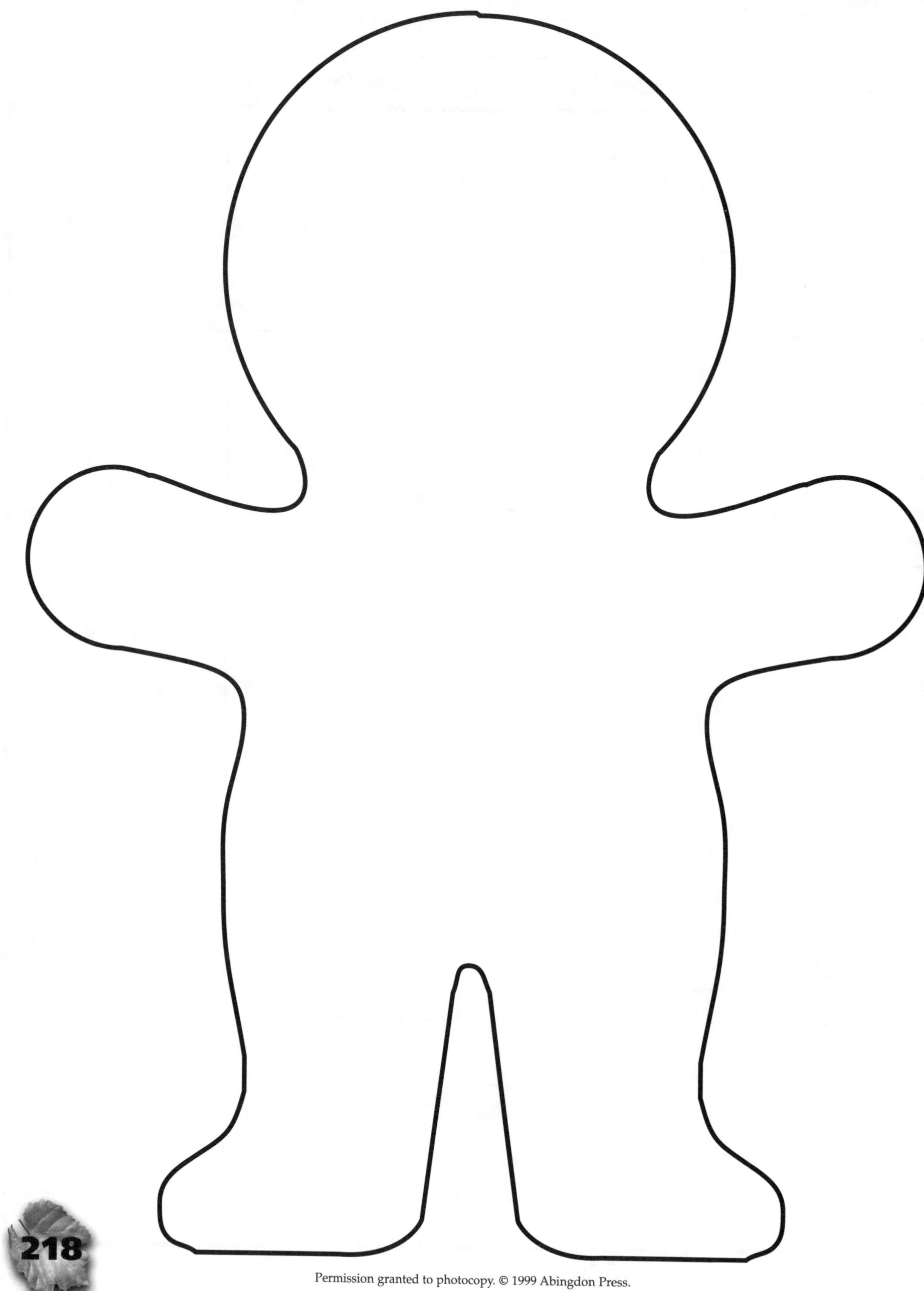

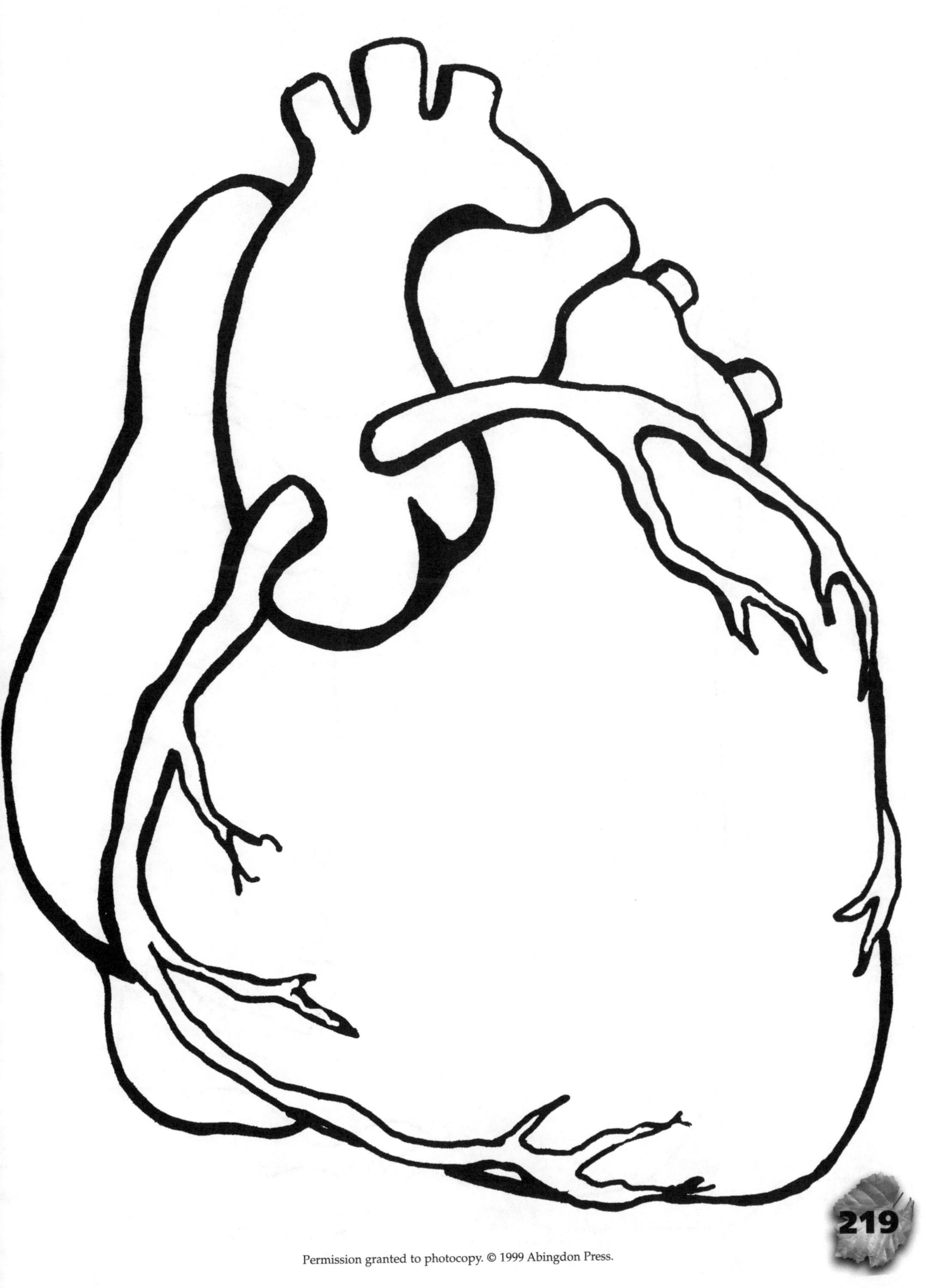

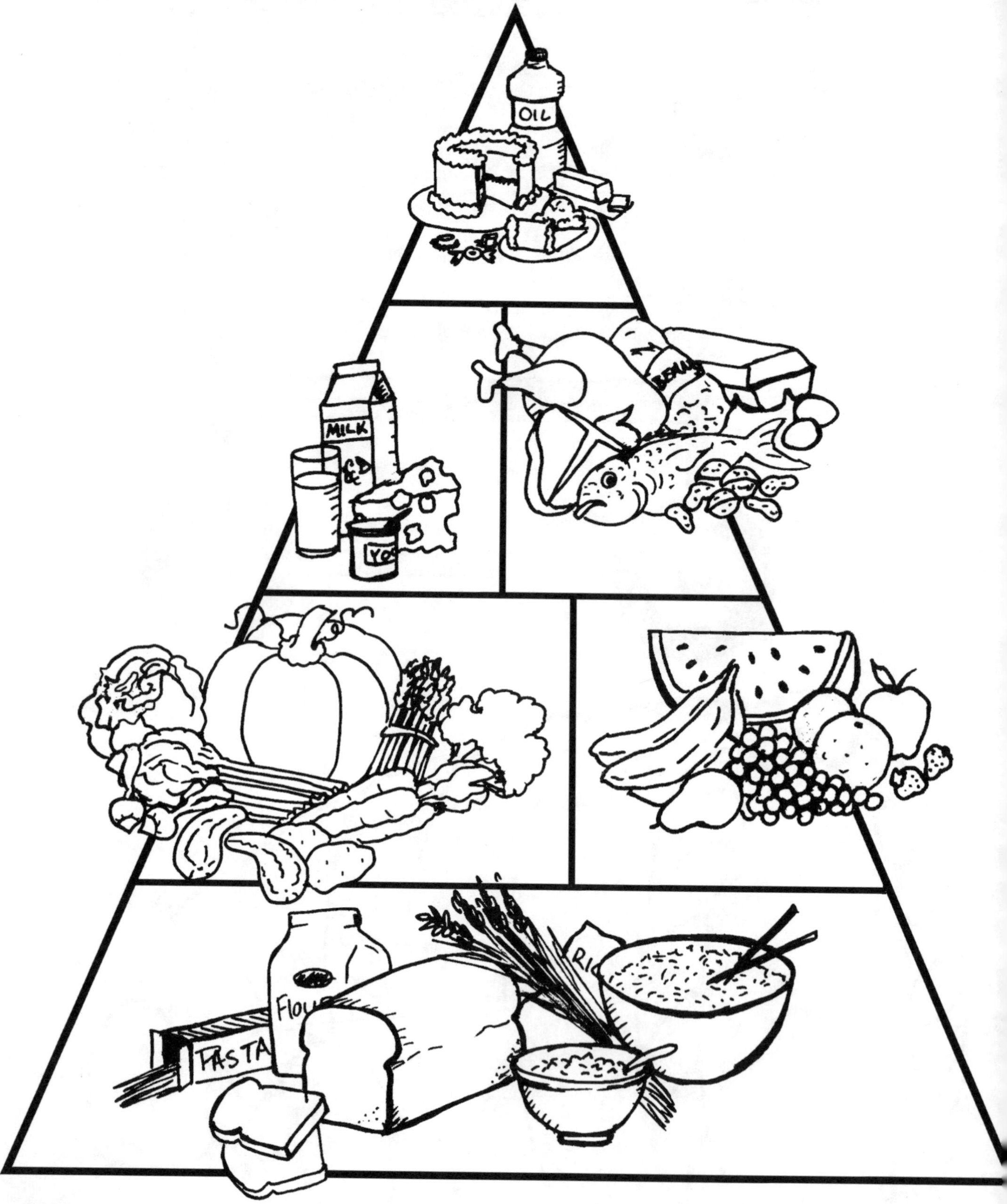
OIL
MILK
BEANS
FLOUR
PASTA
RI